ACCLAIM FOR TRAVEL
BY AND FOR

The Best Women's Trav...
Gold Medal Winner, Independent Publisher Book Awards.
touching and impressive read." —Eva Holland, *WorldHum*

100 Places Every Woman Should Go
"Will ignite the wanderlust in any woman…inspiring and delightful."
—Lowell Thomas Awards judges' citation, Best Travel Book 2007

100 Places in Italy Every Woman Should Go
"Reveals an intimacy with Italy and a honed sense of adventure. *Andiamo!*"
—Frances Mayes

Women in the Wild
"A spiritual, moving and totally female book to take you around the world
and back." —*Mademoiselle*

A Woman's Path
"A sensitive exploration of women's lives that have been unexpectedly and
spiritually touched by travel experiences…highly recommended."
—*Library Journal*

A Woman's World
"Packed with stories of courage and confidence, independence and intro-
spection." —*Self Magazine*

A Woman's Passion for Travel
"Sometimes sexy, sometimes scary, sometimes philosophical and always
entertaining." —*San Francisco Examiner*

Sand in My Bra
"Bursting with exuberant candor and crackling humor."
—*Publishers Weekly*

A Woman's Europe
"These stories will inspire women to find a way to visit places they've only
dreamed of." —*The Globe and Mail*

The World Is a Kitchen
"A vicarious delight for the virtual tourist, as well as an inspiration for the
most seasoned culinary voyager." —Mollie Katzen

Family Travel
"Should give courage to any wary mother who thinks she has to give up on
her love of travel when she gives birth." —*Chicago Herald*

Writing Away
"A witty, profound, and accessible exploration of journal-keeping."
—Anthony Weller

TRAVELERS' TALES

THE
BEST
WOMEN'S TRAVEL
WRITING

2011

TRUE STORIES
FROM AROUND THE WORLD

TRAVELERS' TALES

THE BEST
WOMEN'S TRAVEL
WRITING

2011

TRUE STORIES
FROM AROUND THE WORLD

Edited by
LAVINIA SPALDING

Travelers' Tales
an imprint of Solas House, Inc.
Palo Alto

Art direction: Kimberly Nelson
Cover photograph: © Tom Salyer
Page layout and photo editing: Cynthia Lamb using the fonts
    Granjon, Nicolas Cochin, and Ex Ponto.
Interior design: Melanie Haage
Author photo: Erica Hilton
Production: Christy Quinto and Natalie Baszile

ISBN 1-60952-012-2
ISSN 1553-054X

First Edition
Printed in the United States
10 9 8 7 6 5 4 3 2 1

Soar, eat ether, see what has never been seen;
depart, be lost, but climb.

—EDNA ST. VINCENT MILLAY

For every girlfriend who has ever traveled with me
and
For Dan, who is teaching me about home

Table of Contents

Introduction

Most of us can easily pinpoint the moment we began identifying ourselves as travelers. It was Paris or Jaipur or Chiang Mai—we were perched on a medieval castle wall or sitting cross-legged in a temple at dawn or riding an elephant through a dense jungle. We were someplace entirely foreign, doing something wholly unexpected, when we felt a sudden and overwhelming sense of astonishment, bliss, gratitude—or even horror. And from that instant, we would never be the same.

My defining moment was a little different. I was seated at a cramped kitchen table in Jersey City, drinking gin and tonics with a group of older women who had just announced that they wanted to sit down and have a talk with me.

I'd arrived two days earlier from Boston, where I was working at a Hallmark store while deciding what to do with my post-high-school life. My older sister Blake was visiting her girlfriends in Jersey City, and to my amazement, she had invited me to tag along.

On the first morning of the trip, we took the train into Manhattan, disembarking inside the World Trade Center. We wandered the city for hours, window shopping, squinting into the sun to photograph skyscrapers, hovering over artists as they made sidewalk chalk drawings, listening to street musicians. Eventually we stopped to rest on some steps across from the Hotel Fifth Avenue, and at that instant, a cavalcade of black state sedans, police cars, and motorcycle cops pulled up in front of us with lights flashing and sirens blaring. We watched as Benazir Bhutto stepped gracefully from a limo and hurried into the hotel, escorted by bodyguards. Then Dan Aykroyd sidled up to us. "This is exciting, isn't it?" he asked me.

I ate my first gyro, played the giant floor piano in FAO Schwarz, and strolled through the Museum of Modern Art, where Blake and her friends rhapsodized over the Rothko exhibit and I tried to make sense of what I perceived to be enormous paint swatches. Back in Jersey City that evening, we climbed to the roof of their apartment building and looked out at the Twin Towers and a chocolate factory. We drank, danced, and sang "That's Amore." It's possible I'd never been happier.

But it wasn't until the second day that my moment of travel truth happened. It was late afternoon in Jersey City, but according to Blake, cocktail hour. She made us a round of Tanqueray and tonics and summoned us to the tiny kitchen table by the window. I waited nervously.

My sister and her friends, so wise and experienced at the ripe age of twenty-five, intimidated me. Sophisticated, adventurous, strong, and creative, these women bartended for money, rafted class-five rivers for fun, wore vintage camelhair coats and alligator-skin shoes, dabbled in ceramics and jewelry making and photography. They dated mysterious men, howled with laughter at things I didn't yet understand, and—most impressive—they traveled. They sent postcards from Greece, Turkey, Belgium, Italy, Switzerland, and the bottom of the Grand Canyon, and sometimes brought back small souvenirs. They regaled me with stories of clambering up a spiral staircase to a secret upper section of the Parthenon to drink ouzo under a full moon or of being scolded by women at the Turkish bathhouse for being too thin to ever find husbands. But one thing they did *not* do was sit me down to have talks with me. I was still young enough to worry that I might be in trouble.

Finally, Susie leaned close and looked at me intently, like a doctor about to deliver a critical prognosis.

"We think you've caught the travel bug," she said. "And we want to talk to you about it."

They were serious, and I'm sure they offered up all manner of sage advice that afternoon. Perhaps they urged me to save money or invest in a quality camera, to hoard frequent flier miles or head directly to college, to stay single or marry rich. The only advice I distinctly remember was to avoid buying unnecessarily heavy objects: furniture, art, books.

"That stuff will only weigh you down," they insisted.

I nodded and drank my cocktail, grinning with delight. I wasn't yet a traveler; before this trip, my experiences were limited to spending one spring break lounging on a Mexican beach and moving from Arizona to Massachusetts so I could stock greeting cards. But these women—these *real* travelers—recognized in me a kindred spirit, and that was all I needed. I would not let them down.

Since my visit to Jersey City twenty-odd years ago, I've steadily ignored their advice, carting unnecessarily heavy objects to thirty-five homes in six states, back and forth from one edge of the planet to the other. I've accumulated dozens of boxes of books and art, and despite my best intentions, I invariably return from even the shortest trip abroad with more luggage than when I departed. My desire to nest among heavy objects is as strong as my need to keep moving.

It occurs to me now that my sister and her friends might have done better to advise me against, say, falling for the Balinese painter with the hair down to his knees and the two other girlfriends. Or losing my passport in Thailand, or sleeping on flea-infested mattresses in Cambodia, or inhaling tear gas in South Korea, or drinking the water in Cuba. In the end, it wasn't the advice that mattered. What marked me was the sensation of being invited into a community where I would become what they were convinced I already was. It was my first glimpse of how limitless life could be when I surrounded myself with women who believed that by entertaining the impossible, it became possible.

Many of us grew up hooked on a different kind of tale, one in which the heroine's hardships are ultimately rewarded with true love, a royal home, and an unwavering sense of stability. So a story in which we choose instead to search for our happily-ever-after by wandering off to remote, grubby corners of the planet may read as a bit unorthodox and irresponsible—not to mention daunting. After all, it's not easy to embark on a life of travel, much less continue once you've begun. It takes courage and sacrifice, flexibility, creativity, time, and money.

But first—and most importantly—it takes a spark of inspiration and a fan to coax that spark into a fire. Travelers' Tales' annual collection of women's travel writing is both the spark and the fan. By reading the words of women who have accomplished what we dream of doing, obstacles and implications vanish, leaving nothing but a sisterhood of permission and validation.

Over the years, I've visited thirty-some countries on five continents—more than I ever imagined I would— yet reading the stories in this year's *The Best Women's Travel Writing* makes me feel like I've barely begun. More than ever now, my brain is like a world globe that spins endlessly on its axis, never slowing down, a constant blur of cities and nations and provinces and possibilities.

Suddenly, I want to ride a camel with a Bedouin through the Syrian Desert as Anena Hansen did and take samba lessons in Brazil so I can swing my hips like Jocelyn Edelstein. I want to experience Holikan in India with Kasha Rigby, and Tihar in Nepal with Laurie Weed, and I want Abbie Kozolchyk to take me shopping in Bhutan. Thanks to Angie Chuang, Marcy Gordon, and Anna Wexler, I'm now dying to taste ice cream in Kabul, pork fat in Italy, and even barbecued goat testicles in Serbia. I imagine myself joining the Peace Corps and moving to Niger as Susan Rich did, struggling alongside Nancy Kline to rekindle a love affair with Paris, and moving to Havana if only to be Conner Gorry's next-door neighbor. I wish I were more like Bridget Crocker, who realized that if she could survive that river in Costa Rica, she could survive her broken heart. And I fantasize about leaving it all behind, as Annie Nilsson did, to slop pigs on a farm in Ecuador.

There are also stories in this book that may not inspire envy but underscore why we travel: to pay closer attention, to do more, care more, matter more, to change and be changed, to siphon some understanding out of a confusing world—or simply to bear witness. There's Laura Flynn's first trip to violence-torn Haiti, Sarah Bathum's experience caring for a sick child at a nunnery in Ethiopia, and Kelly Hayes-Raitt's return to Iraq, just months after the U.S. bombings and invasion.

This book will take you from Arezzo to Zinder, Baja to Barcelona, Baghdad, Borač, Belfast, Bahrain, Buenos Aires. You'll have lunch with a mobster and drinks with an IRA member, share your boat with a corpse and get naked with a student. You'll lose your heart in Oahu and shed your inhibitions in Seville, search for your son among the ruins in Cambodia and meet the brother you never knew in France. You'll get divorced and married, sick and healed, lost and found. Such is the way of travel.

If your passport has been stamped a few times, you probably already know that the surest method of keeping your travel fire alive is by reading and telling tales from the road, passing them along like a torch in a relay race. And if you haven't yet traveled but aspire to, I hope this book provides the fan to turn your own spark of interest into a blaze of inspiration. Either way, consider this your invitation into the community of the thirty-three incredible women whose stories make up this year's anthology. They think you might have caught the travel bug, and they want to talk to you about it.

—LAVINIA SPALDING
San Francisco, California

ஃ ஃ ஃ

Masha

Two women, one skirt, and an untold story.

The first time I met Maria Konstantinovna, she was wearing a black leather skirt. It was Italian, brand new, and it was mine.

Masha, as I would come to know her, was a *dejournaya* in Moscow. Women like her sat on every floor in every hotel in the Soviet Union. They performed a range of duties—they served tea from a samovar that simmered behind their station. They ordered your phone call to America and came to wake you if it ever went through. They even washed lingerie and t-shirts, leaving the latter folded like fine envelopes, whiter than they ever deserved to be. They also handed out your room key with varying degrees of suspicion, charm, or ennui, and if you wanted to leave it for safekeeping, collected it when you left the floor. But allegedly, the real purpose of these hall monitors was to observe your comings and goings on behalf of the security apparatus of the Kremlin.

It was my second trip to Cold War Moscow.

One year earlier, I had arrived there with a new degree in Russian Studies and stayed in an old hotel in the center of town. On nights when I drank too much Georgian champagne, I crossed the street and walked alone past the cupolas and red brick walls of Red Square. Now I was back as a tour guide of sorts, a liaison, for groups of doctors who were on continuing education junkets. I was a translator, a babysitter, holder of boarding passes and whipping post if need be when tempers grew hot traveling around the Soviet Empire—which they often did. It was part of my job description to be cheerful, but when my busload of jet-lagged gastroenterologists and I arrived at our hulking mass of a hotel, I despaired.

Our official Intourist guide told us it had been built in 1979 to house athletes and guests for the Olympics the following year. That much was obvious; it was a model Soviet vanity project, from the monstrous scale to the banners out front which erupted with optimism: "Onward!" they proclaimed. Across the street was a giant park devoted to the fruits of socialism, as well as a massive Space Obelisk. Inside, it was as sprawling and noisy as a city, and the air was dense with cigarette smoke and the grease from several restaurants.

Prior to my trip, a fellow tour guide had informed me that there were fiber-optic cables installed in every room, and that the entire twenty-fifth floor was devoted to surveillance. He claimed to have stumbled upon a wall of reel-to-reel tape recorders there. President Reagan had just given his Evil Empire speech, and the country was being run by an ex-KGB chief, Yuri Andropov.

Paranoia was everywhere—in bars and on park benches where we changed dollars for rubles on the black market with people we had no reason to trust and who must have assumed we were listening to *them*.

As my new job paid little and I would depend on tips, I was eager to prove myself. But the first morning I woke up with a foggy head and aching limbs. So with apologies for being sick on day one, I loaded my fourteen physicians and their spouses onto the coach with their Russian guide and then repaired back upstairs, hungry for my bed. I peeled my clothes off and crawled in naked. The sheets were coarse cotton and delightfully crunchy, and the duvet still held a welcoming hint of my own body warmth.

I woke up to the sight of two men going through my suitcase at the foot of the bed. One man's arm was buried in a zipper compartment; the other man was turned toward the window, holding my raincoat up to the light.

"What are you doing?" I asked. Russian literature was full of fever dreams, and I believed I was having one. The clarity was dazzling—two guys in blue shirts, the older one with a pale smoker's complexion and hair all neat like a little boy on school picture day. The younger one had gray eyes that betrayed a flicker of menace, as if I were the one intruding.

Startled, the older man dropped the raincoat into the suitcase.

I was shivering and drew the comforter tightly around my bare body, sleeping bag-style.

"Excuse me," he declared. "We thought you were out."

They scrambled out the door and soon I fell backwards into sleep.

The next day, while my group toured Lenin's tomb, I sat on the bus sweating, too ill to move. I had not spoken of my visitation the previous day. Many of my charges already supposed they were being watched; some were amused and some downright scared. They whispered to each other about the presumed KGB sightings and enjoyed the Cold War folklore. But they were all doctors and their American guide was sick, so they insisted on taking me back to the hotel.

I dragged myself through the lobby, into the elevator, down the hallway that was thick with the rotten-fruit smell of disinfectant. My feet carried me, quicker now, to my room, to that delicious, warm bed. The *dejournaya* station was empty. I had wordlessly passed her that morning, not stopping to leave my key. She had glanced up from her book and smiled, which was unusual for a key lady. I had noticed her wide-set green eyes.

And there she was, inside my room, wearing my skirt. She was curvier than I, and the waistband stretched tightly around her middle. The leather pulled across her hips sexily, as if the utterly random act of wearing a stranger's clothes gave her an air of danger and power. She held a pair of black high heels that I had packed along with the skirt—I knew I would never wear them on my tour of Moscow and Central Asia, but they were new and expensive, and I didn't want to leave them in the closet of my shared New York apartment. Her own satin blouse was unbuttoned; the frayed remains of trim drifted around the cups of her bra, which, at least a size too small, pinched her ribcage and crushed her breasts.

"*Bozhe moi*," she said. Oh my God.

"It's O.K., really." What else could I say to this poor, mortified creature? "I just need to sleep."

"Just a moment," she said. One at a time, with two hands, she bent to place my shoes on the floor, toes pointed straight ahead like loaves on a baking sheet.

"Just a moment," she repeated, unzipping with shaky fingers. I turned my head so as not to see her Soviet-issue panties, hoping at least she wore some. She nodded deferentially, her face creased with shame. In what seemed like one move, she slipped on her wool skirt and stepped into her shoes. She shuffled her breasts around, rearranging them as if to make room in her bra, and fastened her blouse.

I waved her out the door, saying, "Don't worry, don't worry. Please!"

I scanned the room, flipped through my suitcase. Only my make-up case looked disturbed, with pencils, brushes, and compacts strewn about the dresser. Strangely, despite my exhaustion and the fever that addled my brain, I knew I wasn't angry. Rather, I pitied her embarrassment at being caught. Whoever this woman was, she was now exposed and compromised, and I wanted her to know that I, at least, didn't care.

I fell fully clothed into bed.

When I woke up, she was sitting at her station and rose to greet me when I came down the hall. She seemed taller and more beautiful, having regained her composure, and must have been twenty-five or twenty-six, a few years older than I.

"Do you want tea?" she asked.

"Yes, please," I answered. "What's your name?"

"Maria Konstantinovna," she replied, using her patronymic rather than her last name. "Masha."

"I'm Marcia too," I said. In Russian, they sounded the same. "Is there anything to eat?"

She walked me back to my room, where I stripped down to my underwear and slipped into bed. Soon, Masha returned with rolls, cheese, and black tea. I drifted in and out of sleep. At times, I could hear the door swish open and closed or feel her swab my face with a damp cloth. Once I sat up to sip some tea and felt her hands bolster my shoulders, brace me as I lowered myself back to the mattress, and finally tuck the covers under my chin.

"I'm not working tomorrow," she said. I looked at her, puzzled. "I think you will be well enough to leave for Tashkent."

"Thanks to you, I think I will be," I said.

I had not mentioned my itinerary to her, but she knew. The next day would be our last in Moscow, as we were flying to Uzbekistan the following morning. In the room, the shades were drawn. There was still daylight behind them, but I had no idea what time it was. Loud voices erupted in the corridor, and Masha stood to return to her station.

"I'll be back in a few weeks. May I bring you something from America?" I asked.

She pressed the starched napkin that rested underneath the tea glass, and held her finger there while her eyes caught mine. I could see the corner of a folded square of paper, which I later slipped between my fingers and tucked into my wallet.

Within a month, I returned with another group of doctors, this time seventeen thoracic surgeons. At the airport, an agent had confiscated *Vogue* and *Newsweek*, but I still had the illustrated collection of Pushkin fairytales Masha had requested. She wanted the book, she wrote in her note, to read to her young son. At the Russian bookstore in New York City, I had easily procured what was impossible to find in the shortage-ravaged Soviet Union. Of course, I brought a few extra things—a leather handbag stuffed with lip gloss, eye shadow, red licorice. The scene had never left my mind—her open shirt, the tattered lingerie, and her eyes that shifted around mine until that moment of comprehension and convergence: had our fates been reversed, I would have discovered the Italian skirt from the depths of *her* luggage. And I would have slipped it on as she had done to see myself reflected, just once, in something beautiful.

Right after checking in, I hopped the elevator to my old floor and found the on-duty *dejournaya*.

"Is Maria Konstantinovna working today?" I asked.

"She left," the woman answered.

"For the day, or for good?" I asked.

"I don't know," she said, and turned to rearrange the keys, inviting no further questions.

Over the next six months, I was back at the hotel several times with the book in my bag, but I never saw Masha again. In the winter of 1986, I returned to Moscow, this time with an American television network. Change was afoot, Mikhail Gorbachev was in power, and *glasnost* was the order of the day. I was low man on the nightly newscast I worked for, but in those days it still meant I had a car and driver. Snow fell gently, unstoppably, on the black Volga sedan. My old hotel seemed closer to town than I remembered.

She wasn't there.

Rounding the circular drive to leave, I recalled a brief embrace Masha and I had shared at the end of the one day we knew each other. I had recognized her perfume—Amazone—because it had come from my own bottle.

Over the years, I returned many times to Moscow.

I went with Peter Jennings, Barbara Walters, and *60 Minutes*. Each time, I packed that book of fairytales, and each time I journeyed out beyond the Space Obelisk, past the All-Russia Exhibition Center, to the ever-forbidding hotel. Always a fool's errand, to be sure. And each time I got off the elevator, I swallowed harder as I confronted the empty space she once occupied.

After an eighteen-year absence, I recently returned to Moscow. As I packed, I slipped the slim, orange book into my suitcase. I was, frankly, surprised when I found it on the bookshelf, after six moves, a couple of renovations, and decades of neglect. The stories were in Russian so I never read them to my own kids, yet there it was, shelved patiently, a talisman to guilt, gratitude, and unfinished business.

Even though Moscow had changed beyond recognition, I hadn't. Nor had the feeling of dread and sensory overload I experienced when I got to the hotel where Masha worked the day shift twenty-seven years ago. The lobby was still garish, but now it was loud with Italian cafés and gift shops selling nesting dolls and amber jewelry. A large man in a suit would not allow me to pass beyond his checkpoint to the elevators, so I went to the front desk.

"Would it be possible to go to the fifth floor?" I asked the receptionist. "I'm researching a book."

"You are writing something on the hotel?" she asked.

"Not really...." I hesitated. "Well, yes."

"What is the nature of your project?" she asked.

"Actually," I said, "years ago, I met someone here."

Her face softened. "I understand," she said, and turned. "Just a minute."

Within seconds, an official-looking woman approached me at the desk.

"Please leave your passport," she said, "and we'll go upstairs."

I handed it to the receptionist and was ushered past the guard.

"Do you still have *dejournayas*?" I asked.

"Yes, of course. It is not the same as it was. Mostly, they just take care of the floor."

"Can we please stop on five?" I ventured. She pressed the elevator button.

"Twenty-five is the only floor non-guests may see," she stated.

The doors opened.

There was no sign of tape recorders, only a fancy carpet runner and an eerie stillness that bore the echo of empty rooms. There was no *dejournaya*, either, and certainly no Masha. As we strolled back down the corridor, I murmured niceties about the lovely, modern décor.

Back in the elevator, I took out the book and turned to "The Tale of Tsar Saltan," the great writer's most famous children's story about the prince who saves the life of a swan, who in turn becomes a beautiful princess. The illustrations were simple but unremarkable, and I skimmed through the pages, stopping at a drawing of a bird flying across a starry violet sky. I closed the book and put it in my bag. It seemed that Masha had at last given it to me.

For all I knew, she emigrated, and I had passed her on a New York City sidewalk. Maybe she got sick or simply quit her job that day and was somewhere in Moscow now, her son grown. Perhaps she did vanish one night in that hazy time right before her country's sea change.

I would never find out. Masha was in my life so briefly it shouldn't have mattered. But to this day, I have not known comfort like the sound of her footsteps padding in and out of my hotel room as I sweltered with fever. I was twenty-three, in a strange land, nursed by the hands of a woman who, but for the clothes, might have been me.

ℰ℘ ℰ℘ ℰ℘

Marcia DeSanctis spent years traveling the world as a network news producer and is now writing a memoir. Her work has been in Vogue, Departures, The New York Times Magazine, The Christian Science Monitor, More, Princeton Alumni Weekly, *and the* Huffington Post. *She loves to travel alone and her idea of heaven is arriving at a new place, opening the hotel room door, checking out what candy is in the mini-bar, and then heading outside to explore her new, temporary neighborhood. She tries to pinpoint a place to have her coffee every morning and always ducks into a pharmacy. She loves to bring home toothpaste or a jar of vitamins as souvenirs. This story won the Grand Prize Silver Award in the Fifth Annual Solas Awards (BestTravelWriting. com).*

Returning

So you think you can dance?

The last time I lived here it was different. Jessica was sixteen and her dreams revolved around an evangelical pastor who cried during sermons, but now she has a boyfriend. The last time I lived in Val's small house tucked on the hill, I could sleep during gunfire. In the emerald-green city of Rio de Janeiro I spent every night with Val's grandson resting on my chest. Now I wait for the baby who is no longer a baby to remember me—the baby who was born on the crest of December before summer turned the city into a blazing inferno and everyone studied me with concern to see if my gringa disposition meant I would melt, or combust, or simply just die.

Now I wait for the tough skin I had to grow back and I slam my hand against Val's leg when twenty fireworks erupt at once—celebrations for St. George, the patron dragon slayer of Rio, the guardian of drug traffickers.

Some things, however, I don't have to wait for. Things I didn't learn and therefore cannot lose. Things like the elusive, hungry rhythm of samba steps. No matter how many times I attempted them, I always resembled a drunken pretzel. I was a dance major, for crying out loud, trained to figure out steps. But this samba, this prancing, happy-foot, crazy-hip dance—it never rested in my body. Even after hours of placing my hands on Val's hips as she swished and swayed to the samba beat of her stereo, I still hadn't imbued its essence. My samba fate was predestined. I came back to Rio in 2010 with no plans to alter destiny.

In 2006, the baby cried nonstop. We all took turns nestling Jon Pedro into our bodies like a skirt fold, keeping his sharp, defiant shouts at bay. But he was quietest against my beating heart, and I felt a secret pride and a connection I liked to imagine as special. Now he has a full head of kinky curls that shake ever so slightly even when he doesn't move. He looks at me noncommittally. It's been four years, and I am merely another adult in the maze of big people that pepper his world. A white woman his sister refers to as Auntie.

Val is laughing recklessly as I make fun of myself in her high-heeled shoes, pretending to be Brazilian, doing my best impersonation of a dancer at carnival. She calls her daughters in to watch. Tears are streaming down my face I am laughing so hysterically.

Then the music ends and Val's voice is serious, "Jo, don't try so hard. You can't conquer movement. It conquers you."

I take off her shoes and sit by Jessica's boyfriend. I reach my hand out toward Jon Pedro and he saunters off into the kitchen. I listen for more fireworks, but all I hear is gunfire.

Jessica and I walk the hills of the Santa Teresa neighborhood, lined with crumbling blue and pink mansions and the tracks of an ancient streetcar. In Santa Teresa, locals council you to follow the trail of the tracks so you will never end up anywhere deserted. Before this walk, Val pulled me into the corner of the bedroom and whispered fiercely for me to "talk some sense into Jessica, she spends too much time with her boyfriend!" Jessica's coffee eyes glint in the streetlamp and she entangles her fingers in mine. I chew on the weight of Val's words in the midst of her daughter's sweet delight.

"I prayed every day for a man like Daniel. My Mom thinks I focus more on him than on my own life. But I asked for him and here he is. Not paying attention would just be ungrateful."

I nod my head and squeeze her hand. I remember walking into Val's house to find Jessica sitting cross-legged in her underwear enduring the stifling heat with a smile and a Bible spread open at her feet. "I just like to sit with it," she had said. "It makes me feel peaceful."

Two days later I'm at a Mother's Day party with Val, her entire clan, and fifty other people I've never met, but who kiss me right on the lips when they find out I am "Val's Jo." I sit with a can of soda and watch Val and Jessica dance samba circles around each other, hip bones hitting points in the air as if their hip bones had lips and the points were a child with a sweet face or a lover with an open mouth. Four excited senhoras are suddenly at my side, chattering about how they've heard I am desperate to learn samba.

Me? Desperate? "No, no," I assure them. "You must have misunderstood. I desperately can*not* samba—really, don't waste your time." Oh but they are persistent, with voices that rise and fall like waterfalls on rocks in caves and so I let them tug me and nudge me until I please them with my seemingly valiant effort. I don't believe I've learned anything new, but they encourage me as I imagine they would encourage a sweet foreigner who gives their national dance a sincere talking to.

Val notices the commotion and pulls me toward her and Jessica to join their secret samba society. I let her take me farther into the dance, because it's Val and it's Mother's Day and I am in Brazil. And that's when, instead of trying to understand the rhythm, the rhythm all at once understands me. I flash on an image of a little girl in a white dress entering the center of a samba circle. Her dancing parents are in the center of the group when she breaks in to join them. Her dad's head tilts down, and his fingertips tap the rim of his hat. Her mom's eyes are closed, sweat glistening on her breastbone, strappy red sandals cracking against the cement. The girl wiggles off beat for a moment while the drummers cheer and pick up their tempo—and then without warning, a rhythm that has simply been acquainting itself with her teeny body abruptly remembers she is a long-lost family member. It sees her and knows her and so she dances.

Val's excitement makes her voice ring like bells. Her eyes become round as suns as she hollers to her entire family, "Come watch Jo! Come watch Jo samba!"

I feel the difference. The light exuberance of every click-clack that my heel snaps, the cotton-candy weightlessness of my hips. The whole circle of people—Val's family—are clapping their hands and stomping their feet instinctively, the way fellow dancers and onlookers in a samba circle do to encourage the rhythm the sambista is articulating with her body. Instead of shying away, I point frantically to Val's feet. She whips off her high heels and I slip into them in one fluid movement.

I understand now why this rapid trembling, why this deceptively simple-looking step brings so much ecstasy to its worshippers. I feel like a child with a new word that is so satisfying I must repeat it over and over again. As I ricochet the rhythm off my joints and entangle it in my muscles, and as this crowd of people I love roar their celebration, I see a head of thick curls bound into the circle. The baby who is no longer a baby pushes his way through the legs of his uncle and begins shaking his tiny, chubby body at my feet. His eyes shine, sweat drips down the back of my neck, and he claps his tiny hands, saying my name over and over again, like a chant.

♫ ♫ ♫

Jocelyn Edelstein has spent extensive time in Brazil dancing, making friends, and making documentaries. In addition to the samba of Rio de Janeiro, she has attempted maracatu *on Brazil's northeastern coast, tango in Buenos Aires, and flamenco in Barcelona. She currently lives in Portland and teaches hip-hop dance to teenagers.*

✌ ✌ ✌

Elvis Has Entered the Casa

A writer receives a welcome interruption.

"*¡Hay yogurt!*"

"*¡Hay yogurt!*" shouts the man, thin as the daily newspaper, but sinewy strong like most *campesinos* here.

On good days, vendors weave through my Havana housing block peddling homemade yogurt, but also socks, brooms, fresh eggs smudged with chicken shit, squid, and sponge cake. On bad days, it's bleach or peanuts or nothing at all. Such scarcity makes for a unique alertness that has me cocking an ear at every vendor's call.

Mangoes in June, lettuce in January, and calabaza all year round roll up in a wheelbarrow pushed by Luis, a blue-black bear of a man, who is at turns avuncular or chiding, depending on how much you buy.

"Hey cheapskate!" he calls up affectionately to my husband, who rarely patronizes Luis and his rolling produce stand, no matter how voluptuous the tomatoes or the season's first eggplant.

"Hi bandit!" my husband responds with a smile.

"Why would I pay double for the same limes I can get at the market for half the price?" my husband asks me in that maddening, didactic way that burdens even simple queries with deeper meaning. In Cuba, little is ever rhetorical, and certainly not when it pertains to money. As if I didn't grow up poor. As if I didn't know from leftovers and shaving mold off otherwise edible food. Does my husband see me as some materialistic American on whom the value of money is lost and the concept of thrift foreign? I get this from strangers in heavy doses, who assume I've landed in Cuba on a lark, temporarily slumming in socialist scarcity until my real life, abundant and individualistic, resumes somewhere across the Straits.

"Of course we'd rather not pay double, *mi vida*, but without limes we can't make the yucca sauce tonight."

My morning writing session is not going well. The cigarette factory across the street is belching toxic particles into my office and my fancy earplugs are proving useless against the backhoes breaking rocks nearby. My eyes drift. I feel procrastination creeping in. I run a business card between the rows of my keyboard, picking out bits of dust, stray hairs, and popcorn hulls. My mind wanders. The thrum of the backhoe is suddenly cut through by the sing-song of the flower lady.

"*¡Flores!*"

"*¡Flores!*"

I go to the pane-less window, widening the wooden slats for a look. Her bicycle basket is overflowing with wild roses, butterfly jasmine, and heavy-headed sunflowers. I love that a fat bouquet here is just ten pesos—the cost of a pack of gum back home. I'm thinking of buying some jasmine to try to mask the factory's nasty nicotine smell when there's a knock at the door.

It's not the coded *rat-a-tat-tat* of my neighbor, who's convinced that a lone American woman working at home is a prime victim for some hobbyist robber. It must be someone else. The president of the block association with news of our next meeting? The honey man who sells door-to-door rather than pushing his black market wares on the street? Maybe it's the electric company guy here to collect the twelve pesos for last month.

It could be any of these people on any given day, something to which I'm still growing accustomed. Mostly I ignore these intrusions, wishing everyone would just leave me to do all the oddball, possibly suspicious, foreigner things they imagine me to be doing. But unanswered knocks always leave me feeling guilty— like I'm shirking some social(ist) duty. Which is how I find myself tiptoeing around my apartment and turning down the radio. *Can they hear me?* I wonder, before realizing this is how the cycle of compulsion-compliance works. This is what it means to go native.

Cleaning keyboard crud is no reason to ignore the person knocking at my door right now, however. Nor does it matter that my hair isn't brushed or that remnants of last night's celebration are strewn about the living room.

"*¡Momento!*" I yell. Pulling my hair back and clipping it fast to my head, I search for a pair of shorts to exchange for the too-micro mini I'm wearing.

I open the door to a buxom black lady holding a clipboard. Her dark hair is piled high and run through with a wide, white stripe, as if she was shocked by something tragic right before landing on my doorstep.

I recognize her gray uniform with the round blue insignia. She's a public health inspector, part of Project Dengue, which sends teams house to house looking for the standing water that breeds the disease-transmitting mosquitoes. Recently my neighbor warned me about gangs of young men dressing up like these inspectors and being ushered into people's homes, only to walk out with televisions, blenders, and computers, trailing threats of violence. But this woman doesn't look the thieving type.

"*Buenos días,*" she says with a tired smile as she steps through the door. I close the metal gate behind her with a clang.

"Do you have any devotional vessels?" she asks, taking a turn around our living-dining area furnished in a style I call Just Better than Dorm Room.

"No?" I respond in the guessing manner of immigrants still struggling with an adopted culture.

Devotional vessels? Like Noah's Ark or the Holy Grail? Some generic chalice perhaps? At times like these I feel three years old, unable to verbalize what I'm thinking or feeling. It seems my life here is defined by such awkward linguistic exchanges; too often I find myself lurching from one confusing situation to the next with a single thought running through my head: *I have no fucking idea what this person is talking about.*

"Any flower vases?" she asks.

"No."

"May I inspect the back?"

"Sure." Along with becoming a crack interpreter of context and gesture, living in a foreign language has also made me adept at the one-word response.

I lead her from the living room toward the back balcony, passing through the railroad kitchen reminiscent of a Lower East Side squat. The counter is dusted with crumbs from this morning's toast, the sink piled high with dirty dishes. I hope she doesn't notice. Another symptom of going native here is caring—inordinately—what other people think.

Out back, there's a narrow balcony with a concrete sink for scrubbing clothes and a short length of line for drying. The inspector peers into the drain before throwing some powder the color and texture of human remains into the dark, stagnant water. We make our way single file back into the apartment. She asks for the hygiene inspection paper that all Cuban homes have taped to the inside of the front door and makes some cryptic notations.

Putting one hand to her thick neck glistening with sweat, she checks her watch. "It's only 11:00, and already it's been a long day."

To my surprise, I take the cue. "Would you like some water? Coffee?" I'm certain my voice belies my native New Yorker agoraphobic tendencies.

"*Agua*," she says, handing me back the inspection paper with a soft smile.

"It's boiled," I tell her, handing her a glass of water that she gulps down fast, in three swallows. "To savor" does not figure in the Cuban vernacular.

"You should always boil your water, especially in summer," she says.

I surprise myself for the second time today, pulling out one of the iron chairs that in another context would be patio furniture.

"What about this heat?" she asks, accepting my invitation to sit.

I nod.

"Do you have kids?" I ask, sticking to another universal topic.

"Four. I'm a single mother. *No es fácil.*"

"No. It's not easy," I agree, thinking of my own mom. Not easy at all.

She asks if I have kids, and I realize I've set my own trap—even seemingly safe conversation topics aren't always so in Cuba. I find myself groping once again for an answer to the kid question. I'm at that age after all, and here, where children are cherished above everything else, it's strange for me to have none. My reasoning, however, is as foreign to them as devotional vessels are to me: I just don't want them.

"No," I say, smiling, changing the subject. "What's your name?"

"Carmen, but everyone calls me Elvis."

"Elvis? Like the singer Elvis?"

She nods.

"Why?"

"Just a nickname that stuck."

Elvis reaches across the table for the bottle of Cuervo left out from last night's party.

"What's this?" she asks, hefting the square bottle. "Whiskey?"

"No. Tequila. Do you know it?"

She shakes her head. I'm pretty sure she's never heard of the stuff—I don't know if you can even buy Cuervo in Cuba. Certainly Elvis can't: you'd have to be very rich by local standards to afford something so esoteric and imported. Luckily, we have a good friend from Tampico who comes to Cuba every year bearing gifts.

"It's Mexican. Want to try it?" I ask with a sly grin.

"I shouldn't," Elvis says, touching her clipboard, her eyes at once bright with curiosity.

"Come on, *¡aprovechar!*" Seize the opportunity! She laughs huskily, giving in.

I run to the kitchen and grab one of the tiny teacups with purple and pink flowers we use to drink the sweet, dark coffee Cuba is known for. Dumping a mound of salt into a matching saucer, I cut off a wedge of lime (thanks, Luis!) and hustle back to the front room before she changes her mind. Moving aside her clipboard, I fill the teacup and place it in front of her with the saucer of salt.

"Fill that little triangle between your thumb and forefinger with salt. Then eat the salt, throw back the tequila and suck on the lime." I'm miming the action as I explain it, hoping she doesn't insist I go first; explaining why I don't drink is trickier than explaining why I don't breed.

She looks at me questioningly as she grabs the pinch of salt and sprinkles it on her hand.

"¡Vaya!" I say, giving her a wedge of lime and a smile.

She licks her hand and throws back the shot. Her eyes bulge as she sucks on the lime. I can almost taste the sharp, earthy tequila burning its way down her throat.

"Aaach. ¡Fuerte!" she winces. But her eyes are dancing. I can see she's thrilled with the new experience—precious matter in a life that's rote and mind-numbingly dull too much of the time. Elvis thanks me with a few quick shakes of her head as she tries to loosen that spicy echo tequila always leaves.

"I have to get back to work," she tells me, collecting her clipboard and pencil.

"Me too," I agree, walking her to the door.

"Hey Elvis. What's a devotional vessel?"

She looks at me quizzically, her head cocked to one side, as if she's considering a question she's never been asked. "They're glasses of water you put beside pictures of your dead family, so they won't be thirsty in the afterlife."

Elvis is smiling as she makes her way up the stairs to inspect my neighbor's home.

"Have a good day!" I call after her.

I'm smiling too, as the door clicks shut and the back-hoe roars to life.

Я℈ Я℈ Я℈

Havana-based journalist and author Conner Gorry covers Cuban health and medicine for MEDICC Review—*a privileged gig that has sent her to post-quake scenarios in Pakistan and Haiti with disaster relief teams, as well as deep inside the Cuban health system. She has written more than a dozen guidebooks for Lonely Planet and Countryman Press and maintains* Here is Havana—*a blog about life on the "wrong" side of the Straits—on 56Kbps dial-up while smoking her daily five-cent cigar.*

❧ ❧ ❧

Of Mountains and Men

Stuck between a rock and a heart place in India.

*I*t had to be India. Continents and countless countries later, of course it would happen here. I should take my compass and put a heart over magnetic north, the pull is so strong. The impression I give of single adventurous woman—so brave—is just a front. I can navigate myself from Novosibirsk to Mendoza, transcend language barriers, go hungry, and dine with royalty. I can go thirty days without a bath and step out of the trek into luxury. Yes, I am adventurous, independent, not one to be waylaid by something as simple as love. Yet there I was, stopped in my tracks on a sidewalk in India by a mere human, and blue-eyed at that.

Thank goodness he's with a woman, I thought. *I can continue on my journey unfettered.* It's a small town in Northern India. I see them at a restaurant. I see him at a party later, alone. There's an ethereal veil that

India always drapes in front of me, and I am hopelessly seduced by the flickering candles and incense. The candlelight is necessary, of course, due to an absence of electricity, and the cloying incense covers and enhances the smells of something deeper, rotting, animal. I have been terminally seduced by India.

It is Holika Dahan, the night before Holi, a vibrant festival marking the coming of spring. Bonfires are lit across India in a ritual symbolizing victory of good over evil. Maybe it's the beer, the whiskey, the smoke in the air mingled with wild shadows cast by bonfires that catch me off-guard. He is playing with me from across the room and then has me backed against a crumbling stone wall. "A psychic told me once," he says, "that when I met my woman I would look into her eyes and it would be like looking in a mirror."

We were both born into this world with impossibly blue eyes. And *how* I have resisted my fair, Northern European roots, immersing myself first in the heart of Africa, where I experienced man's true capacity for cruelty and kindness, suffering and beauty, beauty in suffering. Later I became hooked on Asia—China, Tibet, Nepal, India—convinced that in past lives these were my homes.

But my first love is the one that never changes—my love for the mountains, some attainable, some eternally humbling in their untouchable majesty. There are the rock stars and the unforgettable first glimpse that grabs your breath, frightens, tantalizes: Everest, Ama Dablam, the Matterhorn. Some of these mountains I will navigate, struggling up their flanks to the summit. Others, it is only that first view—branded into my psyche, permanently tattooed into my core—that remains as much a part of me as my arms and legs.

We have come to India this time to climb and ski a peak just under twenty thousand feet, with radically steep chutes coming down the north face. Hanuman, the monkey god of courage and intellect, the god of wind and hope, will be our spiritual guide as we four women attempt to be the first to ever ski this mountain face.

Usually we arrive in town, buy supplies in the market, stuff ourselves with curries and Tiger Beer, and head out. Never have I been so haunted by a blue-eyed stranger, nor left so off-balance, giddy, and insecure. I worry that he has fed this same line to each of my exotic, beguiling teammates. But I say nothing to them, choosing instead to linger in the tingle of the fragile state of an awakening heart—as risky to me as ice falls and avalanches.

The party is winding down. We have an early start ahead. It feels fortuitous to be taking a helicopter drop deep in the mountains to begin our journey on the first day of Holi. Over the next ten days, we will ascend one side of the mountain and ski its massive face. We're exhilarated, tense, nervous, serious, and acutely aware of the immensity of the mission ahead of us. He presses his face against mine in the shimmering firelight, kisses my cheek with purpose, and asks if, please, we can share a dinner when I return. That is all he wants. The pressure and heat of his kiss linger as he retreats into the shadows.

Holi in India is an explosion of sound and color, one of India's biggest spring festivals. As we head to our launching spot in the morning, we're met with streams of brightly colored dyes and water balloons flung by revelers young and old in the streets. The bombs of color are tossed at passersby with the intention of blessing, but not without a mixture of jubilance and aggression. We begin our journey with hair and faces streaked like brilliant neon rainbows. Loaded in the helicopter with the supplies we'll carry for the next two weeks, he is there, piloting our journey in. Landing us up a steep valley at the base of our climb, he hands me rough hand-knit wool socks, a gift for all of us. Like Christmas stockings, they're stuffed with sweets, a deck of playing cards, and a tiny bottle of whiskey. As quickly as the heli drops us, it's gone. First the flurry of mad rotor wash, then just us, the silence and the looming mountains. As it has been so many times in the past, this is where it begins for us, where our work as a team of strength and determination kicks in.

At first the body is always adjusting. After being in town for long stretches, sleeping in beds, surrounded by electricity and its pulses, we have to return to a more natural state. The first days and nights we are more sensitive to the dramatic change in temperature. We're hot and cold, hungry then thirsty. As the days progress we eventually return to our more adaptable selves. We sleep four spooned in a small tent, and even our breath becomes synchronized.

The nights are starry, clear, sharp, and cold, the days hot. The reflection of sun on snow is almost more dangerous than the frigid black night. Life is reduced to pure existence. We spend evenings melting snow for water, eating, and sleeping. By day we pack up camp and navigate the winding glacier valley, practicing a pace that can go all day, carefully hydrating and nourishing ourselves. We ascend the glacier connected by a rope—our safety, our lifeline to each other, our umbilical cord. We develop an intimate, unerring belief in each other's strength and steadiness. We wind our way up, crossing delicate bridges of snow over gaping crevasses. If anyone were to fall, the others would be responsible for her anchor and rescue. Every day we must trust each other implicitly with our lives.

Nothing is taboo in the tent; all topics are open for discussion. But I am holding this brief flirtation in town secret and sacred. He stays in my thoughts and dreams. In the high clear air, our dreams become vivid—often lucid—and by day we have hour upon hour to break them down in thoughts and conversations. I am so filled with admiration for my teammates, it's impossible to look at them and not assume that any man would choose one of them over me; such are our quiet insecurities. I can't quite believe he hasn't whispered the same sweetnesses in their ears. These woman have traveled the world, speak multiple languages; they have graced magazine covers and been in movies. They're strong and sinewy, beautiful and smart, and I am constantly enchanted. One night I tentatively bring it up over a game of cards. They all laugh at my apprehension and react as only girlfriends can: "Oh, this is very exciting—we finally have something new to talk about!"

The peak towers above us for days, frightening in its enormity yet somehow reassuring in its solidity, the very tip a white granite that changes color with the sky throughout the day. By evening the snow and granite glow impossibly golden pink. The weather stays consistent: hot by day, frigid by night, ideal for travel—but also perfect avalanche conditions. The wide swings in temperature cause crystals to form faceted layers, creating unstable snow conditions. We are approaching the day of our summit, now sleeping and steadily climbing comfortably at over eighteen thousand feet. With one giant face left above us, we decide tomorrow will be the day.

The tent is serious that night, everything a little more difficult in this cold, at this altitude. We melt enough

snow to cook, hydrate, and get us through the night and
conceivably a very long day to follow. We will head for
the summit to ski down a nearly 7,000-foot couloir off
the top, complete with two ice walls that we'll need to
set anchors in and lower over with ropes. There is no
room for error. And no room to think about blue-eyed
strangers.

We set out in the early alpine dark and by sunrise
are frustrated and scared. Hilaree, my adventure mate
for years, battles frostbitten toes and we are wallow-
ing, sometimes up to our waist, in dangerous layers of
unsupportable snow. We regroup to calculate our risks,
evaluating whether to continue to the summit or ski
off a lower shoulder. Reluctantly, we admit we have no
other choice but to ski down to a slightly lower entrance
and drop onto the face from a different angle.

It still proves an undertaking—a first ski descent,
steep and exposed, of over 5,000 feet. It takes us several
hours with delicate and focused determination to ski the
couloir in sections until we reach the end of the snow
line. We take turns at first, going in on rope, testing the
snow conditions. One by one we sidestep in on our skis,
Hilaree coming in last without the rope, the Himalaya
providing a surreal and majestic backdrop. At first, with
so much exposed below, we ski one careful turn at a
time, in soft but ribbed snow.

Time becomes suspended, no past or future—just
purely breathe and turn. This is why we spend ten days
going up for just a few short hours coming down, to
experience true presence of moment. In the morning
warmth, rocks and ice chunks start to loosen and whiz
by us from above, reminding us to keep our pace steady
until we reach the line where snow finally meets rock.

We then hike with packs, laden with our supplies and

our skis, for eight hours more to a village, where we find a rough path that eventually takes us to a mountain pass. We flag down a truck, exhausted and jubilant.

It can be this way on expedition, as in life: one moment is the heat of battle, the next we're showered and drinking tea. How quickly one is transformed from living in perfect symbiosis with self and nature to being thrust back into the world of bright lights and motorized motion. The body that functioned flawlessly in the mountains becomes confused in this world of excessive noise and reflective surfaces. But for a brief time, the experience lingers and its essence protects you like a second, more perfect skin.

This is when he reappears. I am thin and strong from tremendous effort, glowing from hot water and cold Tiger beer. He appears in my sitting room and without hesitation swoops me, envelops me with his arms, smelling of man and tobacco. He's not accustomed to being the one waiting and worrying. It makes us elusive, exotic, erotic, desirable. "Can you stay?" is all he cares to know, and there is no other world that matters to me.

Oh but India, she is so tricky. This diaphanous veil, blown by the breeze, is easily ignited, reduced to ash. When your first love was a towering mountain named for gods, solid and unchanged by mood or weather, and when a man's first glimpse of you is in a moment of candlelit magic and mystery, reality can be unwelcome when it starts to seep in. Maybe it was never meant to leave India.

I haven't returned to the village. This is how I preserve that sweet dream realm of mutual love at first sight, knowing that it has never returned in the form of any flesh-and-blood man. Tricky, lovely India with her gypsy spirit—what makes some of us love her so much we can close our eyes and nearly taste her? Perhaps it's the fine line between mortal and immortal, abject horror and priceless grace, casting illusions that men can be compared to mountains, while behind the veil of incense and shadows, we are merely enchanted lovers full of hubris, trying to fill the footsteps of gods and goddesses.

ॐ ॐ ॐ

Kasha Rigby grew up in Vermont. She has skied since she could walk and began telemark skiing as a teenager. She joined The North Face Ski Team in 1995, which has brought her all over the world, making first descents of some of the most revered peaks, including the Five Holy Peaks in Mongolia. She is one of the few people in the world who has skied from over eight thousand meters. For almost twenty years, Kasha has traveled at least six months a year. Meanwhile, she practices the fine balance of gardening, friendship, music, and yoga. Although she left Vermont decades ago, she still carries a magically refilling bottle of maple syrup in her pack and swears it is the elixir of life.

Naked

In Korea, everything comes out in the wash.

"It's not that I don't like being naked," I had explained. "And I'm a big fan of bathing. Personal hygiene is one of my all-time favorite hygienes. It's just that spending the afternoon showering with my eight-year-old student and her mother makes me a bit uncomfortable, if you know what I mean."

"Of course. I understand completely," said Ji Young, my Korean co-teacher, nodding earnestly.

A few days later, Mrs. Kim is standing at my door holding a gift bag bursting with fluffy tissue paper.

"Thank you," I say, taking the bag. "Should I open this now?"

"Yes, yes," she says with a bright smile.

I rustle through the papery cocoon and retrieve a bottle of jasmine shampoo and a bright pink pouf. I'm confused.

"It for shower." Mrs. Kim says. "You need today."

Panic ripples through me. Why would I need jasmine-smelling shampoo and a bright pink pouf today? I was sure this whole business regarding a trip to the public bath was cleared up when I explained to Ji Young that a more suitable activity might involve visiting a Buddhist temple or taking a nice walk in the woods. Koreans do love their mountains.

"Um, I thought Ji Young talked to you about…"

"Yes."

I wait for her to say more, but she only continues to grin. Maybe she means I'll need to take a hot shower tonight after my long day of hiking and mingling with mountain monks.

"Ji Young say you ashamed body. But O.K. In Korea no problem."

First of all, I never said I was ashamed of my body. I silently curse Ji Young and her habit of misusing dictionary words—I've told her countless times that you can't always translate directly. Secondly, it *is* a problem. In my country taking baths with elementary school students generally results in jail time. I'd never make it in the slammer; my cellmates would kill me for being a pervert. I've heard convicts can be honorable like that.

"We go to sauna. Si Eun wait car. Very happy. Because you come."

"But…um…the thing is…" My stuttering isn't helping my case, nor is it diminishing Mrs. Kim's now Joker-esque grin. With great reluctance but feigned enthusiasm, I pack up my pouf and follow Mrs. Kim to her car.

I've been standing at my open locker for ten minutes, and the only thing I've taken off are my socks.

"Sarah!" Mrs. Kim calls out, and I see her completely naked body rapidly approaching. She walks without an ounce of insecurity, her steps singing a song of normalcy, as if showering with your daughter's English teacher is commonplace, like shopping for melons or hailing a cab.

I have to do it. I have to take my clothes off. Ironically, it's the fact that I'm still fully clothed that's making the situation awkward. I take a deep breath and start stripping with mad ferocity. I pause just briefly when I'm down to my underwear. This is the point of no return: the last barrier between pretending I'm vacationing on a topless beach in Europe and actually *being* naked. I quickly slip my thumbs under the elastic band, fling them off, and stuff them in my locker. I slam the door with a flourish, ostensibly shutting my clothes-wearing life behind me.

I try to wrap myself in the one towel I was given by the stingy locker room attendant, but let's face it—calling it a towel is like calling a pothole filled with rain the Pacific Ocean. It's a glorified washcloth.

"Good you ready. Yogurt. Here." Mrs. Kim says, handing me a little tub of kiwi-flavored yogurt.

"Oh, will we be using this on our skin?" I ask, bewildered.

"Ha ha, you so funny. Yogurt is snack for hungry!"

Of course: that makes sense. I often get hungry in the shower. I don't know why I've never thought to bring snacks before. Why stop at yogurt? Why not an Italian sub or a nice bundt cake? The steam would keep it moist.

"Sarah tee-cha!" Si Eun squeals as she comes barreling at me naked as a jaybird, happy as a lark. Seemingly oblivious to my nudity, she grabs my hand and pulls me toward the shower room.

"Come now, let's go!"

I'm shocked. This is the same child who shrieks in horror at the slightest sight of exposed skin when I lift my arm to write near the top of the blackboard. She has even gone so far as to run to the front of the class, tug at the bottom of my shirt, and give me a look as if to say, "Come on lady, let's keep it decent."

"Tee-cha! This way. *Baliwa*."

The shower room is hot, steamy, and bubbling over with bodies of all shapes and sizes: fat, thin, tall, small, flat, pert, saggy, smooth, round, tan, creamy. They are everywhere, a sprawling sea of sitting, squatting, walking, talking, lounging, scrubbing, soapy, sudsy bodies—an explosion of flesh. A little girl lies on the wet tile floor with her head lazily resting in the lap of her mother who nonchalantly plays with her hair while chatting to a friend shaving her armpits. Bodies are inching into hot pools, splashing in the cold pools, and brewing in the ones filled with green tea.

I try to stand casually but don't know how. My body betrays me with clumsy gestures that are designed to make me appear confident but achieve the exact opposite effect. Usually when I'm naked I'm alone. Or, if another person is involved, we're horizontal and the lights are dimmed. Luckily, I don't have to continue with this charade for long; Mrs. Kim is already leading me through the tangle of naked masses toward a tiny plastic shower stool, on which she promptly plunks me down. To my dismay, I'm now looking at myself in all my barren glory in the giant mirror facing me. I must mention that crouching on a miniature stool doesn't produce the most flattering of angles. I'm still letting the image sink in when I feel someone scrubbing my back, *hard*.

"Many spots. No good. Spots bye-bye," Mrs. Kim says gaily.

"Ouch. Um…actually, those are freckles and they don't come off."

"We make spots come off," she responds with a sudden fierce determination. "Si Eun, help wash tee-cha!"

"O.K. Really, this isn't necessary. Si Eun doesn't need to wash my back. That's just…weird…" I trail off.

But Mrs. Kim isn't relenting. Finally, I jump up, grab the soap, and begin demonstrating that I'm fully capable of cleaning myself, having done it for twenty-eight years now. Mrs. Kim doesn't seem pleased but gives up and instead uses her steel glove of death, similar to a cheese grater, to scour Si Eun's skin raw and red. When her daughter resembles a shriveled red chili pepper, Mrs. Kim is satisfied.

"Tee-cha, we play swimming now!" Si Eun says excitedly.

"Korea have special water," Mrs. Kim declares proudly as we come to a warm ginseng pool. "All baths water different. Secret for beautiful skin," I can't help but notice that Mrs. Kim does have lovely skin. In fact, most Korean women look ten years younger than their age and have a glow to them. This isn't the first I've heard about the "magical" sauna water, and I'm eager to slide into the mineral-rich magic where I can not only hide, but also emerge sleeker, newer, fresher.

Slowly, I begin to feel comforted and even a little liberated by the utter lack of modesty of the women surrounding me. My experience with naked women until now has been limited to my ex-boyfriend's girlie magazines, and it's a relief to see women who aren't

airbrushed or surgically sculpted, who are real and
fleshy and succumbing to gravity. Strange bodies are
everywhere: flat butts, mismatched nipples, jiggly limbs,
and way too much hair down south—yet in the myriad
variations, I feel a perfect sense of unity, because *nobody
cares*.

I suddenly realize that I like being naked. I like being
naked with these women. Instead of quietly slipping
into the next pool, instantly submerging myself to my
shoulders, I surprise myself and begin frolicking and
splashing about with the others, leaping from pool to
pool.

"Sarah, shower time!" Mrs. Kim calls out to me.
Didn't we already do that? I think. But who am I to question the system? They're the ones with the silky skin.

Mrs. Kim eagerly ushers me to another area where we
get to stand and wash the old-fashioned way. The showers are crowded, some sharing two to a nozzle. I stand
back to allow room and wait my turn.

"O.K. In Korea no problem," Mrs. Kim says as she
gives me a shove forward. I'm sandwiched between
two ladies brushing their teeth, talking and spitting
toothpaste down the drain. They're enamored with the
smell of my jasmine shampoo, so they borrow it. They
don't actually ask, but in their defense, they speak no
English—and they do give me cursory smiles before taking it. I don't mind. I smile back—a gesture understood
no matter what country your sauna is in.

"Coffee?" Mrs. Kim asks from the nozzle next to
mine.

"Sure," I answer. "Sounds good. Should we get
dressed?"

"No, no. Coffee here," she gestures toward the dry
sauna room. "With more mothers!"

❧ ❧ ❧

I can honestly say that not once in my life did I imagine I would someday conduct a parent-teacher conference in the buff.

Inside the sauna, the mothers squat shamelessly around a punch bowl on the floor filled with iced coffee. One of them ladles a cup and hands it to me expectantly. They are boisterous, eager, and all at once begin asking about their children. Does my daughter study hard? Does my son pay attention? How is her English progressing? Does he behave? Given the circumstances, I find it easiest to simply say, "Oh yes, very good student," which makes everyone happy.

As the mothers continue to ply me with questions and iced coffee, I squat beside them, sipping slowly. I am content, unhurried, and the thought of putting my clothes back on now seems constricting. I suppose I'll have to do it sooner or later, though. It is winter, after all.

❧ ❧ ❧

After graduating with a B.A. in Sociology, Sarah took a sabbatical from her distinguished waitressing career and traveled to South Korea to teach English. This move proved challenging as she had no formal training in the profession, a disinclination for children with sticky hands, and little knowledge of the basic usage of commas. (A problem, she still, has today.) Eight years later she is still traveling the globe. She has been a television host in Korea, a professor in Japan, a tree house dweller in Laos, a house painter in New Orleans, a sangria swiller in Spain, a dragon hunter in Indonesia, and a fishmonger in Australia. She is currently planning to make a plan for her next adventure.

ℜ ℜ ℜ

Beauty, Beauty

A teacher learns she doesn't have all the answers.

$\mathcal{M}$y students at the May Rodrigues Vocational Training Center are called "out-of-school-leavers," a Guyanese euphemism for high school dropouts. Every morning, eighty teenage girls giggle and saunter up the dirt road to the school, bright blue ribbons woven through their braids. From Tiger Bay, La Penitence, Albuoystown, they come from wooden shacks crowded with ten or twelve brothers and sisters. Without fail, their uniforms are washed and pressed: four pleats in the just-below-the-knee blue polyester skirt. They iron designs onto the backs of their simple white cotton blouses, elaborate geometries expanding out to the sleeve. Breakfast was black tea.

The school has just two full-time staff: a headmistress and a reading teacher. Twice a week, a hunchbacked grandma with thick glasses comes to instruct shorthand;

a young woman arrives two hours late every Wednesday to teach food and nutrition. Students squint in the half-darkened room—electricity is expensive—to complete a crochet chain stitch or thread a thick needle for a straw craft mat. I fill in where I can, calling out vowel sounds in my American accent and chalking the alphabet on a piece of plywood painted black.

Our girls are the ones no one else can manage: slow and sickly, or fast and trouble-making. Some have been expelled for having had "story," incidents with teachers or other students in their old schools. Some have been kept home for years to take care of younger siblings. Most can barely read and must learn a trade to get by. But a few are just too smart for the overcrowded city classrooms and are thrown in with the dropouts because there's nowhere else for them to go. One or two are brilliant. The most brilliant one I met was Onica Belle.

"Miss, Miss!" Onica calls to me as I ascend the wooden steps to the main schoolhouse. She is always out of breath. "Miss, for the swimming this week…" Big inhale, big exhale. "Miss, I have to buy swimming costume and Miss, Finella told me some at Bourda market, a lady selling used ones, Miss, but I didn't see them, Miss, ya seen them? Ya know where to shop them, Miss?"

"Well, I know that the market stalls by the post office…" I start, but she is off again.

"And Miss, for the concert, Miss, I want to do a dance but the other girls sayin' there's too many dances, Miss, maybe I'll read a poem, Miss? What do ya think, ya know any poems, Miss?"

Again, I begin to respond, and again she cuts me off, questions filling her mouth. My brain, already pickled by the searing midday heat, gives up quickly. I lean against the railing, sweating and dizzy.

"Miss, the book, Miss, ya promised me, to understand accounting, Miss, can ya get me the book, Miss? Promise I'll treat it nice, Miss, thanks, Miss. And Miss, I like ya skirt, Miss, the color nice, when ya gone back to New Yark, ya must leave it for me, O.K., Miss, O.K.?"

She is sixteen, bursting with IQ. My other students have boils from malnutrition, yellow eyes from jaundice, welts and scars from physical labor and beatings. Onica has words and energy. Her features are crammed together on her face but wildly animate when she speaks, and her hair is banded hastily at the nape of her neck. But her eyes steady as she copies notes from the board, dropping her litany of gossip. The dim room seems to close in on her body, tensed with curiosity, poised to learn. In class, she calls "Miss! Miss!" and shoots her hand up with the right answers every time.

In another country, another time, Onica would be promoted through the grades and deemed "gifted and talented." In Guyana, her extra brainpower is like a bird caught in a room with no window to escape.

"Belle! Belle!" we hear the Headmistress yell, and Onica skulks into the small corner office of the one-room schoolhouse. Her surname is a legacy of the brief French colonial rule in Guyana, after the Dutch, before the British. I wonder who else realizes that the Headmistress is calling for beauty, again and again.

Onica is talking to other girls' boyfriends behind their backs or tormenting the woman who sells food in the canteen. She seems contrite, but she'll be there the next afternoon for another offense. A few times her mother is called in, a short, rough-looking woman who pulls a tiny girl by the hand. She looks as overwhelmed by her daughter as we are. No one knows what to do with Onica Belle.

In late spring, the Headmistress sends Onica with me to pick up theater tickets, probably just to get her out of the school for the afternoon. We ride the minibus and she prattles on over the blasting music. When we arrive at a wooden house across from St. Joseph's Hospital, a woman comes to the door dressed only in a dirty slip. Two small children and an older girl join her, huddling in the shadows beyond the doorframe.

The woman's eyes are wide and protruding, the bones of her body expressed through her skin. "Thinning disease" the Guyanese call it. I catch myself staring and speak up. "Good afternoon, we have come to find out about tickets for the show," I say. The woman says nothing, and for a horrible moment I think we have disturbed a dying person for no reason.

"I'll send my daughter for them," she says slowly. The older girl recedes into the darkness, while Onica and I stand outside, sun beating down on our faces. She is peering into the squalid house, and the small children are staring up at me, wide-eyed in their ragged clothes. The girl returns and silently hands me the tickets across the threshold.

It is a perfect tropical day, but I'm chilled. I am twenty-two and a foreigner, unaccustomed to meeting death in a doorway. "Onica," I say, in a low voice. "I think that woman has AIDS."

She looks at me and laughs. "Miss, like ya frightened!" she says, then imitates me in a false whisper. "I think she has AIDS." She laughs again. "Nuff, nuff people got AIDS!" She shakes her head as if to say, *dis white lady*.

I have come to Guyana to try to help, but I don't have the medicine to heal this woman. I cannot find the books that will take this girl to college. Everywhere I go in this country, I feel broadsided by harsh realities. The unstoppable bright sun streams down and blinds me, the light and heat burning my skin raw. I shield my eyes as I blink back tears.

Onica doesn't notice. She is talking about the astronomy book she has been reading. "Miss, ya know how many stars in the sky, Miss? And planets, Miss? Ya evah hear of galaxies, Miss? And the moon? Ya know anyone who's been to the moon, Miss?"

❧ ❧ ❧

Katherine Jamieson is a graduate of the Iowa Nonfiction Writing Program. These days, she's traded the balmy tropics of Guyana for a writing life in the woods of rural western Massachusetts. You can read more of her essays, articles, and stories at katherinejamieson. com.

৵৵ ৵৵ ৵৵

I Am

In the desert, you can remember your name.

I still receive emails every few months. *I love you my queen*, he writes. *Please tell me about you, habibi.* And I look out the window and remember: the breadth of the desert, the taste of sand.

I wept, sending my husband off for his second Middle East deployment on a U.S. Navy submarine.

"What will I do while you're gone?" I sniffled.

"Have an adventure, baby," he urged me.

So I did. I packed our belongings into storage, arranged for the mail to be held, and left my dog with my aunt. My plan was to fulfill a forgotten dream and backpack for three months in Eastern Europe and Africa. Years ago, when I'd chosen to marry Josh and settle down, I abandoned my aspiration of a traveling life. Now, with this trip, I wanted more than just adventure—I hoped to reclaim a piece of myself.

Yet when it was finally time to go, I couldn't stop crying.

In Dublin I was lonely. In my twenties I'd back-packed Europe and loved it, but I was thirty-one now, a domestic little woman, and I couldn't find my old travel groove. I missed Josh, even though he'd been at sea for considerably more of our marriage than he'd been home. In Greece I kept crying—not just because he wasn't with me, but because I wished he was. I didn't know when I'd become so useless and frightened.

I wandered Athens like an old lady, in my ergo-nomic flip-flops, studying my guidebook. I ate olives and learned to read Greek by studying billboards and license plates. On a ferry to the islands, a would-be suitor inquired whether I had a "special friend." I did, in theory if not in practice. Josh was a good and kind man with whom I'd struggled to pull together a marriage that was more than just function. As a stay-at-home wife I spent my days quietly, brewing his coffee in the morning, sitting on the couch in my bathrobe deciding whether to take the dog to the park before or after gro-cery shopping. I had dreamed of helping the world and living big; married life could be sweet, but it felt small.

I'd timed the first leg of my trip to overlap with his submarine pulling into Bahrain. I was twiddling my thumbs on a cloudy Greek beach when I got the email that the in-port had been delayed. Now what? Watching movies in my hotel all day wasn't a valid option, so I suddenly changed course and booked a seat on the next flight to Egypt. As I stood in the Athens airport holding the ticket in my hand, a sense of power came over me. I was going to *Egypt*. And I was going alone.

On the plane to Cairo, my seatmate entertained me with tales of lascivious Egyptian men harassing solo-traveling women. As a result I spent the first day hiding in my hotel, terrified to venture out. Finally, that night, I asked the desk clerk to write in Arabic, "I want to buy a phone card," and with deep breaths I walked ten meters to a corner store. The proprietor understood my Arabic pronunciation, which made me proud, but he didn't have phone cards and pointed me farther down the block, to another store that didn't have any. By the time I found one, I was far from my hotel, I was unmolested, and I was *back*. Past families sitting at sidewalk cafés eating fragrant Egyptian food, past storefronts displaying the splashy fashions the veiled women loved to wear, I kept walking and walking.

In the lounge at the dingy, comfortable hotel, I met the Hawaiian woman who visited Egypt every year, the Irish couple who had biked overland from Europe. Our travel conversations filled the room, swirling around me like a vibrant, thumping soundtrack. *This is what it's like to be an active participant in my own life,* I thought. *I remember.*

I rode a camel to the pyramids, had my picture taken beside the Sphinx. In Dahshur I clambered up the side of the Red Pyramid and paid a wizened man five dollars for the privilege of crawling deep into the hot, empty tomb, where I stood alone, enthralled. I caught an overnight train to Aswan and wandered Abu Simbel taking photos on the sly, ignoring the guards ready to pounce on rule-breakers.

I introduced myself in Arabic: "*Ana Anna,*" I said. "I am Anna," a rhyming phrase that was funny the first few times and then grew tedious. I sat in cafés drinking strong, sweet tea, calmly rebuffing the overtures of Arab men and making a mental note to learn "I have a husband" in Arabic. I impulsively broke my vow to never smoke a cigarette when Fatma, the beautiful veiled girl giving me a tour of Cairo, brazenly lit one.

I joined a sailing trip down the Nile on a *felucca,* a traditional craft with a bare deck sheltered by a low cloth roof and captained by a handsome, attentive man named Saber. As dusk fell, we swished silently up the river, while Saber and his two young crewmen scrambled gracefully up and down the mast in their *gabbalahs.* The breeze across the water was hot and fragrant, and I lay on deck chatting with the other passengers, pondering whether this might be the happiest I'd ever been.

In the morning, the *felucca* remained anchored, and we spent the day relaxing lethargically in the heat, chatting and practicing Arabic.

"How do I say, 'I have a husband'?" I asked the crew.

"*Ana ayza zawg,*" answered Saber.

"That's 'I *want* a husband'!" I exclaimed, and we all roared with laughter at their trickery, at my knowing my verbs.

I was in Luxor dutifully photographing ancient monuments when I got the email that Josh's submarine had pulled into Bahrain at last. For two hours I fought airport crowds and offered the first bribe of my life, till I finally got a ticket back to Cairo. The clerk at my hotel had evicted another guest to ready my old room for me. A European passenger from the *felucca* had checked in, greeting me with a delighted embrace. I was part of a community now; I belonged. Why was I even leaving Egypt? I'd found my groove, and I was scared of losing it to be with Josh.

Two nights later I landed in Bahrain.

He was silent in the taxi to the hotel. Reserved. We thawed as the days passed, but it was like looking at him from across a chasm—he seemed so close, yet to reach him an impossible distance had to be traversed. We had low-key arguments. I couldn't bring myself to care. I was completely departed from that girl in Greece who'd wept with longing for him to come along and figure everything out for her. He'd never known the old, powerful Anna and he sure didn't know the new one; did he even want to? The connection on which we'd based our marriage felt terribly flimsy.

He asked where I was going next. A good question. I wanted to return to Egypt but knew it was the wrong choice—too comfortable and safe, another version of my former complacency. *Ana Anna*, I reminded myself: I hold my future in my own hands.

I bought a ticket to Syria. In the Abu Dhabi airport, waiting for my connecting flight, I reflected on the tears I'd cried at separating from Josh again and the contradictory relief I'd felt the moment I was in my taxi: *finally, I'm on my own again.*

At the customs line at 5 A.M. in the Damascus airport, I fixed the official with my most non-threatening smile and slapped my passport on the counter. I knew that as an American, I was required to obtain a Syrian visa through my embassy six weeks in advance, but the Irish bicyclists in Cairo had assured me that I could in fact purchase one at the border if I didn't mind waiting.

"Visa," the customs official demanded.

"I don't have one."

He looked at me with a truly blank expression, and I began to doubt.

"Have seat," he suggested.

When they took me in a back room, three of them questioned me. "Who is meeting you here?"

"No one."

"Where are you staying?"

"I don't know."

"What do you do for work?"

"Nothing."

In another room, more men asked the same questions. I didn't mention being married, thinking it best to avoid the topic of my American military spouse. Nor did I say I was a writer; I'd heard it would be interpreted as being a journalist, another point against me. "Nothing?" they pressed. I shrugged. Nothing. I was wearying of my non-threatening smile but had no alternative act. I waited five hours in the lobby until they granted my visa—and then there I was, an American military wife alone in Syria. Signing the hotel register in Damascus, though, I impulsively left off my married name. *Anna Hansen*, I wrote, for the first time in years.

In that short, sterile time with Josh, I'd lost the hang of crossing suicidal streets, of wandering alone; Damascus left me cold. I saw the magic of the city but couldn't access it. Arbitrarily, I decided to head to Palmyra to see the Roman ruins.

"Your name?" the clerk in the bus station asked.

"*Ana Anna*," I said for the hundredth time.

"Anina?" he questioned, not sure he'd heard correctly.

I stared at him.

"Why yes," I said. "*Ana Anina*."

"Very nice," he nodded.

After weeks of saying, "I am I Am," I thought so too.

ঞ ঞ ঞ

After a three-hour bus ride, I arrived in the quiet, bedraggled town of Palmyra. I forced myself to the hotel lobby to be social and was immediately invited to a "Bedouin party." In a giant pseudo-Bedouin tent, beautiful local men sang and danced for a large group of drunk, clapping, middle-aged German tourists. It was a tacky affair, but I smoked *shisha*, made friends, and watched a sexy, gold-toothed Bedouin leap about athletically in traditional garb then don a leather jacket and roar away on his motorcycle at the end of the night. And suddenly Syria wasn't quite so unappealing.

At 5:30 the next morning I crept from my hotel to catch the famous sunrise over the ruins. I was early; it was pitch black and the town was silent and deserted. A cold wind blew off the desert. I pulled up the hood on my fleece, jammed my hands in my pockets, and skipped down the empty street, giddy. Me! Alone! In the Syrian Desert! I struck off down the cobbled road toward the ruins, pretending it was two thousand years ago and I was a local woman making her way into the city for market day.

I wandered the ruins as the sky lightened and the morning traffic began. An occasional motorcycle bypassed the cobbled road to zip straight through the center of the ruins—glorious sacrilege!—and then, suddenly, as I glanced over my shoulder, right behind me a man on a camel scared the hell out of me.

"Do you want to ride the camel?" he asked. "I will take you to the best place to see the sunrise."

I wavered. But he had a dog, which made me homesick. Then, with great hacking in the back of his throat, he urged the camel to its knees, and I felt *obligated* to

get on. I was immediately glad, as we struck off through
the dawn ruins, this man in the red-and-white-checked
keffiyeh sitting ahead of me on a camel. It was so obvious
that he was a Bedouin prince and I a fair maiden, kid-
napped and carried away to the desert to be his bride.

His name was Rabia, the Bedouin word for spring.
His camel, Casanova. The dog gallivanting beside us—a
dirty diaper proudly clutched in his mouth—had no
name, so I called him Chico and began to fantasize about
moving to Palmyra and getting myself a camel and a
dog. And a Bedouin.

At the ruins of Queen Zenobia's palace, I explored
with wonder, climbing to the top of the tower, queen of
all I surveyed—including that handsome Syrian camel
guide far away down the long plain of ruins. He had
promised to return for me, but I forbade myself to wait,
strolling alone down the pink-lit morning plain, pausing
to lay my hands on the chalky stones, sliding my fingers
in the dental work at the base of ancient pillars. An hour
later our paths converged, and he dropped Casanova to
his knees without asking. As we rode away he lit a cigarette. I took it from his lips. I couldn't help laughing.

"This is the life!" I exclaimed.

"Yes, it's good," he replied. I felt like he understood.

It had been years—it had been Josh—since I'd had a
crush. Rabia took me to his family's home for tea, invited
me on a desert camping trip, then conveyed me home
through the ruins on his motorcycle. Riding behind him,
fingers clamped to his waist, I was drunk on Syria, on
the wide-open potential of my future.

That afternoon I joined a Scottish diplomat's family
and we rode our camels out of Palmyra, past tall crum-
bly buildings, through a pass in the scrubby hills and
across a highway to the flat, rocky desert. At first there

were a few farms, then nothing but wasteland—yet the wasteland was populated, herds of sheep and camels tended by Bedouin men, here and there the corresponding tent of each herder and his family, man and beast scraping out their nourishment from the barren terrain.

We rode several hours to a lone tent pitched in the middle of the endless sand. The Scots were pleasant and the other Bedouin men courteous, but all my senses were tuned to Rabia, smiling at me across the fire as we shared cup after cup of sugary chai, lighting cigarettes from the embers and passing them back and forth. After dinner he beckoned me to his motorcycle and we rode through the starry darkness, chased by wild dogs, silent with delight.

The family slept in the tent but I joined the men outside beneath the stars, stretched under a thick wool blanket stinking of camel. The next afternoon Rabia and I rode his motorcycle again, grinding up an impossibly steep road to the top of a high plateau, the desert spreading below us in a dusty, baking monochrome that overwhelmed me with desire: it felt, for no reason I could name, like home.

And I began to wonder where home was. A little yellow house where my husband, when he was there, played computer games by the hour while I sat on the couch hoping he'd eventually notice me? Or could it be the world, as I'd once dreamed it would be? Could Josh live that life with me?

One morning I left my small hotel and found myself in a dust storm, the town foggy with sand so thick I could taste its grit in my teeth, the sun dimmed to perpetual twilight. Rabia was waiting in the ruins. I climbed on Casanova and we rode out of town to the funerary towers, tall beehives of ancient yellow stone against the dusty backdrop of the desert hills, where bodies were once interred, round and round in inner compartments spiraling up each story of the tower. The tombs were closed, but he showed me one with a broken gate. The bottom chamber was piled with human bones. I climbed the spiraling interior staircase to the roof and stood, barefoot, surveying the dim desert, ecstatic. The rightness of it all was like a balm.

When I came back inside, my ergonomic flip-flops were gone.

"Rabia," I called, "have you seen my shoes?"

"No, where are they?" he called from the ground, three stories below.

"I don't know. I left them at the top of the stairs."

"Must be the *djinnie*," he mused.

I stuck my head out the window. "The *what*?"

"The *djinnie*. Every tomb has one. They like to play tricks."

In this magical land, I was fully ready to believe in the existence of *djinnies*. I looked over my shoulder, glancing around the small chamber and the honeycombed walls with slots where dozens of bodies had once lain. What if the *djinnie* was right here? What if it touched me? I ran down the stairs.

Rabia was waiting at the entrance. "What should I do?" I asked. "Those are the only shoes I have." He shrugged; beyond its trickery, the ways of the tomb *djinnie* seemed to elude him.

"Will he give them back if I ask him?" I prodded.

"Maybe."

"*Djinnie!*" I hollered. "Please give me back my shoes!"

Rabia exploded with laughter, raspy, a smoker's laugh at twenty-three. He gave back my shoes.

We rode Casanova to his garden and I sat in a gazebo beneath palm trees, listening to the buzz of insects in the afternoon heat. Rabia came to me, stood above me, trapped my face in his hands, and kissed me. I resisted, reflexively; he held me fast. I hung suspended for one moment. I thought, *I'll have to tell Josh.* Then I kissed him. And kissed him, and kissed him, and kissed him.

It was the sweetest, most awful thing I'd ever done.

The next day I sat staring out my window at the desert, allowing myself to consider the options outside my marriage. Josh and I had never wanted the same things. For a long time, I'd been silencing myself to make things work—but silence wasn't an option anymore.

Or was this just the high of adventure talking? Sure, I could stay, buy a motorcycle and learn Arabic, make a life in Syria, even shack up with Rabia and have beautiful, coffee-skinned babies. But who could say I wouldn't wake up one day wishing to be back in my living room, the Red Sox playing in the background, watching Josh play EverQuest?

It was a choice I needed to make for myself—not for Josh, certainly not for Rabia. This was about whether I could live in integrity with myself inside my marriage. Only one thing was certain: if I stayed much longer, I'd have a steamy affair with a beautiful camel guide. *Ana andey zawg*—I have a husband! I returned to Damascus and bought a ticket to Africa. Saying goodbye to my husband in Bahrain had been a relief. Saying goodbye to my travel fling in Syria was heartbreaking. Sobbing, I caught my flight to Kenya.

In Nairobi I walked past refuse-filled ditches as buses roared by belching black smoke and mamas strolled with babies slung in brightly colored blankets on their backs. I barely saw it. All I could think of was my next destination.

I could have wandered forever, dodging unhappiness. Anna might have, but I was Anina now; I no longer avoided what frightened me. Instead I began sending Josh long emails written on sticky keyboards in cramped Kenyan cybercafés, the power periodically cutting out, forcing me to wait till the next day and start again. For the first time in our marriage I spoke from my heart about the future I dreamed of, the international life I longed for us to share. I told him I'd kissed a man in Syria and didn't want our one-way marriage anymore. Could he meet me halfway?

He couldn't.

And sometimes marriage is like that.

Weeks after my arrival in Kenya, Josh and I agreed, amicably and still via email, to divorce. With nothing to go home for, I stayed. I wrote to Rabia and told him, but stopped emailing him after that, though I still receive the occasional impassioned letter—*I love you Anena.* Though I kept my new name, the way he spelled it.

Two years later, I do catch myself missing my old life. Josh and I are still vaguely friends, and at times I can't help wondering whether our marriage could have worked—would it have been so bad?

Then I look out my window, at the hustle of Africans walking home in the early-evening sun, at grim Marabou storks poking through garbage heaps and a sly vervet monkey leaping in the branches, at purple jacaranda trees coming into bloom for the third time since I came to Kenya, and I know that, painful as it was, I made the right choice. He could never have given me this. And *this* is what I always wanted.

I understand now why I cried so hard when I left for my trip—on some level, I knew I wasn't coming back. But getting my do-over has been worth it. Living in Kenya is the most challenging, most rewarding endeavor of my life. I'm involved in development work. I'm living life *big*. Maybe I broke my vow to abstain from cigarettes, even my vow to stay with a man till death do us part, but there is one promise to myself I will always keep: never again will I let complacency and security prevent me from living my dreams.

Habibi, I miss you too much. Please tell me about you, Anena.

If I were to tell him about me now, I would say:

I'm not afraid anymore.

ॐ ॐ ॐ

Since 2008, Anena Hansen has lived in Kenya, working with high-risk teenage girls and sex workers and going on a lot of safaris. She's learning Swahili but isn't fluent yet. When her time in Kenya is done, she will most likely move to Syria—and then she'll have to start over with Arabic. She blogs about her life in Kenya at www. hawfield.blogspot.com.

ANNE VAN

❧ ❧ ❧

Going Underground

A curious student in Japan gets
more than she bargained for.

A Suntory whiskey commercial starring Sean
Connery blazed across the Jumbo Tron, the enormous screen suspended in front of the Shinjuku train station. His nose looked even larger than usual as he held a glass up to his face and said, "Suntory time." The words echoed against the skyscrapers, making the buzz of the Shinjuku station even louder.

Someone tapped on my shoulder. "Big nose," Ichiyo said. He always seemed to know what I was thinking—sometimes even before I did.

I'd been a college student in Japan for eight headspinning months and never thought this day would come. Ichiyo was my fun go-to guy and had been promising me a Tokyo underground adventure ever since I met him. Today he was going to deliver. My Japanese was finally good enough to carry on a conversation without embarrassing him.

We walked down the main drag that led into Kabuki–cho, the seedy section of Shinjuku and one of Ichiyo's favorite hangouts. Even with a man next to me, my guard was up. Ichiyo, with his slight build and bookish demeanor, wasn't going to scare anyone away. This was *yakuza* (Japanese mafia) territory, and the police had little influence here. I'd heard you could get shot unexpectedly in the crossfire of bullets—like in the gang-ridden parts of my hometown, Los Angeles. Ichiyo stopped in front of a bright Pepto-pink building with a giant purple sign that declared, "Boom Boom Palace." A porn shop. An impressive window display featured all kinds of erotic delights. The mannequins were stylishly dressed in the latest S&M fashion. This definitely wasn't the adventure I had in mind.

"Ichiyo, if you want to do a little shopping, I'll wait here."

He turned bright red. "Oh no! We're going in to meet my friend. His office is in the back."

I had heard these types of places had unsavory characters lurking in tiny rooms, but as I breathed in the fragrances of strawberry and grape, it seemed about as threatening as a candy store. Then I got an eyeful of the various sex paraphernalia displayed in the shop. The shelves were crammed full of lollipop-colored edible panties, whips, ball gags, and an impressive array of gyrating silicone body parts. I couldn't help but stare when I passed a three-headed dildo: my mind raced.

"My friend has bodyguards, so just keep your hands in front of you at all times," Ichiyo said.

I felt like I was in a Quentin Tarantino movie and had suddenly turned into (a shorter, brunette, more buxom)

Uma Thurman. I kept my hands close to my waist as we
snaked our way to the back of the shop. A striking man
in his early thirties dressed in a tight black suit stood in
front of a door with a sign that said in English, "Enter at
Your Own Life." Two sumo-wrestler type bodyguards
flanked the doorway.

Ichiyo approached the suited man and said in Japanese,
"Nakashimasan, this is my friend Anne from America."

His slicked-back hair accentuated his cheekbones that
jetted out at right angles, and a dragon tattoo peeked out
from underneath his shirtsleeve. Every *yakuza* I'd seen
in the movies wore a black suit, no matter the temperature, and was usually missing a few fingers as punish-
ment for screwing up some hit. From what I could tell,
all of Nakashimasan's digits were intact. He was good
at his job.

My adrenaline surging, I bowed almost to my knees,
deeply enough to show respect for an elder, with a little
extra thrown in for good measure.

Nakashimasan spoke directly to my breasts before
moving up to my face. "Nice to meet you. Ichiyo tells me
you are interested in all the different faces of Japan."

Relieved that I could keep up with the conversation
so far, I still chose my Japanese words carefully. "Yes,
within reason."

Nakashimasan laughed. "You don't have to worry. I
am small time. Just run this shop and produce porno-
graphic movies."

I hoped he wasn't going to offer me a job. Thankfully,
I had worn one of my usual student outfits, jeans and a
faded UCLA t-shirt—looking frumpy was a plus in this
situation.

"Actually, I would like you to see the movie I am
working on. I want to take it to America."

Perfect, I thought. *Now politeness dictates that I have to watch hardcore porn. Thanks a lot, Ichiyo.*

"Don't worry, Anne," said Ichiyo, once again reading my mind. "It's an art movie."

Art movie? Who were they kidding?

We followed Nakashimasan down a small hallway filled with the pungent smell of sweat, which led to another section of the store. He opened the door into a closet-like room used to view XXX-rated films. I sat on a stain-covered chair and suppressed the impulse to gag. Shifting nervously in my well-worn seat, I promised myself that the first thing I'd do if I ever made it home from this was burn my clothes.

Nakashimasan snapped his fingers and the screen lit up. The scene opened with a *yakuza* staggering wounded across a street. Another gangster chased him through a series of smaller and smaller alleys until the injured man was cornered. The story was about a *yakuza* trying to retire from his gang because he didn't want to kill anymore. It had the makings of a good movie, and with a running time of only an hour and twenty minutes, it gave fast-paced a new meaning.

Nakashimasan turned the lights back up. "What do you think? Will they like this in America?"

Grateful that the film actually had possibilities, I told him I liked it. "People in the U.S. are very interested in the *yakuza*. They're much like our mafia, but with a longer history."

Nakashimasan nodded. "Some think we descend from the Samurai who were left to fend for themselves after the Shoguns lost power; others say we were like Robin Hood, protectors of the villagers." He smiled. "I pick Robin Hood."

Maybe he was right. I'd read that after the big earthquake in Kobe, Japan, the Japanese mafia gave financial
aid to the homeless and even used their private helicopter to help evacuate victims.

A serious expression crossed Ichiyo's face. "Japan
needs the *yakuza*. They keep our government in line."

I had somehow touched a nerve: Ichiyo felt com-
pelled to defend the mafia. I wondered if he'd sought
Nakashimasan's help at some point—but I decided I
didn't need to know about their business relationship.

Ichiyo sprung from his seat and turned to me. "Let's
get lunch."

I hadn't eaten since breakfast but until then hadn't
even thought of food; I'd been too nervous.

"Can I join you?" Nakashimasan asked, already getting up from his chair.

Terrific: now I was going to be seen in public with
a *yakuza* and his bodyguards, and people would think
I was a prostitute who worked for him. Not that I
hadn't already been accused several times; I was stopped
by police whenever I hung out with a group of male
friends. In Tokyo, a lone white woman with a group of
Japanese men is assumed to be a hostess, also known as
a hooker. This would just about seal it. But I couldn't
refuse Nakashimasan's offer. I dutifully followed behind
the men.

Ichiyo and I climbed into the back seat of a slick black
Mercedes sedan and were quickly sandwiched between
the two bodyguards. We sped away from Kabuki-cho
toward the trendy part of Shinjuku. The car reeked of
cigarette smoke and men's cologne, so I was glad when
we soon stopped at a cute café called the Dollar Monkey.
I only hoped Nakashimasan's favorite dining spot didn't

dish up its namesake—live monkey was a Chinese delicacy, and I'd heard of Japanese restaurants that served it.
I let out a sigh of relief when we walked inside the café;
the air smelled like freshly baked bread, and the menu
listed sandwiches and noodle dishes.

I felt like a celebrity walking in with an entourage.
The people in the restaurant tried not to stare while the
staff hurried about, preparing Nakashimasan's favorite
corner table. They put on a fresh yellow-and-white
checkered tablecloth and dusted off the black wrought-
iron bistro chairs while the waiter ran to the kitchen
to alert the chef. I could see why Ichiyo might enjoy
being friends with a *yakuza*; the attention made me feel
important.

I'd been fascinated by the Japanese mafia ever since
seeing the movie *Black Rain*, starring Michael Douglas
as a New York cop who had to escort a wanted *yakuza*
back to Japan. The film opened my eyes to the Japanese
underworld, and since then I'd devoured what little I
could find on the subject. Now here I sat, next to the
real thing. *I need to learn more about the gangster life*, I
thought. *This is my big chance. I might not get another.*

The question flew out of my mouth before I could
consider the consequences. "Can I ask you how long
you've been in the organization?"

Nakashimasan's bodyguards leaned forward, their
shoulders forming a protective barrier around him.
A slight grin spread across their boss's face, and they
relaxed a bit. "If you weren't so pretty," he said, "I'd have
you killed for asking me such a question."

Sweat began to bead on the back of my neck as I eyed
the bodyguards. Nakashimasan paused, then let out a
robust laugh. "I was making a joke. I joined when I was

just out of high school. They recruited me from a street gang—I was the leader. I had a very romantic view of the *yakuza* and thought it was an honor."

"Thank you for being so honest," I said, more intrigued than ever. "If you don't mind my asking, how did you prove your loyalty?"

"That's a good question," Nakashimasan said, his eyes measuring my cup size before casually leaning back in his chair. "I went through a special ceremony where I drank a cup of fish scales and shared it with the Boss. This bound me to him."

"I guess drinking something that disgusting at least proves you have a strong stomach?" The bodyguards sat stone-faced, but Nakashimasan laughed.

I was in now. There was no stopping me: "What about the tradition of cutting the little finger?"

Ichiyo's furrowed brow looked like two angry bats fighting. "Anne, let Nakashimasan eat his lunch."

Nakashimasan ignored Ichiyo's outburst and took a sip of his beer. "No, it's fine. I like that she's interested in my world."

The two businessmen sitting at the table next to us quickly moved their chairs away from our table as the waitress rushed over to see if there was anything else her special guest wanted. Her hands shook as she picked up an empty Kirin bottle. Nakashimasan waved her away. "When someone offends the Boss by breaking a *yakuza* code, he must show regret. He does this by cutting off the top joint of his little finger. If he makes another error he cuts the next section. Once that digit is gone they move onto the ring finger. But usually there's no need."

I didn't want to push my luck, but I was dying to know why. "Is there a reason they cut the little finger?"

Ichiyo shifted nervously in his chair while Nakashimasan ran his fingers through his slicked-back hair. No doubt about it—he had all ten.

He leaned forward, forcing the bodyguards to follow suit. "Another good question. In the days of the Samurai, the little finger was important for holding the large *katana* sword. If the Samurai disobeyed his Shogun, he was punished by having his little finger cut off. This made him a weaker swordsman and dependent on his master for protection."

Listening to Nakashimasan was better than any textbook. Although I had read about the modern-day *yakuza*, I knew nothing about their ancient history; now I understood why their sense of loyalty ran so strong.

It was surprising how comfortable I felt with him— and how harmless he looked munching away on his *wagyu* beef sandwich. Even the bodyguards seemed more at ease as they leaned back in their chairs and watched their boss eat his lunch. In fact, the mood of the whole restaurant had shifted. The people around us no longer stole quick glances at our table or leaned in to hear what we were saying. Instead, they enjoyed their lunches and concentrated on their own conversations.

Yet as I watched Ichiyo continue to squirm in his chair, I knew that Nakashimasan's charm might be a cover for something far more sinister. He admitted to having been in a street gang as a kid; maybe he'd even killed someone. Plus, I couldn't help but wonder if there was something hidden beneath his harmless-looking porn shop. I'd read that the *yakuza* went into the construction business so they could hide the bodies of their victims in the concrete foundations of the buildings. Was the Boom Boom Palace really a graveyard? The thought gave me goose bumps. But as I stared at Nakashimasan's handsome face, I chose to believe that he was just a small-time gangster selling nothing more menacing than love dolls and Hello Kitty vibrators.

Thinking about the store brought up another question. So far, Nakashimasan had been a good sport—and his smile seemed to beg for more. Besides, I wanted to know if another myth I'd heard was true. "Do the *yakuza* sell foreign women?"

The color drained from Ichiyo's face as the bodyguards stood up and moved toward me.

Oh shit. Now I've gone too far.

Nakashimasan waved them away and took a swig of beer. "Are you implying we deal in sex slavery?"

What the hell had I been thinking? "No sir. Sorry... bad joke."

Ichiyo's legs fidgeted, causing the table to shake. "Look at the time. We should be going."

Nakashimasan held up his hand like a stop sign. "But Anne hasn't finished eating."

In all the excitement, I'd barely touched my sandwich.

Ichiyo kicked me under the table.

All eyes were on me as I grabbed my veggie special. In three big bites it vanished. Swallowing hard, I managed to squeak out, "Very delicious." Thank God I wasn't fibbing; with his piercing gaze, Nakashimasan was like a human lie detector. "And thank you so much for lunch and answering my questions."

Nakashimasan glanced at his watch and got up from his chair. The bodyguards rose in unison like a military drill team. "Sorry, but I have to attend a meeting." He reached out his hand and took one last look at my breasts. "So nice to meet you," he said. "Thank you for watching my movie. And if you ever need help while you are in Tokyo, you know where to find me."

I let go of his hand as the bodyguards moved to form a shield around him. As he got ready to head back to his car, a smile flashed across Nakashimasan's face.

"Oh, and to answer your question, Anne, I think you might be worth a quarter of a million dollars."

I froze, somewhere between standing and sitting, and watched his black Mercedes drive away.

"Two hundred fifty thousand? Not bad," joked Ichiyo, much more at ease once Nakashimasan was gone.

I dropped into my chair. *No*, I thought. *Not bad at all.*

Anne Van has always heard stories in her head. It's in her DNA. The storyteller gene was passed down from her grandfather, known in his small town as King of the Whoppers. Majoring in art, she attended college in Tokyo, Japan, and learned a lot more than how to paint a koi fish. Currently Anne splits her time between painting the next Mona Lisa *and putting her whoppers on paper.*

◦◦◦ ◦◦◦ ◦◦◦

A Hundred Unspoken Rules

In the embrace of extended family, a woman
reconsiders the ties that bind.

Inside Uncle Anna's house, the women are swathed
in nine-yard saris, gold and colored silk wrapped a
dozen times around their aging bodies, which move more
slowly than they used to. They set up an altar with two
banana leaves, a mirror, fresh flowers, and a gold necklace. An oil lamp burns in the corner. They draw designs
in rice flour to mark place settings on the floor. They
bend down and wipe turmeric paste on their feet.

My Uncle Anna has lived through a thousand moons,
and to celebrate, Anna—literally "big brother" in his
native Tamil tongue—and his wife Manni will spend
the next few days reenacting their 1951 marriage. But
today is not about him. Today is about the women. It is

mangali pondugal, the Brahmin ceremony to remember, honor, and seek the blessings of the women who have come before. Three of my uncle's sisters and all his brothers' wives have gathered at their house. There are some extended family members and a neighbor. The few men in attendance sit outside, reading the newspaper and sipping coffee, ignored.

I watch the preparations, unsure of when I can participate and when I can't. This motion is for the married, that one for the eldest, this for the woman of honor. There are a hundred unspoken rules I don't know, details neither my American mother nor my Indian father, a long-ago lapsed Hindu, ever taught me. With each return visit to India, the years creep up on me at the same relentless pace as for my elderly aunts, and my ignorance of what to do during the Hindu ceremonies seems more glaring. As a child, and even a young woman, I could play at the Hindu rituals in a way I never could at my friends' Catholic churches and Jewish synagogues on the Jersey shore. In the Hindu temple, redolent with the scent of oil lamps and incense, it all felt exotic and removed. Now, on the brink of my fortieth year, I am a grown woman, and the same motions feel fraudulent in any culture, in all the religions I don't believe in.

I sit on the couch next to Nitya, a cousin's cousin through marriage, her eight-and-a-half-month belly prominent beneath her sari. Beside her sits her ninety-eight-year-old great-grandmother, frail and tired and about to add another "great" to her familial title. It is the most natural thing, this continuity of lifelines, blood and birth and memory in an endless procession looping back upon itself, each time seeming a singular event. Miracle upon miracle. What used to be a quaint anomaly, my

resistance to marriage—or my dull inability to find
someone to undertake it with—turns into something
sadder and more unspeakable here with time. To be
single in New York City is the stuff of hit TV shows.
To be single in south India is to create an uncomfortable rift in the Order of Things. The poking jokes from
previous trips about finding me a husband are now
conspicuously absent.

I am lost in these thoughts when my aunt Santhi
draws me into the fray. She comes and kneels before
me, wiping the turmeric paste across the smooth tops
of my feet. Then she draws a line in another paste, a
deeper red that will dye the skin for days, encircling
my long, bony, half-south Indian feet. I ask her what it
means, and she laughs, tells me it's for decoration, nothing else. She brings me over to where the sisters have
gathered tightly in the corner of the room, as though a
wind has swept them there like leaves. We turn toward
Manni as she swishes red water around in a shallow
stainless basin and repeats mantras, aided by her sister's
prompts. We bow toward her as she tosses flowers upon
us, the calendula petals landing on the crowns of our
heads—bright yellow against hair black, silver, degrees
of black and silver.

Aunt Akka remains on the couch, the only sister present who has lost a husband. Though she is a modern-
day widow—ignoring the ancient edicts to shave her
head, shed her jewelry, and forgo the bindi on her forehead—she will not participate. It seems wrong that I can
partake more than she can, when she has brought four
children into this world, walked seven times—one for
each vow—around the marriage fire, known the smell
of the funeral pyre. I have only known campfires, helped
my farmer friends deliver kid goats, breathed the deep

musk of many men. I have buried dear friends and one
lover, but the closest thing I've had to a husband is alive
and well, although I don't talk to him much these days.
I am from some other world than this tribe of women
who have known me all my life. I am at once connected
and separate.

Their beliefs guide their rituals which guide their
beliefs, completing some perfect circle that starts with
the start of life and ends with the end of death, which
they know is yet another beginning. I only believe in
reincarnation through compost and daisies and the circular path of water from cloud to sea and back again. In
the ability of a baby falcon to fly the first time it leaves
the nest. I don't believe in their gods, though they are
colorful and enticing, nor the godheads of the western
world, whom I find morose and unappealingly asexual.
I don't believe that Hanuman jumped to Sri Lanka
or that Vishnu shape-shifted into a woman to lure the
bad guys away from the ambrosia or that Moses parted
the Red Sea or that God recited anything to anybody
anytime.

But I understand the aching need for ritual. I believe
in my grandmother, who I can imagine somewhere
between the heat of the oil lamp and the smell of the
rice and curry wafting from the kitchen. She has died
all over again, with this return to India, my first since
her death two years ago. I was in Brooklyn then, alone,
without ceremonies or gods or belief in anything other
than the harsh biological knowledge that the generations
had shifted up a notch, the family tree growing skyward,
leaving me stranded by my own clumsy will on a branch
that was rising higher from the ground with time. I have
cousins who are grandmothers but I now have no grandmother on this earth. No god can change this fact.

Everyone else here—the aunts clustered in the corner, the one contentedly alone on the couch, the uncles who will come in later to eat—witnessed her final days. They spread her ashes where they spread my grandfather's ashes, at the union of the stagnant waters of the Adyar River and the salty waves of the Bay of Bengal. They fed her spirit food for fourteen days and then left out the salt on the fifteenth day, signaling that it was time for her to go. They waited a year and marked the passage with more of these Hindu rituals that all seem the same to me. Oil lamps. Platters of fruit and flowers and gold. Food, eaten and offered. A priest.

But there is no priest today. The *puja* is short. After the decorated feet and the tossed flowers, it's time to eat. There are women cooking in the kitchen and women around the table, women on the couch and women sitting cross-legged on the floor before bright green banana leaves wiped clean with a handful of water and glistening in anticipation. The cooks make the offerings at the altar before passing down the line to serve us—steaming rice, ladlefuls of a half dozen vegetable curries, and golden, deep-fried *vadas*, crispy on the outside and soft in the middle, which we dip into fresh ground chutneys of cilantro, of coconut, of tamarind.

The sisters are loud and talk on top of each other, mouths full of food and tumbling Tamil. They reminisce about when their father, fed up with the noise of his eight children, decreed silence during mealtimes. For months the quiet dragged on, nothing but the slurping sound of curd rice and curries lapped up through fingers, until one day my cousin Kumar, who was just a baby, peed straight into my grandfather's pile of basmati rice. "In those days, they only put nappies on girls, not boys," Santhi tells me in English as she catches her breath between bouts of laughter. They laugh now as they must have then. The silence ended, then and there.

The cooks clear the banana leaves, sweep the floor clean by hand. And then we make one more motion, lining up in pairs. We get down on our knees, curling our bodies to the floor, closing our eyes, and bowing to something or someone that resides in the altars of our own making. With our *namaskarams*, we bend, all of us on our knees, shared blood and belief and disbelief.

♪♫ ♪♫ ♪♫

Meera Subramanian writes about culture, faith, and the environment for The New York Times, Wall Street Journal, Smithsonian, Audubon, Discover, Salon, *and others and is a senior editor for the online religion magazine* Killing the Buddha. *She frequently flees her Brooklyn brownstone under the auspices of "work" but is really in search of birds of prey, skies without contrails, and animals that might eat her. Visit her at meerasub.org.*

BONNIE STEWART

෴ ෴ ෴

The Wind that Shakes the Barley

A tourist gets an insider's glimpse
into a shadowy world.

*I*reland in July is a lesson in why autumn is the perfect
time to travel. It's a tourist destination, a place that
turns itself inside out come summer to present a smiling
face to a world that lines its pockets in return. I do not say
this with cynicism; it's simply a fact.

I should have known better than to travel in tourist
season. I'm from the same type of place: a summer spot,
a land where inner and outer circles are indelibly, com-
plicatedly demarcated. We are all friendliness in July on
my little summer island. But if you visit, you will only
see our parlour face, our best self, all genuine cheer and
clannish closed-ness, a paradox. It is simply that we have
only so much energy and there are so many crowding in

to see whatever spectacle they have in mind of who we are. In high season, you will not really get to know us.

And so it was with me in most of Ireland that green, wet summer. I wandered streets and cobblestones, ducked into pubs, hitchhiked on the wrong side of the road. I struck up conversations with old men who lay half-prone on bus station benches, red-flowered noses far less poetic in person than in the storied romance of a nation's manhood, self-sabotaged.

Mostly, I was alone. Hostels in small Irish towns are not necessarily hotbeds of wild conversational nightlife. In Sligo, I had the run of the place but for one elderly gentleman in town for the night for a job interview. I settled into my chair with my tea, keen to chatter. He stared at me, took his teeth literally out of his mouth, and gummed, "Goo'nighd."

Chastened, I went to bed.

And so it unfolded. All around the cheery, busy coast, I danced on the periphery of a culture I could not break into. Then I got to Belfast. If you should ever need a straight dose of reality after a month of feeling like a bloody tourist no matter where you turn, I recommend Belfast. Don't mind the pipe bomb warnings or the grim, Dickensian buildings with their squat red-brick tops and their razor wire. Go. Walk. Skip the Black Cab tour and take yourself up the Falls Road and down the Shankill. Open your eyes to the human hands that painted the sectarian murals that decorate the brick. A paramilitary war zone for generations and neighborhoods, homes. Both are true.

Belfast doesn't have much of a tourist season. The gap-toothed kids I met didn't mind at all that I was taking pictures. But one wanted to know why I only saw the murals? Why not take a picture of him in front of the fish shop? There was only Kodachrome, then. The boy turned out blurry, and I felt I had lost something forever.

I bellied up to the oak bar of a pub and watched the barman pour Guinness, noting the flick of his wrist, the art of the proper pint; I like watching people do what they do well.

A young man—not much more than a kid, really, smooth-cheeked and gangly—came up to me. We chatted. His name was Conor. He spoke with the Belfast accent, all flattened vowels and dropped gerunds, and I told him, laughing, that I was homesick for Irish music because where I'm from the pubs are full of ti-deedly tunes and the long, sad ballads of the Olde Country. I'd been in Asia for a year, nearly. This was as close as I could get to home.

And so he took me, that kid Conor, across the humid city that night, through alleys and down wide thoroughfares that were strangely empty, past the glorious Hotel Europa: the most bombed hotel in Europe, he informed me, half-smiling, half-testing. I asked if he'd ever been in it.

"No," he said.

I marveled at how we end up inside our skins. I was as seamless a fit here—a foot in each world, my Scottish-Irish mongrel genes marked all over my fair freckled face—as anywhere on the planet. We could have been brother and sister, he and I. But with the impunity and innocence of a tourist, I was able to go places that he did not dream of setting foot. I knew in that moment that even if I tried, I'd never see the city as anything but an outsider.

Conor took me to a tiny den of a bar, nestled down low in the ground, dank and warm and strangely

welcoming. There was an upright piano in the corner
and a man with that most oddly Irish of instruments, the
bouzouki. He warbled and plucked, and then my new
friend and another man got up and joined him in an old
ballad called "My Bonny Highwayman," for me. The
liquor made me brave, and in return I took the stage and
regaled them loudly with all the verses of "Farewell to
Nova Scotia." They were remarkably kind. There were
perhaps six people in the place.

As I sang, a man came in, older than the rest of us
twenty-somethings by perhaps fifteen years. He stood
watching, and I saw Conor nod and go over and shake
his hand.

The newcomer was a bear of a man in a black trench
coat. His hair was longish and wild, and the matching
beard and his sharp blue eyes made me think at first of
Rasputin. I bowed. A few hands clapped. And then I
wandered off the stage at the very moment Conor asked
the bear how he was, and I saw the man's face crumple
in front of me. It was no time to introduce myself. Tipsy
and fey and far from home, I took his arm, his giant
arm.

"Sit," I commanded.

We sat, the three of us, in a round corner booth under
a single incandescent bulb. The big man began to talk.

His love had died. His wife—or not really his wife,
he conceded, but his partner of twenty years, older than
him, his *trooo luf*—had died of cancer perhaps a month
before. Words and sorrow and shame spilled from him
like music, about how her body wasted, and he was so
afraid, and he had not known what to say to her and in
the end it was she who lay beside him and told him it
would be alright. I have never seen a man so big seem so
small. I asked her name. It was Diane.

I no longer remember his.

We sat, and the drinks kept coming, and then as suddenly as he had arrived, he was off, paying the tab as he went. Before he left, he enclosed me in his arms, in the depths of that great coat, and I think I touched his face. He shook Conor's hand again, and he was gone.

The music was over. We sat, suddenly in silence, and I realized I had no idea how to get back to the hostel. I looked at my host, curious.

"Who was he?" I asked. "How do you know him?"

"Everybody knows him," Conor answered. "He's a legend. He's one of the big boys; he's been around here since the old days. My brothers knew him."

Then, wry and gentle, because my puzzled face must've given me away, he said, "He's a knee-capper, girl, an enforcer." He strung off a list of acronyms and adjectives that meant nothing to me.

He continued slowly, as if I were a child. "He's IRA. IRA? Get it?"

I'd known the whole time I was in the city that a fissure ran beneath it, invisible despite the murals. I'd walked the streets, shot my photo essay, humming Protestant hymns from my childhood when I'd realized my raincoat was bright Republican green. But I hadn't understood. I'd been a tourist, nothing more. And then I sat down with a bear of a man who did terrible things, a broken man in his grief and grace and whisky.

I felt my cheeks flush. Tears stung my eyes. The spectacle I had wandered the streets with my camera trying to capture was no spectacle after all. Only human, all of us. I met Conor's eyes and nodded.

ᔓ ᔓ ᔓ

Bonnie Stewart is an educator, writer, and social media researcher with a penchant for jelly beans. On her blog, crib chronicles, *and in her academic work, Bonnie writes about not looking away. Mother to Oscar and Posey, and to the memory of Finn, Bonnie has lived on all three coasts of Canada and in Asia and Europe. She has, however, achieved the Nirvana of her people and come home to the red mud of Prince Edward Island without having to work in the Anne of Green Gables industry. Her roots in the tightly networked habitat of PEI inform her doctoral studies in social media communities, connections, and branded identity. Her life's goal is to be on* Celebrity Jeopardy.

❧ ❧ ❧

The Labyrinth

Weep, pray, paddle.

"Get your shit together, Flaca, we're going boating." Roland bursts through the bedroom door, his shirtless, wiry frame hardly blocking my swollen eyes from the early-morning light.

I've been awake for hours listening to flocks of parakeets circling the nearby rainforest. Their shrieks harmonize with chirping crickets and weave around the rhythm of lonely surf breaking onto hard, dry sand below. Outside, laughing Ticos shuffle off to school and work in the Pacific town of Quepos amid chords of Costa Rican frogs and roosters.

Beads of sweat have been forming in the hollows of my upper lip and temples since before dawn, converging with the dripping stream of tears that pool in my ears before spilling down my neck toward my drenched, matted hair.

For days, I have lain listless like some forsaken Ophelia, staving off the recollection of how I came to be assed-out in a foreign country, effectively dying from heartbreak.

"I can't get up, Rolly," I say flatly, burrowing deeper into my sheet, sinking into the drone of overhead fan. I dismiss him with a shaking sob.

"Get up." Roland's stern, like a reprimanding father. He strides across the room to the closet and digs out my tattered river mesh bag, filling it with my helmet, paddling top, lifejacket, and a few carabiners before zipping it shut. Throwing me a bathing suit, he carries my gear off to load onto the flatbed. "I'll wait for you outside. Get up now, girl."

Slowly, I swing my legs over the edge of the bed and slip them into my bikini bottoms, resentful that Roland is hell-bent on staging this ridiculous paddling intervention. It's only because we've known each other for a decade and have guided countless rafting trips together that I listen to him at all.

I struggle into my top and slide on sunglasses and cracked river sandals before shuffling across the tile floor, out into the harsh daylight. The idling truck's passenger door is open, and I hoist myself onto the searing seat like a child being dragged to Sunday school.

The truck bounces over potholes, scattering chickens and packs of mangy, homeless dogs as we hurtle upward into the outlying mountains east of town, toward the headwaters of the Naranjo River where Roland's farm is. Raised in east L.A. by a Colombian mother and Tico father, Roland moved to Costa Rica after graduating college twenty-five years ago. He's so completely *tranquilo* at this point, it's nearly impossible to tell he's from the

States; only a die-hard allegiance to Steely Dan gives
him away.

We drive in silence, winding along the jungle-bound
road lined with pink, red, and orange impatiens. Cicadas
trill in oppressive, building waves that vibrate through
the truck cab until Roland finally turns to me and asks
the inevitable, "Well, what happened with you and
Nano?"

I look out at the blurred forest through fresh tears,
shaking my head before answering, "He's married."

"Yeah? So?"

"So! I never signed up to be the mistress."

"Who told you he was married?"

"You knew?"

"Everyone knows," Roland delivers the news softly,
like he's telling me my cat's been hit by a car or my house
burned down while I was away.

Shame and rage boil from my core to the surface of
my skin until I'm outwardly shaking. I sit on my hands
to keep from opening the cab door and jumping out. An
audience witnessing my humiliation seems unbearable.

"I found a letter from his wife," is all I can manage.

"Breathe," Roland squeezes my shoulder.

I want to come clean—tell him how for months before
moving to Costa Rica, I'd dreamt of finding a love letter
from someone else in Nano's bed. I'd ignored my intu-
ition, just as I had when, back in the States, Nano casually mentioned obtaining a green card through marrying
a friend. "It's not like it's a real marriage," he'd said.
"We haven't been together in years." It wasn't until I'd
stumbled upon the heartfelt words of another woman
(an American river guide like me) intent on saving her
marriage that I was forced to snap out of it.

Dammit, why won't Roland turn the truck around and let me get on with my earlier plan of hurling myself off Cathedral Point? Why does he insist on casually driving toward this godforsaken put-in?

"I wish someone would have mentioned that my boyfriend was married before I liquidated my life in the States to move down here." I'm glaring at him now, like it's his fault I'd given away my own marriage, a house, a business, and three cats just to chase a fantasy.

"You didn't ask."

I'm still sitting on my hands, wheezing.

"Look, you hooked up with another river guide." He shrugs. "You drank the Kool-Aid."

It's true—after twelve years of guiding on four continents, I had seen this scenario played out often enough. I knew better.

We pull up to Roland's farm and gather a two-person inflatable shredder from the shed, along with two paddles.

"Nano and Sandra were the last ones to take the shredder out," Roland tells me. "Just before you arrived, actually. They seemed pretty cozy."

"Like I need to hear that, Rolly."

"I don't want you whining later that no one told you."

Roland tops off the dual catamaran tubes of the shredder with air before stashing the pump back in the shed. He climbs in the passenger side of the rig and pushes me over to straddle the stick shift. Felipe, Roland's unlicensed teenaged son, appears from inside the farmhouse and hops behind the wheel of the flatbed. Felipe's sporting the same annoyingly affable smile as his father, which I find highly inappropriate considering I've hit rock bottom.

We hobble along the dwindling road, forging our way upstream along the river past a sparse scattering of homes. Near the top, where the road becomes more like a horse trail than a vehicle byway, we unload the shredder and our mesh bags. Felipe skillfully, and smilingly, ekes out a nine-point turn. He throws a shaka before disappearing down the hill, leaving Roland and me to the jungle.

"This is the way to the river." Roland stands before a steep, overgrown trail and hoists one end of the shredder above his head. He motions for me to follow suit.

"Watch your step," he warns.

We grunt our way down through the foliage, pausing occasionally to admire a passing toucan or epiphyte hanging from a vanilla tree. I put one foot in front of the other, balancing the shredder on my head while trying to match Roland's rhythm ahead of me until finally we reach the bottom of the gorge and rest on a fallen ceiba tree. Sweat clusters, unabsorbed by the steamy rainforest, glisten on our skin.

"Remember that time on the Upper Kern when you got caught in those horrible strainers?" Roland asks as he passes me his water bottle.

A whisper of a laugh escapes through my nose. "Yeah, I remember. I was highsiding an oar boat on a tree island while those poor Japanese folks clung to the bow crying. If you hadn't pulled my ass out of there with a Z-drag, I would have been screwed."

"In twenty-five years of guiding, that sticks in my mind as some of the gnarliest river carnage I've ever seen," Roland declares. "I hiked up to where you were stuck, saw you highsiding and thought, *How is that skinny girl keeping the boat from flipping?*" He laughs and shakes his head, beginning to pull gear out of his mesh bag.

"This upper section is called 'The Labyrinth,'" Roland says, cinching down his frayed lifejacket. "It's been run maybe three or four times before today. I've seen it a couple times and I'd say it's pretty solid Class V. Lots of steep drops through tight chutes. There are a few slots we have to make—it's not an option to miss them. I think I can remember them all, but we'll have to scout as we go. There's no way out of the gorge once we start."

Normally I would be anxious about taking a flaccid shredder down a little-run Class V boulder garden without the safety of other boaters along or even an evacuation route. Plus, Roland forgot his helmet and we have no throw bag. Oddly, I couldn't care less. I feel no hint of the usual Class V jitters or concern for our lack of preparedness. It occurs to me that I may be spared a trip to Cathedral Point, as our little daytrip down the Labyrinth is suicidal enough.

We climb into the tiny craft and immediately drop into a sizeable chute cascading onto exposed rocks. It's continuous maneuvering from there; the maze is relentless and we're teetering and spinning off boulders, fighting each other's rhythm. We catch a small eddy and Roland, who's sitting on the left side of the shredder, shouts out, "Do you guide from the left or right?"

"Left," I say.

"I guide from the right, let's switch sides."

We start to click after switching, powerfully stroking across current lines and straightening out for the drops. Paddling becomes like meditation; there's only the hum of frenetic water and our focused concentration on the line.

We park on a rock cluster above the first big rapid, "Stacy's Lament." Roland explains that the last time

he ran down the Labyrinth, he escorted some kayak-
ers from Colorado who were insistent that Costa Rican
Class V was really like Class IV in Colorado. After
spending a good portion of the upper section upside
down, the group became disheartened while scouting
the first "real" rapid. One of the more intrepid Colorado
paddlers probed it first, hitting the narrow, eight-foot
drop on the far left side next to the gorge wall. Just
below the drop, he inexplicably veered and smashed
headlong into the curving monolith. He swam out of his
kayak and was pushed by the funneling current into the
collection of sieve rocks stacked against the right wall of
the gorge. Submerged for some time against the rocks,
he surfaced in a pool of blood minutes later, his face
badly lacerated from the impact. That's when Stacy, the
least experienced of the group, began to cry uncontrol-
lably, realizing that there was no way to portage or line
around the rapid. There was only one way out: through
the guts.

"Don't swim here," Roland warns as we push off the
rock island and head for the left side.

We make it to the slot and straighten out for the drop,
noticing too late that there's a doinker rock poking out
next to the wall. It grabs the left front tube of the shredder and spins it so that we smash full-on into the jutting
left wall with the force of the waterfall folding the boat
in half against the rock. As the angled boat floods with
water, I spin around and slip two of my fingers through
the back D-ring, and my feet flutter outside of the boat
in the downstream current. From the corner of my eye,
I see Roland flush out, propelling headfirst into the rock
sieve below. He disappears underwater, exactly in the
spot where the lacerated Colorado boater had been.

Hanging from a keychain-sized metal ring by the inside crooks of my knuckles, I tuck my long legs up to my chest against the current and wrap them firmly around the pinned back tube. Legs secured, I use my hands to push the boat away from the rock wall, inching the plastered shredder along the wall slowly until it unwraps and pops free. Somehow, my paddle has survived inside the boat, and I use it to draw-stroke my way across the current until I'm downstream from where Roland has surfaced. I quickly yank him into the shredder, spy an eddy and draw us into it while Roland fishes his floating-away paddle out of the drink.

We sit in the eddy, breathing and looking up at Stacy's Lament; Roland's rubbing his head with an eerie, frozen grin on his face.

"You hit your head?"

He nods.

"Did you see stars?"

"I think so, yeah."

"Do me a favor and bring your helmet next time," I scold. At least there are no bloody lacerations to deal with; we didn't bring first aid supplies or even duct tape.

With miles left to go, the sun slides below the canyon wall. We push on through the twilight, navigating the maze of downed logs, bus-sized rocks, and steep chutes. We do our best to read-and-run from our low vantage point, not wanting to waste any of the dwindling gray light on scouting.

Near the bottom of the run, we come to a severe horizon line; white froth shoots skyward from the force of the drop.

"This might be the rapid that has a big strainer blocking the entrance on the right," Roland yells over the roar.

We park on a flat rock at the top and climb around a house-sized boulder to get a full view.

Roland's remembered correctly—there's an enormous, fallen ceiba tree braced across the only feasible entrance in the rock-riddled rapid. Everything looks distant and two-dimensional in the flat light. We scooch like crabs across a series of mostly submerged boulders over to the downed snag and try to kick it free without success. Standing next to the drop, we study the current, noting that there's more clearance if we pass under the tree on the right side of the chute. If we hit the left side, we'll be tangled in the scoured ceiba branches and either get pinned against the knotty obstacles or swept out of the boat. Below the chute, there's a nearly river-wide death sieve of rocks that's completely impassable; a swim here would be heinous at best. We simply have to clear under the tree on the right, then haul ass over to the left side of the river to drop down and out of the Labyrinth.

I start to feel it then: adrenaline buzzing in tune to the thumping of whitewater, flooding my body until I want to thrash out of my skin, kicking and punching. Looking down at the water rushing under the tree, I realize that more than anything I want to live. My survival switch has been kicked, and I suddenly become the girl who highsides huge oar boats on strainer islands, who hand-walks shredders off rock walls to rescue friends. I am the creation of all the rivers I have known and the knowledge they've instilled: I am constant, adaptable, and strong-willed.

I lean out and put my hand in the water as I always have, and ask the Naranjo River for safe passage. "My hands are your hands," I say. "Use them."

As I'm bent over, a Blue Morpho butterfly lands on the log in front of me, just above a slight crease in the current. I look closer and see that the water to the right of the crease drops down and clears the log. The water on the left side of the crease spills under the nastiest part of the strainer. Gently, I touch my wet fingers onto my forehead, knowing the way out of the Labyrinth.

"Look at the crease," I call over to Roland. "If we put the left tube on it, we'll clear the log."

His eyebrows lift, then he nods. We walk back to the shredder and push off the flat boulder. Gently paddling forward, we ease alongside the crease and effortlessly slide under the right side of the log. Hitting the bottom of the chute, we charge over to the left where we drop down and out of the gorge.

We float in silence to Roland's farm just downstream, the sky ablaze in crimson. Howler monkeys bellow from the forest canopy, noting our passage.

"They say in Costa Rica, 'Las cosas son como Dios quiere, no como uno quiere'—things are how God wants, not how you want," Roland whispers, his strong profile outlined in the fading orange glow.

He touches my arm and we paddle for shore, where Felipe is waiting for us. Smiling, I dip my hand in the water and say a silent thank you to the Naranjo for teaching me how to survive.

❧ ❧ ❧

Two years after their journey down the Labyrinth (a.k.a. the Chorro), Bridget Crocker read this story to Roland Cervilla just before he died of cancer. Shortly after, Roland's longtime girlfriend, Kris Krengel, gave the shredder as a wedding gift to Bridget and her new husband. Happily married with two girls, Bridget lives on the coast near Ventura, California, and works as a freelance outdoor travel writer. Her narratives have been featured in National Geographic Adventure, Outside, Paddler, *and* Trail Runner *magazines and she is a contributing author for Lonely Planet guidebooks.*

✂ ✂ ✂

Belle of the Ball

A fiery traveler exposes the crown jewels
of the Balkans.

The sizzling testicles weren't as round as I'd expected
them to be. Instead, they'd been sliced in half and
looked like lumpy pieces of chicken breast. Next to the
pan, which was propped up over a fire, a man crouched
on a wooden stool, eyeing the delicacies to make sure they
didn't burn.

I pointed at the meat. "Kangaroo?"

He nodded, prodding the testicles with a metal
spatula.

If it weren't for the words printed in big letters across
his t-shirt—WORLD TESTICLE COOKING CHAMPIONSHIP—I
might be forgiven for thinking that I was at any old
barbeque festival, albeit in the middle of Serbia: canvas
shade structures housed folding tables littered with
plates of sausages and half-eaten white bread, empty

beer bottles lay in haphazard piles on the grass, rock music blared from portable stereos, people sipped wine from plastic cups, and at least a dozen plumes of smoke emanated from cooking fires, creating a permanent white fog that settled in the camping area.

I'd found out about the testicle festival the same way I find out about all other important things in my life: by browsing the internet late at night. I came across an online cookbook entitled "Cooking with Balls: The World's First Testicle Cookbook." The preview video shows a middle-aged man with wire-frame glasses wearing a chef's hat and sitting outdoors next to a brass pot. He bangs the spatula once, then again, and looks directly at the camera. "Chello my friends! My name is Ljubomir Erovic, organizer and creator of the annual World Testicle Cooking Championships here in Serbia."

There was something magnetic about Ljubomir. Maybe it was the strange way he spoke, putting extra emphasis on each word, or maybe it was the lack of irony in his voice, as if he were giving a lesson on the principles of neurology, not a primer on how to cut testicles into diagonal slices. Even before I bought the e-book, which contains recipes for everything from ostrich testicles to goulash with bull testicles, I knew I couldn't miss the testicle festival. He'd had me at Chello.

I emailed Ljubomir, informing him of my plans to attend. I offered to put on a free fire dancing performance, a talent I'd cultivated over the years from a hobby to a part-time profession. A fire show in central Serbia sounded like it would provide me with a much-needed adventure. Ljubomir wrote back, accepting my offer and promising to buy the necessary fuel, and I began searching for the perfect song for my performance.

A few weeks later I was on a dilapidated bus headed from Belgrade, Serbia's capital, to Kragujevac, an industrial city 150 kilometers to the south. At the bus station I was picked up by Zoran, a friendly thirty-year-old local I'd contacted on couchsurfing.com, a travel-oriented website that facilitates connections between locals and travelers. Neither Zoran nor the five other people I'd emailed had ever heard of the World Testicle Cooking Championship. In fact, Zoran was so surprised I was coming to Kragujevac—"We don't get any visitors here!"—that he took off work just to drive me to Borač, the village where the festival would be held the following day.

The drive to Borač only took twenty minutes, but it felt like we traveled back centuries in time: the two-lane highway narrowed into a single-lane road, which wound through rolling green hills dotted with small homes crowned by red shingled roofs. The paved roads gave way to a rough dirt track that cut through rows of tall cornfields, and suddenly our car seemed odd among tractors and pick-up trucks hauling loads of pumpkins. The testicle festival was being held *here*?

Even Zoran was incredulous. "We'd better call," he said, picking up his cell phone to dial Ljubomir. We drove down what appeared to be the main street in Borač—the single shop had a poster for Nestlé ice cream—and soon were facing an even rockier dirt road. Zoran looked hesitantly at the road, and then at me, but we went on. After a few bumpy moments, we saw a two-story white stone house on our right. In the adjacent yard were a dozen small wooden tables. And there, in the midst of this rural nowhere, five people milled about, all wearing t-shirts that proclaimed "World Testicle Cooking Championship."

A white van drove up moments later, and Ljubomir half-stumbled out of the driver's door. He looked exactly like he did in the e-cookbook, only much taller and a little chubbier. He was wearing a red t-shirt with navy cotton shorts and sneakers, and his close-cropped hair was graying at the sides. In a swift motion, he puffed on his cigarette, stuck it between his lips, grabbed my hand, and shook it firmly. "Anna! Pleased to meet you," he shouted. He continued shaking. "I have been waiting."

Before I could say, "You too," Ljubomir was gone. He'd practically done a nosedive back into the van. He rummaged furiously through some plastic bags, procured a one-liter bottle of fuel, handed it to me, dove back into the van, flipped through more bags, and without turning his head, called out: "What size t-shirt you like?"

"I don't know. Medium?"

"Ahaaa, ahaaa," he said excitedly, in what I assumed was his version of "Uh-huh." He continued noisily flipping through each plastic-wrapped t-shirt, checking their size tags, and hurling each non-medium shirt, one by one, toward the passenger seat.

All this happened quickly. It took me a moment to realize that there were hundreds of t-shirts in the front seat—and Ljubomir was going through each one. This could take all day.

"You know what," I said, "any size is fine."

"Ahaaa, yes?" he said, finally looking up at me. "I find you a medium later. It is promise."

Ljubomir noticed Zoran. He got out of the van, shook Zoran's hand, said something to him in rapid Serbian, ducked back inside, and slammed the door. He turned to me through the open window—"See you in one hour!"—and the van jolted forward, its tires kicking up a dust storm in its wake.

I exchanged a look with Zoran, my eyes wide. This man was a tornado. "This is Serbian people," he said, by way of explanation. We got back into the car—Ljubomir had found accommodation for me at a farmhouse just up the road—and Zoran dropped me off. An hour later, as promised, Ljubomir picked me up, and this time I noticed that the back of the van was crammed full with amplifiers and speakers.

"Anna, please, get inside," he said. I jumped into the passenger seat, brushing away dozens of shrink-wrapped t-shirts.

"Do you smoke?" he asked, lighting the cigarette that dangled from his lips.

"No."

Ljubomir burst out laughing. He laughed too loudly and too long, as if I'd cracked a brilliant joke.

"I must ask you something," he said.

"O.K."

"I have very much honor that you are here. And I like you to be President of the Juru."

"Juru?"

"Juru," he repeated, searching for the word in English, "Jury, jury. You must taste all testicle dishes and decide which is the best."

"I'd love to."

The following morning I was sipping the last of my Turkish coffee when Ljubomir's van came to an abrupt halt in front of the farmhouse. He walked purposefully through the gate and slapped a paper the size of an index card on the table. "You must wear this," he said. Printed on the card was my name, and underneath it the words *Expert Juru*.

We drove to the site of the festival, where at least a hundred cars—mostly Yugos and similar rickety-

looking cars—were haphazardly parked on the road-
side. On our right was the house, and to the left, a
narrow path descended sharply to a creek, passable by
a small footbridge. Across the footbridge, on a patch of
grass the size of a baseball field and hedged by woods,
the festival was in full swing: sausages crackled on the
grill, music blared from a five-piece band with tubas and
horns, and men removed their shirts to cool off in the
stifling heat. Ljubomir marched me through the crowd
as if I was a movie star and he my bodyguard. A dozen
journalists and cameramen were gathered in a semi-
circle at one end of the field, and when Ljubomir spoke
into the microphone, the crowds gathered round. Then
I heard the words "Anna" "Izra-el" and "Ah-mer-eeca."
Everyone looked at me and clapped. "I told them you
are ballsy for coming here," Ljubomir whispered as he
handed me the microphone. "Say something."

I glanced at the expectant crowd. The lenses were
trained on me. "I am very proud to be in Borač for the
sixth annual World Testicle Cooking Championship," I
said, pausing for my words to be translated into Serbian,
"I have traveled very far to try your testicles. Let the
cooking begin!"

Actually, the cooking had begun the evening before;
I'd caught a glimpse of the teams getting set up as
Ljubomir had driven us past "Balls Camp." We'd
continued on to some kind of tavern—picnic tables
arranged in front of a horse stable—and Ljubomir had
ordered us a few beers.

He had leaned in closely. "I must tell you something
about me," he said gravely, looking me straight in the
eye. "I am chef, musician, and sport pilot." He pushed
his glasses up his nose. "But now I want to do just music.
Rock 'n' roll music. Like Djanee Cash."

At forty-seven, Ljubomir was a rock musician and an inventor (of, among other things, a tub that enabled nurses to massage their patients more efficiently), and he regularly worked to fix medical and dental equipment. He ran a restaurant in the nearby town of Gorni Milasovic, where he was born, but he was planning to open a restaurant in London in a few months, where he could cook and play music.

"Anna, I must ask you something. Please," he said, again in that dramatic way.

"What do you think of my website?"

Ballcup.com was spectacular, mostly for its complete disregard of all website design norms. At the top, the fluorescent green words WORLD NEEDS A GOOD BALLS OFFER accompanied a headshot of Ljubomir, wearing a yellow baseball cap, light glinting off his glasses, head tilted slightly and looking off into the distance, as if he were President Obama talking about the future of America. The rest of the homepage was a chaotic jumble: a cartoon illustration of a mustached chef with his balls inside a boiling brass pot, a bizarre excerpt from a 2004 article about kangaroo testicles, two videos of Ljubomir on a Serbian cooking show, red ticker tape announcing the August 2009 date of the championship, videos demonstrating how to peel the skin off frozen testicles, a BBC weather logo linking to the forecast in central Serbia, a video from the U.K.'s *Daily Telegraph* about Ljubomir's e-cookbook, bold-faced headings like VERY IMPORTANT and IDEA followed by Ljubomir's journal-like musings, scrolling text listing festival rules such as "Strictly prohibited to bring Viagra," and my favorite, a fifteen-picture thumbnail collage of Ljubomir at different stages of his life, from the late 70s through today. Each thumbnail linked to a larger image, and when there were multiple people in the photograph, a thick Microsoft-Paint-style red arrow pointed to Ljubomir's head. In today's age of template-style blogs and neat navigation bars, ballcup. com was a refreshing bomb blast.

"It's great," I said, "very unique."

I directed the conversation to the matter at hand: testicles, and how Ljubomir became interested in them. He told me that when he was a young boy, around eight or nine, his grandmother fed him goulash and told him it was made with rabbit meat. That night, he was incredibly aroused—"very chot, much energy, you understand?"—but he didn't know why, until he found out from friends that he'd consumed testicle goulash, not rabbit goulash. Since then, Ljubomir has promoted "testes food" as an aphrodisiac and a healthy alternative to Viagra.

"For women, too?"

"Yes." He nodded emphatically. Most of the people who bought his e-cookbook were women, judging from the list of names sent to him by his publisher. "I don't know if they buy for themselves," he said, laughing, "I think is because their chusbands need chelp!"

I asked Ljubomir how many kinds of testicles I could expect to try tomorrow. He said that he didn't know for sure what each team would bring, but probably boar, bull, stallion, pig, maybe kangaroo, ram, maybe ostrich, goat, donkey, rooster, turkey, reindeer, buck, bear, deer and elk. And what, in his expert opinion, were the tastiest testicles?

"Stallion," he said. "And bull."

It was the bull testicles that attracted my attention immediately after the opening ceremony, mostly because the platter was particularly eye-catching: a dozen testicles, each the size of an apple and the color of a well-done steak, were arranged in a circle. Topping each was a smattering of cheese and a sprinkling of green herbs, with a single grape crowning each ball, like the cherry atop an ice cream sundae. To complete the phallic symbolism, a green chili pepper stood erect in the center of the circle, stuffed inside a scooped-out tomato.

I couldn't gape at the testicles unnoticed. I was President of the Jury, the only person with dreadlocks, and, it seemed, the only young female attendee: by default, a rock star. Team Aptem was thrilled to have drawn my attention to their bull testicles. A man in a cowboy hat led me to the platter, and I smiled politely for a photo-op. I was handed a shot glass of *rakija*, the homemade Serbian plum brandy, and we clinked glasses to cries of "*Jeevoolay!*"

I wandered—or was half-dragged by men with *rakija*-breath who grabbed my arms—from team to team. Beneath the sign for Team Knjaz Milos was a pair of fleshy testicles that looked like two fatty chicken thighs dangling from a string. It was unsettling seeing the organs unattached to any kind of body. One team member guided my hands to the balls. The flesh was cool and jiggly, and covered by a layer of skin. Dark veins ran across the surface, squiggling around but never crossing, like elevation lines on a topographic map.

Then I noticed the poor (former) owner of the testicles. It was a goat, and it was being roasted, whole, near my feet. The metal spit pierced its length and ran through its mouth, so that it looked like it was choking on a pole. What an awful way to go, I thought. Castrated and cooked, balls hovering above your head.

But that goat was tasty. One team member grabbed a butcher's knife, cut off a chunk from its shoulder, crammed the moist meat into a piece of white bread, and offered it to me. Once the others saw that I'd eaten, I was rushed with offers of homemade white cheese, roasted peppers topped with a cream cheese-like Serbian specialty called *kaymac*, chocolate truffles, pound cake, and sausages. It's not every day that people trip over themselves to bring me the best of their home cooking, so I happily indulged—at first. But soon I realized that I should probably stay neutral, seeing as how I was President of the Jury and everything.

"*Kosneyia*," I said, in response to the remaining food offers, using the Serbian word for "later." I also wanted to save my appetite for the testicle dishes that would be presented to the jury, which was supposed to convene at 4 P.M.

Still, it wasn't easy. Testicles were everywhere: some were being marinated in bowls, waiting to be added to stews, while others sizzled in frying pans. A heavy brass pot seemed to be the cooking utensil of choice, adding a medieval touch to the whole atmosphere. Most teams had at least one brass pot, suspended from a tripod-like device so that it swung freely over a fire. But some teams had two: the elderly members of Mz Verelec, dressed in white overalls, were bent stiffly over their two pots, one brimming with sliced onions and the other with testicles.

The most innovative testicle-cooking contraption, by far, was the bicycle wheel constructed by Team Loza. They'd turned the spokes into skewers onto which they had artfully arranged testicles and peppers. This genius bicycle kebab wheel, which had been stripped of its rubber tire, was connected to a motor and spun rapidly over a fire. One team member constantly doused the testicles with a cloth soaked in oil. A nearby Serbian sign read

"Balls on Wheel" and the English-speaking journalist who translated it explained that this was a popular Serbian phrase, "he's got his balls in a wheel," used to describe someone who is completely confused. The whole thing was brilliant.

I really took a liking to Team Mirsha. They were an earnest father-and-son team, and the only ones who weren't drunk. The head of the team, probably in his forties, had a big nose, deep-set black eyes, and a face that looked kind of sad. He showed me what his team was cooking for the jury: a pot full of bubbling reddish stew with testicles, vegetables, and chopped herbs. Then he pointed to a brass casserole dish that was layered with tomato and meat, and topped with cheese.

"Testicle moussaka," he said proudly, wiping the beads of sweat from his face.

Throughout the day, Ljubomir was in constant motion: shaking hands here, talking to a journalist there, and running from place to place with an entourage. He'd put me in charge of holding his keys, cellphone, digital camera, and camcorder, and every so often he'd find me and give me something new to hold.

At some point he motioned for me to follow him, and I was introduced to his "good friend," a thin, serious-looking man who held a manila envelope protectively against his torso. We sat down at an empty table and the man solemnly handed both Ljubomir and me felt-tip pens. He procured an official-looking stamp pad. We all took shots of *rakija*, nodded seriously, and got down to business.

Of course, I didn't know what the business was—I figured this guy was a lawyer, and that I'd be signing some official Serbian documents—until he opened the folder and revealed a stack of certificates, each printed on thick glossy paper and containing the official logo of the festival, a McDonald's "M" that's been stretched, as if on a balloon, to look like a pair of testicles. The man licked his index finger, carefully separated the first certificate, stamped it with an official "Mudrijada" (the Serbian name for the Championship) stamp, and gently passed the certificate to Ljubomir, taking care not to crease it. Ljubomir stuffed his cigarette in his mouth, signed on the bottom, and I signed after him, beneath the words "Presideanje de Juru."

Soon after, Ljubomir rounded up a bunch of people— a Bulgarian journalist, the guy who provides internet for Ljubomir's village, a few others and me—and with a wave of his hand, gestured for us to file into the back of the van. When we got out a few bumpy moments later, we were in the main street of Borač.

"Press conference," Ljubomir declared.

We were standing outside an open-air restaurant, and the tables were full of journalists, all drinking beer and *rakija*. Ljubomir immediately disappeared—I saw him off to one side, giving a television interview—and I, touted by Ljubomir as the next most important person, was suddenly in the spotlight.

An English-speaking reporter from *Serbia Today* asked me how I'd found out about the festival, and when I said "the Internet," he raised an eyebrow, probably wondering what the hell I had been googling. A journalist from *Vreme*, the Serbian version of *Time*, acted as a translator for a tableful of journalists: "Why are you qualified to be President of the Jury?"

Good question, I thought. I muttered something about never having tasted testicles before, so I had a "fresh tongue."

It got increasingly surreal. I was thrust in front of a

television camera, where I was asked to tell the Serbian nation what I thought of them ("very hospitable"), if I'd eaten testicles before ("no, only liquor fermented with goat testicles, in Vietnam"), and finally: "As a young person coming from Israel and America, what is your message for the young people of Serbia today?"

I considered comparing my upcoming fire show to the U.S. fire that rained down on Serbia ten years earlier, but decided against it. "I know that America and Israel and Serbia haven't had good relations in the past," I stated confidently, "but I would like my visit to represent the start of a new era for these three nations. An era of friendship and peace." As the translator translated my words into Serbian, I marveled at the grandiose bullshit I'd just spewed. But the interviewer smiled happily; he loved every bit of it.

Then Ljubomir gave a self-aggrandizing mono-logue ("Jamie Oliver is just a chef, but I am a chef and a musician"), after which a half-hour of chaos ensued. Should we return to the festival, or stay at the restaurant as Ljubomir had instructed? It was after 5 P.M., and the Bulgarian journalist left in frustration, wonder-ing whether or not the jury would actually convene. Eventually, the rest of us decided to walk back to the festival. We heard Ljubomir singing before we saw him, on a sound system so elaborate it would have been better suited to Bonnaroo than a field in central Serbia. Then, finally, the moment I'd been waiting for: I was called into the top-secret jury room.

The World Testicle Cooking Championship is not the only testicle festival in the world. The Rocky Mountain Oyster Festival—which showcases its namesake, bull testicles—is held every year at a lodge in Montana. The

festival has a raunchy party atmosphere, featuring topless women, wet t-shirt contests, lots of Budweiser, and,
of course, the quintessential American festival experience, the eating competition: in 2007, a guy named Matt
Powers ate forty bull testicles in four minutes.

Smaller, less-lewd testicle festivals take place throughout the U.S.: the town of Eagle, Idaho, hosts one as a
fundraiser for its firefighters, and the Turkey Testicle
Festival in Byron, Illinois, donates its proceeds to hos-
pitals and charities. The Cowboy Museum in Oakdale,
California, puts on an annual testicle dinner, and other
testicle festivals take place in ranch towns like Olean,
Missouri, and Watsonville, California. In Oklahoma
and Kansas, fried bull testicles are called "calf fries,"
in Canada they're known as "prairie oysters," and
internationally, "white kidney" is the most popular
euphemism. And the practice of testicle eating is nothing new: testicles are considered a delicacy throughout
Asia, in countries like Iran, Afghanistan, Taiwan, and,
of course, China.

But what sets the World Testicle Cooking
Championship apart is not its supposed international
character—I was the most international guest—but the
variety of testicles (from more than a dozen different
animals) and the atmosphere in which they are cooked.
Only natural ingredients are allowed and all dishes are
cooked over a wood fire. Participants are a mix of pro-
fessional chefs and amateurs, mostly from Serbia and
nearby Balkan countries. Ljubomir told me that this year
a few international teams cancelled due to the economic
crisis and concerns about swine flu. Each team pays an
entry fee of fifty euros, and that money, combined with
t-shirt sales, allows Ljubomir to break even on expenses.
The teams compete for bragging rights and the first

prize, which is an all-inclusive vacation for two in the Serbian mountains. And whatever remaining doubts I had about the culinary seriousness of the festival, the jury room—and the dishes themselves—put them to rest.

The jury room was on the top floor of the house, in a bedroom decorated with paintings of stone-faced Czars and mustached Serbian heroes. The lawyer sat near a window with his manila envelope, and two women and two men, each wearing an EXPERT JURU badge, studied the fifteen testicle dishes spread out on the table.

"Do you work with animals?" asked one man as he introduced himself.

"No. Why, do you?"

"Yes, we three are veterinary doctors and he"—he pointed to other man—"is in the food business."

The man's wife introduced herself as Boyana and handed me a spoon. I dug into the first dish, pieces of testicle meat swimming in a brown soup. Using the thin edge of my spoon, I cut a piece in half and was surprised by how readily the meat gave way. I savored it on my tongue and tried to identify the taste: it was moist and tender, not sinewy or chewy, almost like a very soft sausage that had been simmering for hours in a thick gravy. I nodded my approval.

Boyana, pencil in hand, asked me to rate the dish, five being the highest mark and one the lowest. The dish was good, but it wasn't out-of-this-world spectacular. But didn't I have to taste a five dish to know which was a four? I decided to quickly try a bite of each dish, just to get an idea of the range. I began to hurriedly work my way around the table, wolfing down a spoonful of each.

Apparently I'd adopted an incorrect strategy. The two men looked at me sternly, indicating with their outstretched palms that I should slow down. "We have time," one said. And Boyana laid her hand gently on my shoulder. "Testicles high caloric," she said.

Eventually we narrowed it down to five or six contenders. The platters of grilled or barbequed testicles never really stood a chance—they drew wrinkled noses and scornful looks from the jury—but their arrangement was impressive, like exotically carved fruit platters at a wedding.

Then it was down to two entries: one with testicles and onions, seemingly stewed together for hours. The two flavors balanced each other perfectly, leaving a smooth, savory taste on my tongue. The other entry was a roller coaster ride: first I tasted the meat, soft and bursting with flavor, then the olives, which slightly dampened the meat taste, and then I recognized hints of basil, which added to the already growing cohesion of flavors, and when I chewed the peppers and olives and pickles, everything combined in a sort of joyous symphony of flavors, and finally, the peanut flavor carried it out, and just when I thought it was all over—I'd swallowed and everything—another taste floated up, an entirely different aftertaste, which hung in my mouth like the ending violin note vibrating away after a spectacular concert.

But when Boyana asked us to vote on that dish, only another woman and I raised our hands. The onion dish garnered the other three votes.

"Really?" I looked at Boyana in disbelief.

She shrugged: "Too many vegetables."

I considered inquiring about veto power—after all, Serbia has a rich history of leaders doing whatever they please—but seeing as I was vastly underqualified in my Presidential role, I kept my mouth shut. Boyana picked up the two winning dishes and beneath them, hand-written on scraps of paper, were the team's names: the team of older white-haired guys had submitted the onion dish, and Team Mirsha, the ones with the testicle moussaka, had submitted the mind-blowing dish. Boyana conferred with the lawyer, who removed the cover from his special pen. When I glanced over, I saw that he was elegantly drawing out the name of each team, and only then did I understand: this man was not a lawyer, he was a calligrapher.

While he worked on the certificates, I continued eating, in some vague attempt to hold onto this transcendent hour of culinary wonder. One stew-like dish had moist, spongy balls that relented perfectly to my teeth. I wondered if they were the testicles of a smaller animal, like a turkey or rooster. Then it hit me: they reminded me of matzah balls from my Bubbe's chicken soup.

"Wow," I said, pointing with my spoon, "that one has excellent texture."

Boyana's husband didn't understand. "Texture," I repeated, rubbing my thumb and forefinger together.

He scooped out a ball from the bowl and ate it. "Ahh, textura?"

"Yes," I said, "it is very good."

He said something to the others, and they, too, tasted the dish again, murmuring to each other as they rolled the testicles on their tongues. Then the husband turned to me: "We have agreed with your idea of making a new prize for testicle texture."

"Oh, it was just a comment."

"What?"

"Nothing." I smiled. "Yes, prize for texture is good."

When the calligrapher finished, Boyana grabbed my hand and led me downstairs to the yard. Ljubomir and his bandmate were still singing—a mix of Serbian songs and classic rock covers like Creedence Clearwater's "Proud Mary"—and a large crowd had assembled, anxiously awaiting the awards ceremony. The sun was slowly dipping behind the hills, and it cast a golden hue across the people drinking and dancing in the evening light. I started to walk off to join them, but Boyana drew me back, gesturing—because the music was too loud to make herself heard—that I would be presenting the final awards. And so we waited, next to a gigantic cake frosted with a pair of flesh-colored balls, for Ljubomir to finish his performance.

Ljubomir didn't care that everyone wanted him to finish the concert. This was his festival, and if he wanted to play music for three hours, he was going to play music for three hours.

He was a curious mix of genius and drunk. Half the time I marveled at his brilliance, coming from the middle of nowhere in Serbia, managing to publish a testicle cookbook and market the championship to domestic and international media. But despite the fastidious attention to detail, the overall impression was that of chaos. The festival seemed to barrel forward on the backs of Ljubomir's energy and charisma, but also with his attention span. No one knew when, how, or why things were going to happen. In the end it all worked, though, and the result was something brilliant: a gonzo-style festival led by the Serbian version of Hunter S. Thompson.

If it was that novelty that drew me here, it was never clearer than now, minutes before the awards ceremony, that this festival was anything but a joke. The mood had shifted. During the day the teams had mingled and shared food, but now they huddled in groups, stealing nervous glances toward Boyana and me. The tension was palpable.

When the awards ceremony began, Boyana did the talking and I did my best to look important: I smiled and congratulated each team with a handshake as they came up to accept their certificates. But apparently my handshake was not appropriate. Ljubomir quickly corrected me. "You must kiss three times," he whispered in my ear, "this is Serbian way."

And so I did. At first I thought I'd owe just a handful of kisses; as the ceremony stretched on, however, I realized that each team was being awarded for participation—and I'm pretty sure a few unaffiliated drunks snuck in, too.

 Middle-aged men couldn't hide their excitement as they came up, beaming, shining in their individual moments of pride. Nor could they hide their disappointment. I'll never forget the crestfallen faces of Team Mirsha when they learned they'd placed second. And when the old guys were awarded first prize, they ran up, jumping up and down like kids.

Then it came time to present the trophy. Ljubomir had explained to me that the World Testicle Cooking Championship trophy was just like the World Cup trophy—held by the winning team until a new champion is crowned. The trophy featured the wooden figure of a man, naked, his penis erect. But last year's team had crafted a sheath that slipped over the penis, doubling its size and giving it more definition, so now it was a detailed head and shaft instead of a nondescript rod. I presented the trophy with its new sheath, kissed everyone again, cut the balls cake, and relaxed with a beer until it got dark enough for my fire show.

I changed into my fire clothes in the jury room, the only semi-private spot. The testicle dishes were still on the table, so I helped myself to a few more spoonfuls. Outside, I took hold of my fire poi and gave a nod to the sound guy. Someone held up a lighter to the poi, and two big balls of fire lit up the night. On came the drumbeat, and I waved the fireballs tantalizingly close to the audience, illuminating their faces. I swung my hips in time to the beat, slowly, waiting for the music to build. Ljubomir crouched in the corner with his camcorder.

Say, anybody ever seen my balls they're big and salty and brown growled the deep voice of Isaac Hayes over the speaker, blasting into the Serbian countryside. I'd choreographed my fire routine to "Chocolate Salty Balls," which turned out to be my private joke, because no one here understood the lyrics. No matter. For the climax (*Baby you better get back in the kitchen*) I kneeled on the ground (*'cause I got a sneaking suspicion*) slowly brought my head down (*Baby! You just… burned my balls!*), and swung the poi close to my face, so that the fireballs came within inches of my chin and nose. When it was all over, I bowed and walked off to cries of "Bravo, Anna!"

The night ended quietly, with a handful of us drinking *rakija* around a folding table. When there was nothing left to drink we piled into Ljubomir's van. Just then the storm that had held itself back unleashed, and I ran from the van to the farmhouse under torrents of rain.

I was awakened by a knock on my door early in the morning. Ljubomir was on the phone for me. Groggily, I stumbled to the living room, marveling that this farmhouse had a landline. My head was pounding, and I wondered why Ljubomir was calling so early. Do Serbians not get hangovers?

"Hello," I croaked.

"Anna, hello! It is me, Ljubomir."

"I know."

"Anna, please, I must tell you something. Last night you forget your certificate."

"Oh no, really?" I'd been awarded a certificate—for what I wasn't exactly sure—and my name had been drawn out in swirly calligraphy.

"You must take it. I come now."

Ljubomir was at the farmhouse within the hour, chatting away on his cell phone as he walked up. "Radio interview," he explained as he clicked the phone shut. We drank coffee and talked about next year's festival. Ljubomir told me that the people of Borač hadn't been happy about this year's festival—"They don't like rock music"—so he had found a new site fifteen kilometers away. He had already set the August 2010 dates and was counting on my presence, since I was now an important part of the World Testicle Cooking Championship. I promised to do my best to attend.

Then it was time to go. Ljubomir gave me a lift to an intersection where I was to meet Zoran, who'd offered to drive me all the way back to Belgrade. On the short drive, Ljubomir became emotional. "I a lot of like you," he kept saying. "You are like daughter to me." I thanked him for everything and told him I hadn't expected to have so much fun. As he gave me a final hug, his mouth quivered a bit, and I saw that he was holding back tears.

Zoran, ever the interpreter, noticed Ljubomir's emotion, and perhaps my surprise at the outpouring of it. "Serbian people," he said. "We are very open."

On the way to Belgrade, Ljubomir called Zoran several times, urging us to check out the newspapers. We finally stopped at a newsstand and picked up a Serbian daily, and sure enough, there I was: Ana Veksburg, noted the blurb accompanying my photo, President of the International Jury.

But the biggest surprise came when I returned home and logged onto ballcup.com to see if Ljubomir had posted pictures. At the top of the page, squeezed into the space between "The Scots have Scotch, the Swiss have cheese, and we Serbs have balls!" and the BBC weather logo, was a video of my fire performance and below it, in fluorescent green lettering: "Anna Wexler star of WTCC 2009."

☙ ☙ ☙

Anna Wexler is a writer, documentary filmmaker, neuroscientist, and adventure traveler whose trip ideas are a continual source of concern for her friends and family. She has yet to top the solo bicycle ride across Mexico, but volcano boarding in Nicaragua, motorcycling through northern Vietnam, and seal hunting in Greenland all came pretty close. When Wexler isn't on the road, she writes about science, travel, and food from her sea view desk in Tel Aviv.

🦋 🦋 🦋

Unsilent Night

An expat finds the Christmas spirit
even when it's ninety degrees.

O n Christmas Eve, I wandered Accra aimlessly, taking minibuses that I knew would get caught in traffic jams. Accra, the capitol of the West African nation of Ghana, has a seemingly endless fleet of converted passenger vans in varying states of dangerous decay that run mostly on hope and glue. It was not hard for me to walk down my dirt road, past hawkers selling hibiscus-flavored water sachets and coconuts, and board one.

The hot, wet, malarial air rising off the Gulf of Guinea seeped into the rust-punched minibus whenever we stopped in traffic, which was all the time. I didn't mind. I had nowhere to go, and previous travel experience had taught me that it's nearly impossible to feel lonely in an overcrowded minibus. My frizzy blonde hair stuck to my neck in damp tendrils, and a little

girl with sleek cornrows sitting next to me touched it
with curiosity. Women wiped sweating foreheads with
folded handkerchiefs and adjusted babies bound to their
backs with bright printed wax cloth. Passengers perused
motivational pamphlets and religious literature. We
all stared straight ahead as the exhaust fumes and heat
began to overtake us.

I ended up at Koala, an air-conditioned supermarket
owned by a Lebanese family. The store, which catered to
expatriates and wealthy Ghanaians, had hired a bubble
machine to simulate wintery weather in the parking lot.
The bubbles fell confused to the ground, approximating
snow in a place that had never seen a single snowflake.
Inside the front doors, women were dressed in felt Santa
costumes, handing out pieces of hard candy shaped like
Christmas trees and stockings. It was at least ninety
degrees outside. The shop was abuzz with preparations for the holiday: diplomat wives and Ghanaians
with shiny pomaded hairdos and expensive handbags
ransacked the aisles for imported chocolates and bottles
of Canadian whiskey. They crowded the meat counter
to buy up sausages and beef for Christmas dinner; they
scooped up packages of peas and perfectly cubed carrots.

For months I'd known that I would be spending
Christmas alone in West Africa. No big deal, I'd thought.
I'd be working. I'd be busy. It would be an adventure.
My loneliness was almost ornamental, until suddenly
I was stranded in Accra, and it wasn't. Standing in
line with a comforting Coca-Cola, I wondered if the
crowds could actually see my loneliness. Travel is about
being brave, I reminded myself. I watched customers
walk out the door loaded with groceries. Their drivers
waited out front, watching the snow bubbles fall to the
hot pavement.

And then another bus, another hot hour on a grid-locked road. A man climbed onto the bus and did not sit down. No one noticed him at first. He faced us, filling the aisle. Young and handsome, wearing black dress pants, a shiny belt, and a vest over a crisp blue shirt and tie, he was a bus preacher—a common phenomenon from Kenya to Nigeria. Since it was the day before Christmas, he had come to tell us a Very Important Story about a man named Jesus. He didn't say this in any language I could understand but I knew it from the Bible in his hand. His voice rumbled over the low valleys and high peaks of the tale. The story was familiar. Even though I couldn't understand the language I could pick out the words Jerusalem, Nazareth, Hallelujah. Everyone paused to murmur Hallelujah in response, and to my surprise I joined in.

The man was shouting and sweating by then, his own personal crispness sacrificed to do justice to the story of Baby Jesus. We were getting close to the market. Commerce spilled into the street, and people started trying to sell us dog collars and plastic bowls for washing and batteries and cell phones and soap and televisions through the windows. But we were transfixed. The street preacher reached the climax of his story. Sweat rolled down his forehead and he pumped his fists in the air. How lucky we are, he said, to have been saved by that sweet Jesus, born in a manger, just as common and low as any one of us! He said all of this in Twi but we, even the frizzy-haired white lady, knew and understood the same thing. He kept on.

"What's he saying?" I whispered to a teenage girl clicking a cell phone. "He is saying that God cannot ever leave you alone," she said. And then he was done, spent. We gathered baskets and babies, preparing to splinter into this Christmas Eve in the syrupy, exhaust-filled heat of Accra. We did not say goodbye to each other, but some of us handed the rumpled, satisfied street preacher a wrinkled bill or coins. I walked into the dusk and made my way home.

In Ghana, a place where Jesus and cell phones are equally popular (which is to say that Jesus is very, very popular), Christmas can feel like an unnecessary extra. After all, Jesus is already worshipped in churches and weedy empty lots and at all-night prayer encounter sessions in every corner of this city at any given hour. The hairdresser is called Jehovah's Love; the snack bar that sells fried plantains has been named Let Us All Clap for Jesus. (Or would have been if not for a particularly tragic typo that changed the name to Let Us All Crap for Jesus.) Everywhere there are Signs and Prophecies and Revelations relating to the figure Ghanaians call our Big Man, our Boss, Jesus. His face—white, black, whatever—is on posters and billboards and His name or advice has been painted on the rear of nearly every taxicab and minibus. Jesus is not a once-a-year preoccupation couched in Santa Claus and shopping: in Ghana, He is everywhere, all the time. I had kept my distance. After months in Ghana I'd never even been to a church service. (I was terrified to hear they sometimes went on for nine hours.)

Later that night, I sat on the roof of my hostel to escape the heat. I called my family on a cell phone, and it sounded as if they were an ocean and two continents away—which they were. Every other year of my life, Christmas Eve had featured the same predictable elements: Scandinavians gathering in a dimly-lit Seattle apartment, pickled herring, the clink of ice into a gin and tonic, and the lights of the city beyond the inky

Puget Sound. I thought of being a child in the back of an old Ford Bronco, driving home to the foothills of the Cascade Mountains with my parents after Christmas Eve gatherings. I remembered drifting to sleep looking out at the lights, silent and twinkling on the edges of the lake, knowing that Christmas morning was hours away. On the tape deck, my mother would play an old Nat King Cole Christmas album. We listened to "Silent Night" again and again.

Outside my window, boys played soccer in an alleyway, hiplife music thumped from a bar with a palm-thatched roof, a feral cat spoke to the moon, and two women argued. The stars peeked through the pink haze of wood smoke. I could hear the loudspeaker of an "All Night Prayer Encounter" session I'd seen on a billboard in the neighborhood. I thought about what the woman on the bus had said: God cannot ever leave you alone. Maybe that was true. I'd been on my own all day, but I had the distinct and unfamiliar sensation that I was followed by some force, maybe even the Big Man. Here in Africa, it was an unsilent night, and I went right to sleep.

ॐ ॐ ॐ

Michelle Theriault Boots is a journalist and essayist whose work has taken her from truck driving school in rural Oregon to the slums of West Africa. She's reported for the Associated Press from two continents and has published articles and essays in literary journals, newspapers, and magazines and on public radio programs that include the High Country News, Oregon Quarterly, *the* High Desert Journal, *and the* Alaska Public Radio Network. *When she's not traveling, she lives in Anchorage, Alaska, where she writes and works as an adjunct professor of journalism. She's at work on her first book, a nonfiction account of the lives of a handful of the world's billion urban poor.*

❦ ❦ ❦

The Boy with the Green Blanket

Compassion is sometimes all you can hope for.

Sometime after lunch as I sit grading papers, I hear an unfamiliar engine chugging slowly through the hot and lazy afternoon. It isn't often that an unexpected visitor arrives at the mission and, mind not on my work, I am easily distracted. I peer out the window of my little house into the compound of tin-roofed schoolrooms, chapels, and outdoor kitchens efficiently run by a handful of the Salesian Sisters of St. John Bosco. An unforgiving dry season has left the once green hills of southern Ethiopia cracked and thirsty for rain. The giant trees are losing their leaves, one by one falling to the ground like withered cornhusks. The ubiquitous swamps of shoe-sucking mud have disappeared into so many clouds of orange dust.

A worn minibus appears, laboring along the dirt

road past my little house and down toward the clinic. Curiosity gets the better of me. I slip on my sandals and go outside, following the trail of dust and squinting in the harsh sunlight. "*Ciao*, Sara!" A group of children sitting along the playground fence wave at me. "*Ciao, lejoch*," I smile back. Desta, one of my favorites, hops up to take my hand and walk with me.

Surprises are a welcome disruption to the busy routine of the compound. In addition to my daily English classes, I help with a feeding and bathing program for the malnourished children of the poorest of the poor. I sew and play volleyball with the young girls who attend Sister Igina's Saturday activities and monitor a study hall every afternoon. Sister Meaza gives me Amharic lessons. In the evenings after dinner, I sit in the main house with the sisters, listen to local news, and knit. Compound life shapes my days.

Having little truly in common with the nuns, however, and speaking only limited Amharic, loneliness too shapes my days. On bad days, it sticks to me like my white skin, like foreignness. With each wave of homesickness, loneliness beats down upon me like the East African sun and calls to me from the trees like raucous hornbills just after sunrise.

On good days, most days, my heart is as wide open as the great blue sky and I have never felt so blessed. I try my best to ease into the rhythm of compound life—the simplicity and peace. On good days, I delight in the thousands of little things that make life here a happiness that fills me near to bursting: the bright, eager faces of my students, mobs of Sister Elizabeth's kindergartners quarrelling over who gets to hold my hand, stunning Dilla sunsets, and sweet avocado pudding.

When Desta and I reach the gate to the clinic, a small crowd of nearby villagers has already gathered to welcome our unexpected guest.

"*Dehna nesh*, Sara?" Woinshet asks me in greeting. Woinshet is one of two local women who work full time at the clinic, assisting Fulvia, the Italian doctor, and saintly Sister Ines, our nurse.

"*Dehna egzi abehear amesegen*," I reply. I am fine, thanks be to God. "*Dehna nesh?*"

Woinshet smiles a wide, toothy smile, still unable to resist grinning at my Amharic. "*Dehna.*"

A playmate calls to Desta. He lets go of my hand and takes off into the bush.

"Woinshet, *lemen?*" I ask, pointing at the locked gates. Usually the clinic is bustling this time of day, tending to a long line of patients.

"Saint Gabriel Feast Day," Woinshet explains, politely switching to English so I will understand. "Few patient so close early."

The minibus chugs to a halt at the clinic gates and Woinshet and I turn to watch with the others. The passenger door opens and Rachel climbs out. Her blond hair is pulled back in a ponytail and she is wearing one of her school-teaching skirts. Rachel is British and teaches English at the small college down the road from the mission. She spots me easily in the small crowd and quickly turns back to the van. In the front seats sit two Ethiopian men I do not recognize—friends from the college.

The men emerge, doors creaking, and walk with Rachel around to open the back hatch. I squint into the dimness of the interior and understand immediately why they have come.

She has brought him.

Yesterday, Rachel dropped by the mission while I was having a cup of tea between my afternoon classes. She was brief and to the point. There is a boy, she told me, lying on the side of the road near the college. He has been there, in the same spot, for nearly a week. She was ashamed for not taking action sooner.

"Can we bring him to the clinic?"

"I'll ask the sisters."

Today Rachel has brought him.

The boy is a small dark mound curled up on the folded-down back seats of the minivan, like an old sack of bones in a forgotten graveyard. A filthy blanket is wrapped around him, covering all but an elbow or a knee, the top of his head. The yellow glare of the hot afternoon sun makes it difficult to see him.

"Woinshet," I turn back to her. "Sister Ines, *yeat allech?*" Suddenly I am frantic to find Sister Ines. Where is she? Why must the gates be locked this afternoon of all afternoons? It is always a feast day. It is always something.

"*Alawokum*, Sara." Woinshet doesn't know. "*Melabut, iza.*" She points to the main house.

"*Ow, amesegenallo*," I thank her and rush to the sisters' house. I am sweating in an instant.

I pull open the screen door to the kitchen and stick my head inside. Lomi, who cooks breakfast and lunch for us everyday but Sunday, is up to her elbows in dishwater and dirty pots. "Sister Ines?" I ask.

"*Ie*," Lomi shakes her head. Seeing the anxiety in my flushed face, she points her chin out the window toward Sister Ines's chicken house.

"*Amesegenallo*." I hurry through the back field to the chicken house, cursing my sweat, the sun, the dust, the flies, the blisters on my feet, and Saint Gabriel.

I find Sister Ines, coaxing dirty eggs out from underneath cross chickens, murmuring something soothing in Italian. She is cradling half a dozen against her ample grandmotherly bosom and, as usual, doesn't notice me right away.

"Sister Ines."

She turns to look at me standing in the doorway. "Eh, *ciao*, Sara. *Ciao*." She smiles a plump friendly smile and blinks slowly at me from behind her thick enormous glasses, as if trying to recall just who I am and why she knows she likes me. Wisps of soft silver hair have escaped her oversized veil and she pushes them around distractedly.

"*Ciao*, Sister Ines." I swallow and tell her about the boy. Sister Ines and I communicate in a broken combination of Italian, English, and Amharic, choosing words from all three we know the other will understand. At the end of my brief story, Sister Ines sighs and carefully puts down the dirty eggs one by one. She wipes her hands on her apron, muttering in Italian. She seems annoyed but saintly Sister Ines is never annoyed and I feel sudden tears of confusion well up as I stand helpless in the smelly chicken house.

"*Va bene*, Sara. *Andiamo*." Bewildered, I follow Sister Ines as she wobbles slowly toward the clinic. In an instant, her frustration with this interruption to her egg collecting has turned my little Ethiopian world upside down. When one of the other sisters kicks a stray cat (shocking because nuns do not kick animals), Sister Ines takes it in and feeds it bread and milk. Without her distracted bottomless goodness, I am suddenly lost. I brush the tears from my hot cheeks.

As soon as we reach the clinic and the small crowd surrounding the minibus, Sister Ines becomes her saintly self again and I am relieved. She unlocks the gates and shouts for one of the workers. Beyene is there in an instant, hollering at the crowd and clearing a path to the clinic's front patio. I can't explain to Rachel why it took so long.

The sack of bones lies still in the back of the van. Then there are hands upon him. Many pairs, dragging him into the sunlight. The men from the college wear latex gloves they have brought with them. Best not to touch him too much. Who knows what illness accompanies this strange boy, but there are certainly fleas, lice, jiggers. God knows what.

Carefully, awkwardly, they carry him. One at each of his elbows, two more with his legs. Rachel steps back, watching. The men shout at each other, steering their way through the crowd, trying not to trip or pull their fragile cargo in too many different directions.

Weakly, the boy protests, mumbling incomprehensibly. His ragged, filthy clothes are more holes than anything. He struggles to cover himself, conscious of his nakedness and a crowd of curious, peering eyes, but his arms are being held by strong hands in latex gloves and he can't reach his blanket. It falls to the ground. His wild and vacant eyes roll loose and broken in their sockets. He writhes, pitifully twisting and turning, desperately trying to free himself from these well-meaning strangers, but it is hopeless. He long ago lost his strength to fight. Delicate curtains of orange dust jostle loose from the folds of his rags and settle gently on the ground. He closes his eyes.

I stare in silence.

Gently the latex-covered don't-get-too-close hands lay the boy on the red tile floor outside the clinic. His body is deathly thin, all bony angles and hollows where there should not be hollows. His cheeks are fallen in like slackened sails. But his hands and feet and belly are swollen, clear signs of severe malnutrition. His skin is not brown, but nearly gray, a sick-looking dull color of gray, and peeling in great patches all over his body. There is angry pink skin underneath. It is difficult to tell how old he is. Maybe as old as eighteen. Maybe as young as twelve.

Again I search the crowd for Rachel and find her standing silently at the edge. Her cheeks are flushed pink and a few damp fingers of hair have escaped her ponytail. Her eyes pull away from the boy to meet mine.

She has brought him.

"I've got to teach a class in ten minutes. I have to run."

I nod.

"Will you be all right?"

"Yes, of course. I'll be fine."

"You sure?"

"Yes. Go."

"I'll come 'round tomorrow then, first thing?"

"O.K."

"Thanks, ya." Rachel disappears inside the minibus and her friends pull away.

I turn back to the clinic and see that the crowd has gathered in a circle around the boy, safely two steps back. But Sister Ines hobbles right up to the edge of his filthy blanket and gracelessly bends down to poke and prod him, pick aside his rags, and make disapproving clucking sounds.

"*Ma signore*," she mutters. "*Ma signore pieta. Si, si, pauverino.*" She shakes her head in disgust, her two-sizes-too-big veil threatening to slip down over her forehead and come to rest on the tops of her two-sizes-too-big glasses.

The boy twists away from her in protest and more sounds come out of his blistered mouth, but he is powerless against Sister Ines's relentless, bumbling goodness.

"*Si, si. Guarda*, Sara." Without turning from the boy, she beckons me with one hand to come and look. I obey.

"*Gobez*, Sara. *Guarda*." Despite his weak protests, Sister Ines continues her systematic inspection, picking up and turning over his swollen hands and feet. "*Izi*." She points to a series of open sores on the underside of one arm. "*Izi*." She shows me where the jiggers have made a feast of the worn and dirty skin between his toes. "Very seek, Sara. Very seek." She brings the fingertips of one hand up to her mouth. "No food." She shakes her head. "No food."

"*Si*, Sister Ines," I respond lamely.

Gradually the other onlookers lose interest in the boy and wander back into the hot afternoon. Suffering they know.

Beyene approaches, unraveling a stubborn green hose. The boy drinks clumsily and greedily for long moments. When Beyene turns his drink into an unexpected bath, the boy swats ridiculously at the water with sudden energy, wriggling to escape its cold and unwelcome touch. Beyene throws the rags from the boy's body into the clinic incinerator, picking up what is left of them with a stick and holding it aloft like a rotting flag. He stabs the filthy cloth into the hot brick mouth full of dirty towels, band aids and used strips of foul-colored gauze. The boy's blanket is spared; Sister Ines will no doubt press a few birr into the hand of one of the village women so that she might wash it. It will return to

him as if given new life. Bright green. Cheerfully green.
Resurrected from the dust and stink and piss and mango
peels of the side of the road.

Sister Ines hands me some bananas and tells me to
take them to him. He sits slumped over, awkward in
new clothes, gaudy and bright against his dull skin.
Water from the harsh scrubbing drips down his temples
and elbows making gray pathways, like sweaty fingers
drawn across a dusty chalkboard, through the delousing
powder still stuck to his skin.

"*Mus tefellegalleh?*" I ask, holding out a banana. He
takes it without looking at me, immediately fumbling
with the peel. I stand there next to him, smiling stupidly.
He has trouble maneuvering his mouth around the
banana at first. I wonder when he last had something to
eat. Has it been days? A week?

The boy pushes pieces of the fruit into his mouth. He
still doesn't look at me. He will never look at me. He will
never say another word. And with the exception of the
time Sister Ines will give him a piece of candy, he will
never smile. I will never touch him. No one asks it of me.
My paleness makes me fragile. I have been delivered to
this place wrapped in cellophane, a dainty porcelain doll
who must be fussed over and guided by the arm to the
shade of a nearby tree when her cheeks flush pink like
strawberries in the sun.

When he finishes the banana, I hold out a second one.
He doesn't take it.

Sister Ines comes to stand beside me. First Fulvia will
test the boy for malaria, TB, and AIDS, she explains,
in order to rule out disease. Perhaps he is only starving.
Only. Then he will be moved to stay with one of the
families down the path from the clinic. It has all been
arranged.

"Dilla hospital, *bazoo chigger alle. Teru idellum.*" There are many problems at the hospital, she says. It is not good.

In fact, the hospital in town is a nightmare. Without enough beds, the sick and dying lie on homemade pallets on the dirty floor. Without screens on the windows, the sick and dying weakly swat at the flies and mosquitoes boldly feasting on what is left of their flesh. Without nearly enough medicine and supplies, the sick and dying will die simply because they are poor and Ethiopian.

"Ees no good, Sara," Sister Ines assures me. "Ees better thees way."

"*Eshi*, Sister Ines."

Weeks from now, when the boy has not improved, we will try taking him to this nightmarish place nevertheless, dreaming beyond our wits that they can somehow do a better job of saving him.

During our visits to the hospital to check on him, people will pull shyly at Sister Ines, with low murmurs and entreaties for blessings. The women will uncover their starving babies with wide eyes, silent cries, and arms and legs like sticks. Sister Ines will stop, lay a hand on each child's forehead, and whisper her prayer, bobbing her head with the mother's hope and with her grief. The women will look at me, in my jeans and sandals, as if simply being near this saintly woman endows me with some similar power to heal. Or is it my white skin in this nightmarish place? My come-from-a-land-of-plenty-ness that might bless them somehow as well? Might rub off? During these visits to the hospital, it is the only time in all my six months with the sisters that I will wish I was closer to God.

Shortly after we take the boy to the nightmarish place of the sick and dying, we will take him away again.

Without enough doctors and nurses, some among the sick and dying go entirely unnoticed—including our boy. Not even the white women, one of them wearing God's clothes and a cross around her neck, can pull enough medicine and doctors out of the clear blue sky.

Shortly after we bring him home again, we will discover that Rachel was right. We should have taken him to a hospital in Addis Ababa as soon as she found him. Perhaps then he would have lived.

But for now, a woman named Tamirnesh will care for him and, in return, Rachel and I will pay her fifteen birr every week. One dollar and seventy-five cents. The money will buy food and medicine for the boy and help provide a little extra for the household in exchange for his care. It has all been arranged.

On bad days, loneliness is as much a part of my life in Ethiopia as the pink of my cheeks and the blue of my eyes. It is reflected in the worn and weary face of a lost boy who never even told us his name.

On good days, I imagine him released from his suffering, from his poor and ravaged body, set free from the dust and stink and hunger and hopelessness of the side of the road.

ॐ ॐ ॐ

Sara Bathum now lives back home in Seattle with her husband and son. This story is for Rachel, Sister Ines, and our lost boy.

ERIN VAN RHEENEN

❧ ❧ ❧

Up the Río Frío One Last Time

In the end, they were all in the same boat.

*S*omething launches itself out of the bottle-green river, traces a silver arc in the air, and slaps back down with a report like a rifle shot. Whatever it is, it's big. The locals waiting with us at the crumbling cement dock don't even look up.

"*Sábalo*," a man says. Tarpon.

I've heard that this fish fights like a prehistoric devil when it's hooked. Tarpon can grow up to eight feet long and 150 pounds. They swim here in the Río Frío but are bigger and more plentiful a short boat ride north, on the Río San Juan, the fluid border between Costa Rica and Nicaragua.

We're not here for the fish, though we are heading for the San Juan, which runs from Lake Nicaragua, one of the largest freshwater lakes in the world, to the Caribbean Coast. The boat that was to take us there is two hours late. We thought we had all bases covered—we'd either be picked up by the riverside lodge where we're staying, or we'd take the *bote público*, which is supposed to run a few times a day. Neither boat has shown.

I've had my fill of rental cars and tour operators and realtors. I'm taking a break from a tightly scheduled crisscrossing of Costa Rica, researching the third edition of a guide I wrote about moving here. The last time I did this sweep I thought the new national bird should be the construction crane. This time, the machine's creak has been silenced by the world economic downturn. Mammoth cranes sit idle on razed hillsides.

Costa Rica was my home for a while; now I'm not sure where home is. I live and work in San Francisco, but part of me feels like I'm waiting for the next big move, the next time I launch myself, like a fish leaping out of the river, into some unfamiliar element.

Meanwhile, I wait. A few boat captains lounge at one end of the cement pier, buying cold soda and plantain chips from a bicycle vendor. One wanders over, his belly hanging out of his t-shirt, and half-heartedly tries to convince us to take his boat to Nicaragua instead of waiting for the public ferry or the lodge's *lancha*. He wants more than $100 for the trip; the *bote público* charges $10.

The day started off deceptively easy with immigration in Los Chiles—it was the fastest I've ever left a country. We filled out a short form (the clerk loaned us his pen), got our passports stamped (there was no line), and were on our way to the town dock. We've been waiting here all morning and most of the afternoon.

An *aguacero* sweeps in—a downpour. Even under a corrugated tin shelter, it feels as if we're in the eye of the storm. It bounces hard off the cement and onto our legs, and then a sudden wind blows the sheets of rain horizontal. Water floods the slab that is the pier, and we have to move our bags onto a narrow metal bench right on the water. The corroded pole that serves as a backrest barely keeps the bags from toppling into the river.

A young man with copper-colored skin smiles and shrugs. I wonder if he's Costa Rican or Nicaraguan. Near the border, everyone looks like they're from the same mestizo stock, but elsewhere in Costa Rica the difference is more pronounced. Costa Ricans tend to be lighter skinned than Nicaraguans, but even if skin tone is identical, Nicaraguans are more likely to be found working the jobs Costa Ricans don't want: harvesting bananas, doing manual labor on building sites, caring for the kids of two-career households. Nicaragua is to Costa Rica as Mexico is to the U.S.—people from the poorer country stream into the richer one, become a crucial part of that country's labor force, and often suffer discrimination. Ask any Costa Rican taxi driver why crime is on the rise here, and he'll have the "answer." It's the Nicas, goes the argument, inured to violence by decades of civil strife.

The rain lets up a little. A man peddles by on a bicycle, one hand holding a big black umbrella. A few minutes later, an old pickup truck with wood-plank sides putters by with an oblong box in the back. So much action in so little time! The box in the back of the truck is swaddled in plastic tarps so it's hard to tell what it is, but I imagine it to be a casket.

Such are the ways we entertain ourselves when there's nothing to do. With no wi-fi here, I revert to the oldest form of entertainment available—enhancing reality by making up stories about what's in front of me.

Half an hour later, another diversion rolls up. Two muddy teenage boys hoist themselves out of the back of a pickup full of sheep and make a run for the river, yelling and laughing. They dive in fully clothed, no doubt to rinse off the sheep dung and mud. They scramble back out and, dripping wet, help the driver of the truck load the animals into a *lancha*. One unhappy sheep gets in a good kick, and when the boat motors off upriver, the truck driver yells, "*Bon voyage, hijueputa!*" Have a good trip, you son of a bitch!

When the boat from the lodge finally arrives, it's laden with a group from the U.S. who have been tarpon fishing on the Río San Juan. We're catching a ride back to the Esquina del Lago Lodge, but first, the crew will help the returning clients through Costa Rican immigration (easy as *pan dulce*), get something to eat, and have a good long smoke or two.

An hour later, the captain saunters over. "*Hay un problemita*," he says. There's a little problem.

How little? I wonder.

"*Hay un difunto*," he says in a low voice. There's a dead person.

So it *was* a coffin in the back of the pickup. And it seems the *difunto* needs to go where we're going. In our boat.

"*No hay problema*," I say. "*Pero espero que no tenemos que conversar con el.*" No problem. I just hope we don't have to make conversation with him.

The captain cracks a smile. "*Los difuntos son muy serios*," he notes. The dead are so serious.

It's not quite as funny when they start to load the coffin into the boat. It takes up a whole row—six molded plastic seats and the aisle—at the back of the long and narrow *lancha*. A young man accompanies the *difunto*, and the expression on his face looks like something just pierced his chest and he doesn't know whether to pull it out or leave it there.

We learn that the dead man, the young man's uncle, was a Nicaraguan who crossed the border to work in Costa Rica, in Puerto Viejo de Sarapiquí. He died of a *puñeleado*—a knife wound—he suffered in a bar fight. The young man came down to Costa Rica to claim his uncle's body and to bring him home.

We start up the Río Frío at dusk. Swallows swoop close to the water, picking off mosquitoes. A flock of parrots flies overhead. Herons and egrets stand sentinel along the river. Howler monkeys contribute their deep-throated call. As we pass under a leafless tree full of black cormorants, it feels as if we're part of a waterborne funeral procession.

I think fleetingly of rivers and rituals the world over, of the Ganges in India and of the River Styx. But it's the here-and-nowness of this rite on this river that really hits me. This, I realize, is what I've been waiting for: to be smack in the middle of the moment, in the thick of something I could never have predicted or imagined. Streaming up an unfamiliar river with a body in the back of the boat, a body traveling in a closed box that will never open again.

Suddenly the air feels supercharged with oxygen. The last of the day's light fans out horizontally, illuminating the riverside trees from the inside out. The breeze has dried my rain-soaked blouse, and I catch the scent of some night-blooming flower starting to open. It feels so good to be here, so very good to be alive.

Soon we've arrived at the confluence of the Río Frío, the Río San Juan, and Lake Nicaragua. The boat noses up to a rickety wooden immigration station right on

the water in the town of San Carlos. There's no line
to enter Nicaragua here, and the only other action is a
policewoman in heavy eyeliner and dangling earrings
asking the nephew of the dead man for his paperwork. I
wonder if they've kept the office open late to receive the
coffin—the place is all but deserted.

A soft breeze, smelling of fish and mud, comes off the
water. Out of the corner of my eye I see a short but solid
middle-aged woman emerge from the dockside shadows; she pulls the grieving young man to her tightly. He
slumps into her, losing several inches in height, finally
letting down after single-handedly bringing his uncle
home.

As we fill out forms in the dim light and pay our
$7 apiece entry fee, a tall, pale man appears, floating
over the heads of the smaller, darker Nicaraguans. It's
the Frenchman who runs Esquina del Lago Lodge.
There's silver stubble on his cheeks, and his blue eyes
are kind. "Do you understand what happened?" he says
in English softened with French. He's talking about our
fellow passenger, *el difunto*.

Yes, we assure him. We understand. People die, and
they need to be brought home. All we did was share a
ride with someone who needed it much more than we
did.

I look out over the water. With two rivers and a lake
meeting right here, it's hard to tell which way the current is flowing. But a few wavelets roll toward us, moon-
light riding their backs. They gently rock the boat we
arrived on, which is maneuvering to another spot along
the dock. For the first time I notice its name: the *Amen*.

ℛ ℛ ℛ

When she was three years old, Erin Van Rheenen's parents moved the family from Portland, Oregon, to Lagos, Nigeria. This two-year stint was the start of a life of travel and living abroad. Erin loves to go away but she may love even more the week or two before she embarks, when the trip is still just a dazzling idea. Erin is the author of Living Abroad in Costa Rica *and the creator of MissMoveAbroad.com. She also works as a writer at San Francisco's Exploratorium.*

ॐ ॐ ॐ

Blue Gates

In the middle of nowhere, there was nowhere to hide.

*M*ost days, water arrived for a maximum of three hours—that is, if the Peace Corps had supplied a house with running water. Women clamored to collect the giardia-free liquid in tall red clay jugs called *kwanos*. At these times, my shower stall transformed into a water station, as did the spigot to the right of the garden. These two patches of mud flooring were the only ones where a *kwano* could fit, where afterwards I could easily roll the heavy container back to the ground where it belonged. Sometimes the compound guard's daughter Mariama and I engaged in a battle of *kwanos*, but the water flowed from only one source at a time, and she usually won. For homes without a spigot, there was the *mai ruwa*, the water man. This man, usually tall, always attractive, would for a small fee carry metal tins of water to anyone's front door. The *mai ruwa* was Niger's version of the milkman.

On the shores of the Sahara desert, in the region known as the Sahel, the city of Zinder—which is not a city—claims one grand mosque and two mediocre bars. During the two years I lived there, the mail arrived once a week, the early call to prayer pulled me from sleep at four o'clock each morning, and repairmen smoked stubs of cigarettes as they greased and re-greased the ancient engines of their motorcycles and cars, all of which had been imported from France more than a decade before. Zinder was my own personal middle of nowhere.

But even there, love found its way through washboard streets. I came to the West African nation of Niger as an idealistic young Peace Corps volunteer apprehensive about my place in the world. I left two years later, forever changed.

The blue gate leading into my compound creaked each time a visitor arrived. The guardian's wife Habiba knew everyone in town, and they all came to call each morning just after sunrise. I'd look out my bedroom window to see a man clasping the legs of an upside down chicken; he'd wander over to her corner of the compound, singing under his breath, or perhaps praying.

Flocks of neighbor women would appear as Habiba pounded the family's millet or plucked the feathers off of her freshly killed chicken. The women would laugh uproariously, drunk with joy. My Hausa never became good enough to understand their storytelling, but I found their mood infectious all the same. I'd join them and we'd sit on our haunches, knees up, bottoms wide, never touching the hard, pink ground.

School days, however, there was less time to sit and listen to a language I could barely understand, less time to watch the constant comings and goings through my gate, less time to feel like the sister from another planet.

My identity as a Bostonian, my world of take-out and telephones, receded and was replaced with shortwave radios and beautiful women covered head to ankle in brightly colored fabric. Slowly, I became a part of this place—a place where the floury scent of beignets sold by street vendors wrapped around the neighborhood; where little boys learned to embroider their skullcaps in stitching circles under the yellow glow of a streetlight. Here, time swayed in a gentle rhythm, comfortable within its own sensual design.

At midday, when I returned home for lunch, there was always a small cluster of kids waiting for me. Covered in a layer of dust, their clothes frayed and torn, these gorgeous boys on the brink of adolescence never sat inside a classroom. They were Fulani nomads, and any type of education beyond the tribe was forbidden. Yet from them I learned that trust and beauty need no words, that Beatles music holds more global appeal than Vivaldi, and that my M&M's were no longer mine alone. The Wodaabee Fulani are famous for their male beauty contests and their absolute indulgence in the pleasures of the senses. Even the kids here in nowhere knew the score.

I'll never know whether it was the American food or the novelty of hanging out in a house with water flowing from a ceiling pipe that brought them back week after week. What I do know is that three boys, Sa-a, Dari, and Yabide, eventually became my close friends and protectors. They explained to me, as if I were the adolescent and they the twenty-something adult, that everyone in town knew where I hid my house key; that not every nomad who came to my house for lunch was as wise or honest as they were, and that from now on, they would like to work for their M&M's.

Their cool kid confidence appealed to me; after all, I was alone on a continent I couldn't begin to understand. Often, a man I didn't know would call at my house in the evenings and sit expectantly on my couch, a glass of water in his hands. He was not the only one. Moussa, Habiba's husband—the guardian the Peace Corps had assigned to watch my house—had propositioned my friend Martha by grabbing her crotch and whispering *café café café*. Even at the high school there was little clarity—a law had recently passed requiring teachers who impregnated their students to marry them. Everyone was in an uproar. One French instructor was sent back to France with less than twenty-four hours notice for (it was rumored) sleeping with several students. Taking the advice of a few preteen nomads seemed as good a plan as any I could think of. In nowhere, all the rules changed.

Even love in nowhere took on new proportions. Never before had I seen a man jump out of a truck and known that he was mine. Never before could anyone's eyes alone transform me into another self, into a woman I didn't recognize. I should have run the other way. Instead I set out like a private detective to learn everything I could about him.

Benoit Lizee. French. Eccentric. Obsessed. Obsessed with work, with ideas on how to improve the lives of West Africans, with himself. Only three days out of Paris, Benoit persuaded the organization he had volunteered with that he should travel the length of the country—at their expense, of course. He'd create an assessment tool and evaluate all of the other volunteers' projects. Anyone else with thirty-six hours experience in-country would have been laughed out of the office. Not Benoit. He wrote his own job description and was soon touring Niger village by village in his white

Toyota truck, a fabulous perk unheard of even for French volunteers.

When we were introduced, I merely nodded. My French skills were still those of a six-year-old, so I kept my distance, held my breath. Niger had created a sort of blank slate for all the internationals. We were a more enlivened and at the same time, more vulnerable, version of our former selves. I didn't feel ready to handle the level of intensity I already felt. But in nowhere there was nowhere to hide.

Months passed and I moved out of Niamey, the capital, into the smaller city of Zinder. Benoit became merely a passing fantasy, relegated in my mind somewhere in between Johnny Depp and James Dean—until one Saturday night, six months later. I'd gone to bed rather early with a book, a bowl of popcorn, and another Peace Corps volunteer. A Peace Corps boyfriend came with the territory: a little patch of home, a touch of the familiar in all that was foreign. It was a rite of passage, one to embrace and then release, like any coming-of-age ritual.

Visitors arrived at all hours of the day and night in Zinder, and the only way to prevent your house from taking on the feel of a busy train station was to lock the doors. Even with the lights turned out, it wasn't unusual to hear insistent knocking, especially on a weekend night. Nor was it unusual that it would continue for some time—even that the door would rattle a bit. It could be Habiba wanting to borrow ice or another curious Nigerian man coming to see what the unmarried American woman did on weekends. What was unusual on this particular evening was that the knocking moved around to the left side of the house, to the French doors of my bedroom.

When I opened the door, I first only noticed Yvette, the wife of the French teacher at the lycee. Her French was far too clipped and quick for me to understand much of what she said, and whenever we met she was always extolling her love of *la cuisine Française*—not my kind of woman. However, French food, or the promise of it, was what brought her to my door. A week earlier I had bumped into her in town, and she mentioned something about my coming to her house for authentic French crepes. The light gray flour flown in from France. The butter burnt *comme ça*.

This, it seemed, was the night she'd chosen for her dinner party, and Benoit was with her. Our first meeting in Niamey already relegated to history, he was introduced to me and my Peace Corps boyfriend, Chris. It seemed Benoit's agency had relocated him to Zinder to be closer to the villages he toured.

Twenty-two years later I still remember Yvette's menu. The crepes with a thin layer of gruyere finished with sweet cream; the shrimp, single malt whiskey, strawberries, and vanilla sorbet. This was the only time in my two years in Niger that I came in contact with such pleasures of the tongue. They appeared on plates and in bowls before me like phantoms from some former life, precious and rare as new love.

But my strongest sensation that night was of how open the world had become. The five of us were joined together as if tied by one ball of twine—a tug that brought us out into the tipsy embrace of the night. I remember trying to keep track of my hands, my cheeks, my eyes—of Benoit's eyes, on me. The sense that this man with tangled curls and a body that never stayed still would be my partner for life was overwhelming. If only I had a *gris-gris*, an amulet to protect me from such

stupid spirits. If only Sa-a and the other Fulanis had
been able to protect me from my own false future.

Then, months of tangling and disentangling our lives.
The usual push and pull of inexperienced lovers, the
problems of an unexpected pregnancy, the bike accident,
the miscarriage, the medical evacuation, all complicated
by how far apart our own worlds were. How hard it is to
know who you are when you're living in the middle of
the desert, half out of your mind in love and its concur-
rent, grief.

When I think of this man now, I remember a long
series of arrivals and departures. After a few days or
sometimes weeks, the once gleaming white truck, now
cloaked in dust, would pull up outside my front gate.
I soon learned the sound of his engine, the slam of the
driver's door, his insistent knock.

Where had I been blindsided? What crucial scrap of
information did I miss? For many years these questions
suffocated me. Rejection is never fun, but this was rejection on a global scale involving three continents and at
least as many countries. We'd traveled by freight train
through Bamako to Dakar, swum in clear-glass water,
made love every night.

I left Niger in my third month of pregnancy. I
remember the Russian doctor who examined me at the
local hospital scolding me for bicycling when I was *con
bebe*. I remember friends coming over to help me pack,
as I wasn't supposed to lift heavy objects. I remember
that before the helicopter touched down on the tarmac,
I said my good-byes to Habiba, and that she cried at
my leaving with such intensity that today I feel sure she
knew I was just at the beginning of a nightmare.

Our parting wasn't clean cut. Benoit and I traveled
back and forth between Niamey, Paris, and eventually

my hometown of Boston trying to imagine a life together. Or at least that's what I was doing. "We're not on the same path," was all he would say when he decided to forgo the part-time teaching job I found for him, when he said no thanks to the Ph. D. program at M.I.T. When he said no thanks to becoming a father.

In my dreams, Benoit comes back to me far too regularly. He sits at the end of the bar, at the edge of the party, behind me as we cross-country ski. There's very little—if anything—he has to say, but I know why he's there. He's come back to watch, to listen to my conversation, even evaluate my friends. He wants to know if he made the right choice when he left me pregnant and on my own twenty-some years ago.

Recently, these dreams have diminished. In their place is a dream of the blue gates outside the house where I lived. Habiba and the other women are pounding millet, filling the compound with laughter. Mariama is sauntering by, her gentlemen callers already lining up to visit with her, but she'll have none of them. They don't seem the least bit surprised to see me, nor I them.

By the back door, next to the kitchen, Sa-a, Dari, and Yabide greet me with a soft "*Ina ƙwana*" and wait patiently for their lunch. Even the cats Ecoute and Zarma are resurrected for my return. I know that the visit will be short, but that it's as important as any trip I've ever taken. The water is running, and as we fill the *ƙwanos* with cool clear liquid, splash it over the top and let it spray our bodies, I know this joy is what I've returned for; this joy that connects me to that younger woman, the one whose life was just about to start.

❧ ❧ ❧

*Susan Rich was a Peace Corps volunteer in Niger, West Africa,
where she somehow survived two years without fresh ground coffee
or a good rain. Her first book,* The Cartographer's Tongue:
Poems of the World *won the Peace Corps Writers Award and
the PEN USA Award. Her next books,* Cures Include Travel
and The Alchemist's Kitchen, *continue her focus on the tension
between travel and creating home. She now makes her home in
Seattle, Washington.*

ɹɞ ɹɞ ɹɞ

Aloha, with Love

Confessions of a Couch Surfer.

arta wants a husband so she can get a green card. She has two degrees from one of the universities in Austria but can't seem to get out of the International Marketplace, which is an open-air mall. This part of Oahu is like a miniature Disney World, or Hong Kong. Signs flash around the clock offering fluorescent fish bowls of food coloring and alcohol and foot-long plastic straws for thirty dollars a pop. People stop to snap photographs of hanging baubles strung together and driven into town from twenty miles away, in the middle of the island where chickens run in yards, where the massage parlor signs aren't as bright.

"You ever read any Dostoevsky?" Marta asks me, picking up a silk pashmina from the kiosk and draping it around her shoulders, over her bathing suit.

"I hear Leningrad is a dump." I rub my hands and sigh.

"I cannot drink this water," her voice hardens. "No one here understands my humor." She walks toward the back of the cart to redisplay the ukuleles and canisters of fake snow powder. She shakes the flakes out onto a display mirror.

"This looks nothing like snow," she says.

"You in line?" a tourist asks.

Out in the middle of the island you can take a hairpin turn off of Highway One and go nut picking, but after dark the one-lane highway becomes treacherous. Now the papers are reporting that copper thieves have been running amuck above the macadamia grove because the wiring's selling for five dollars a pound. They're climbing up the poles, stripping the rubber insulation, and shipping the copper off the docks before dawn, leaving long stretches of highway dark. All the scrap the bandits have left behind is stuck in the banyan trees, causing pile-ups for the morning drivers coming to work downtown or to drop off their baubles at the kiosks in the International Marketplace.

We're waiting for Jessica at the kiosk where Marta works. Jessica is from here. Her grandfather ran the island's prostitution ring, and years before that her great-great grandfather was involved with the very first hotels on the island. Her parents met on the beach and took the inherited hookermoney and opened the island's first French restaurant. She was raised on the North Shore, where Pipeline happens—where once a year the gods open up the earth and create the most intense waves on the planet, and thousands of people come to hang out on her sandy front yard. Jessica grew up bare-foot in a schoolhouse with four pupils, encouraged to be daring, surfing after dinner. Her long, platinum lemon hair dances the sun back onto the paved street while she shakes her hips and fingers her crucifix necklace. She knows all the streetwalkers; they nod at her out of respect.

"Sup, bitches?" Jessica asks us, immediately thumbing through Marta's stock. I have known these women for twelve hours.

"This man," Marta shouts at me in her Austrian accent, from behind the lit-up miniature Santa Claus figurines on the cart, "he is like quicksand?"

"Have you ever seen quicksand?" I kid.

"In John Wayne," she answers.

"Movies," Jessica says to me, applying lip-gloss in front of the now-empty snow mirror from the table. "She means in John Wayne movies."

Jessica has come to give me the key to her place because last night I produced the cash. She'd answered the "Woman Needs Temporary Place" ad I posted on the Internet, after I moved all my belongings into a hotel—the same night the wind from the mountains blew our door completely off its hinges.

Our apartment was in an area one might refer to as "legit"—up in the mountains, removed from tourist attractions, closer to the gangs and people who didn't want us there. Beautiful, but the Goddesses are constantly reminding you who's in charge, blowing doors off or starting a rainstorm when there are no clouds in the sky, forcing you to question whether you should really be there in the first place.

The geology of this island is the basis for countless legends—volcanoes formed from flying body parts, healing waterfalls, a constant system of superstitious checks and balances. While I was having a relationship crisis, at least one academic, I was certain, was wondering about ritualistic offerings over a campfire in the heat, in the shadows. I could almost hear him taking notes in the distance.

The wind was howling as I'd packed, sitting on my knees on our freshly carpeted, newly leased bungalow floor.

"Who is she?" I asked.

"Somebody else," he answered. "Everything that you're not."

"You're crazy," I said.

"Yeah, but for somebody else."

"Girl," the woman at the hotel front desk said, giving me a Kleenex and checking her computer, "is he white? It's always a *haole*. We get like five of you a week."

She paused and handed me a button. "Integrity, Respect, Contract." All the hotel workers on the island were on strike, she explained. It was all I wanted to tell him—he'd like that. "Hello? The hotel workers are on strike."

"I have one suitcase," I sniffled as she checked me into the hotel. I tried to focus my eyes on the countertop—it was the only solid thing I could see.

I spent the next day packing boxes and walking them from the apartment down to the post office in a shopping cart I'd taken from the supermarket parking lot where shirtless men with long hair hissed at me. I wondered if I could ever get my T.A. job at City College back. I took a deep breath and tried not to think about my last week teaching in San Francisco, or the students who looked up at me wild-eyed and wondering, with so much hope: "You're going *where*?"

"We have extra bikinis," was how Jessica, Marta, and Lori responded to my online ad.

Lori is a tiny twenty-one-year-old redheaded girl who rents out the other room in Jessica's apartment. Her parents think she's going to college, but she splits her time between the liquor store downstairs from the apartment and her job at Burgers in Heaven up the block. She sends her parents emails about how wonderful her classes seem and how much she's learning about the weather and how difficult her student loan repayment's going to be and how high her grades are. There are hundreds like her on the island. She brings home Marines, sometimes two at a time, and a man who plays *mahjong* in the back of the liquor store in intervals. She runs around like it's the fifties and she's waving at the docks. I'm certain she did originally come here to study. She has a secretive way about her, almost like a writer—as if she's collecting details to use for something else later.

I walk with the three girls down the strip to the apartment, wearing the largest sunglasses I could find at Marta's kiosk, wondering how much longer I can take the heat. Jessica stops to say hello to a streetwalker, long, brown-legged and leaning in a doorway, wearing incredibly expensive-looking shoes and a bathing suit. Then she runs in her flip-flops to catch up to us, stopping again to stub out her cigarette. This would become routine, Jessica stopping to say hello while we sweat and roll our eyes.

We walk past vendors and street performers who have

made their way here from afar. Tired faces, shoulders
peeling, they come from harsh Oregon winters, abusive
parents. Their eyes are puffy, their skin dehydrated.
They left that snow, that person, that drug, to come here
and feed alcoholism, to end up standing beside a silvery
dragon painted on a wall in Chinatown. But I get the
feeling they're better looking now than they've ever
been, and I think about when we first arrived. Because
of his work transfer, I left my own job behind. Now
I'm veering between distraction and dizzy spells, and
he's building sandcastles somewhere with a girl who is
everything I am not.

Jessica's apartment is full of surfboards with women's
underwear hanging from them to dry, and antique
radios occupying every windowsill—dusted off, they
give the appearance of being the only thing not haphazard in the apartment. Junk food wrappers and Ho-Ho
packages litter the living room, and a vase of wilting
roses is sweating on the coffee table next to a tiny note,
unopened, with Jessica's name on the envelope. The
carpet reeks of stale smoke and possibly lemon carpet cleaner—I can't tell for sure because the inside of
my nose is still raw from last night's sob-fest with the
Kleenex-dispensing hotel receptionist.

"Jacov is coming," Jessica says, plopping onto the
couch, sighing like she's bored. "He'll be in my room."

Lori giggles, standing in front of the freezer eating a
Popsicle. I join Marta at the kitchen table, creaking into
a straw chair.

"He owns the kiosk," Marta tells me, lighting a cigarette.

"Israeli," says Jessica. "All the kiosks are owned by
Israelis. Lovers, they are the best." She thumbs through
a beauty magazine, sighing again.

"Why are all of the kiosks owned by any particular cultural subset?" I ask.

"I think it's because whole countries of men got word Jessica's here to sleep with them all!" says Lori, and everyone giggles.

"He has a girlfriend in Italy, they live together." Jessica's voice and eyes become a warm puddle. "But he always comes back to me."

The dizziness returns, and in one wave an image comes crashing of them surfing; maybe he's wearing the swimsuit I bought him last month and left in our closet. Marta sees me lean into the side of the couch, tilting my head forward, staring into nothing.

I wake at six P.M. to the sound of a parked car alarm going off and a man and woman fighting in the street. The sun is just setting and through the screen window, the sky looks like an Easter egg of blue and purple cream. They're yelling in a dialect I can't quite make out from the distance between the window and the liquor store beneath us. I roll over on the couch and stare up at the ceiling, listening to the two spew their vitriol into the air.

Jessica appears in the doorway of the living room, twitching a knee and unfastening an earring. Grinning, she says, "C'mon bitches, we dance tonight."

I stretch my arms up at the blue-cream darkening sky and wonder about the constellations. I haven't even looked to see if they're differently angled on this island.

In between their shower turns, shoe swapping, and eye-shadow handoffs, Jessica and Lori seem to have forged a succinct Little Women system of getting dressed for the evening. I'm lying on the couch watching the local news on mute while the girls run back and forth in front of the television screen like kittens.

"The gray or the gold?" Jessica asks me, standing in two different strappy high-heeled shoes.

"The gray." I sigh, moving my head to watch the footage of the copper wire coverings all over the highway. Though the sound is off, I can tell by the newscaster's face that none of the thieves has been caught. They show footage of SWAT teams with dogs, sniffing the steps at the pier.

"Let's go," says Jessica. "You're not even going to shower?"

"I'll stick my feet in the water," I answer her. She rolls her eyes and runs back to the bathroom. Marta storms through the living room, throws her bag on the floor next to me, and rifles through the fridge for a Miller Light.

"Rough afternoon at the office?" I ask her, using the remote to turn off the television, ungluing my face from Jessica's couch pillows while her hairdryer roars from the bathroom.

"I'm leaving," Marta says to me, lighting a cigarette. I reach over and take one from her pack. I light it and attempt to smoke it without hacking.

"To where?" I ask, hacking.

"Anywhere," she says. "I have been trapped here for seven years. I am sick of looking for a husband."

"Will they let you into anywhere else?" I stand up.

"If I leave I can't come back here." She inhales. "Maybe they let me in but they never let me back out. It's a difficult thing in my country. It's a difficult thing everywhere." She exhales.

"Who wants Schnapps?" Lori asks us, holding a peach colored bottle, smelling like a mall beauty store.

We clop down the three flights of stairs to the gate and meet with flashing police lights. Marta turns her back to the car, lighting a cigarette and quickening her pace ahead of us.

"Don't look up," Jessica says to me. "He's watching from the ninth floor of the hotel." She adds an extra sway to her hips and catches up with Marta.

"Jacov. He always watches for us before heading to the bar," Lori whispers.

We walk through The International Marketplace, past kiosks draped in cloth and tied with cord, past men in hotel uniforms sleeping before the midnight rush of drunken tourists return from the bars. We cut down a paved sidewalk onto the beach, and for a moment I am breathless as my shoes touch the sand and I hear the sound of waves hitting the shoreline. We're on an island, and there's no other coast for three thousand miles.

The bar is removed from the resort space where people are barbequing and performers throw fiery batons while parents clap wide-eyed and their children play in the sand. The moon is almost full and that means nobody goes in the water, as the jellyfish will be coming to nest.

The sign above the bar front says, "Anyplace." The inside isn't as glamorous as I might have expected had I given it any thought at all. I'm exhausted and missing a would-have-been husband. Dark brown wood paneling covers the walls, and televisions are mounted at the top of two corners. We take our place on the tall barstools and wait for the others to join us. Jessica waves aloha to most of the people in the room and starts a tab under the name Jacov.

Fifteen minutes and a gin and tonic later, Lori is already tickling a man in a chair when three tall, dark men appear in the doorway. One is wearing a leather jacket, and they're all standing like they've been here before. Jessica turns, forgetting herself—or maybe remembering—and runs into the tallest man's arms, wrapping her legs around his waist, letting her bathing suit bottom show under her skirt. I watch them kiss and again feel the world spinning out from under me. She takes hold of his hand and pulls him over to us, leaning into the bar and our shoulders.

"This is Jacov," she says to me, smiling. "And these are his friends Oren and Ari."

Jacov is undeniably beautiful. He's in his thirties and he looks healthy, solid; testosterone oozes from the wells of his black, shifting eyes. Oren is tall and thin, with a mass of thick curly hair like a seventies rock star. He's wearing cowboy boots under his expensive worn-wash jeans. Ari, shorter and stockier, has to stretch his neck to kiss Marta's cheek.

"Hello, gentlemen, see you later, gentlemen," Lori says, drunk yet delicate. Holding hands, she and the man she's been leaning into saunter out of the bar. Marta and Jessica sip from their drinks, unfazed.

"You are new here?" Oren asks me, holding my hand longer than necessary.

"Sort of," I answer.

"She's been ditched," Jessica says, tossing her hair into Jacov's olfactory line.

"Ah, yes, the do-gooder ladies club works again," Jacov responds. I suddenly wonder how many people have taken refuge on that couch.

"What are you drinking?" Oren asks me, smiling.

Two hollowed-out pineapples of rum later, I throw my mini umbrella on the bar and ask him, "If you could have anything you wanted on this island, what would it be?"

He laughs and answers without blinking. "Well, that one's simple. A woman."

"You know, I...I am a really good woman," I answer toward his entire gender.

Marta grabs my arm and takes me outside the bar for a smoke.

"You are losing," she says to me.

I look up from the concrete I'm squatting on beneath the shadow of her pencil-thin shoulders in the lamplight. "What am I doing here?" I ask her.

We hear the smash before anybody else because we're fifteen feet from the parking lot. I can see shards of glass under a car, and then I hear the bat hitting another. I drunkenly reach an empty hand into the warm air before Jessica and company come running toward us.

"Come on," she says, picking me up by the arm, scowling at Marta who has turned to watch. "Islanders out *haole*-hunting."

We walk from the parking lot as a set of couples in rows, just out for a stroll, incognito in our supposed tourism.

"There are copper thieves climbing up poles," I say to the group.

"We've heard," says Jacov.

"He's in the navy," I say back to them, pointing a finger. "You were in the army, in Israel, right?" I am fairly drunk.

"Yes, we were," says Ari. "Greatest experience of my life." He lights a cigarette and blows smoke into the warm air.

We wander back toward the kiosks, already reopened and laid out for the midnight tourists. The carts hold oil in tiny brown glass bottles, medicine made of plant roots from the countryside, cell phone jewel cases. Reds and magentas and yellows. One of Jacov's kiosks carries light catchers, plastic pieces hung from fishing wire that turn in the breeze, reflecting the electricity of the streetlight with waves that undulate like sex.

Jessica stands under one, angelic. Her nose touches the bottom tip, and it slows its rotation above her. She lifts a foot like a movie star being kissed in an old black and white film. A psychic in the booth two kiosks over blushes, sighing happily at the humanity of it all. My chest is sinking but I swallow hard, turn to Oren and ask, "What the hell is Oren supposed to be?"

"It means pine tree in Hebrew." He sips from a bottle of water, also watching Jessica.

"Pine tree," I answer, rubbing my fingers to my forehead, "I know those."

He takes my hand slowly, and I realize it's been six weeks since anyone else has. We walk from the marketplace toward a stone wall covered in white blossoms that reach toward the hang gliders above the ocean in the night.

"Moonflowers," he tells me. "They bloom before the jellyfish come."

I turn my head toward the water, past the concrete and the pearlescent sand. I want to run to it and drop to my knees and ask, "Why? How does something like this happen?" but Oren takes hold of my arm. I watch a calico cat sleeping on a doorstep under a sign. They sell bongs and shaved ice in the yard, it says.

"I can't," I answer, and begin to walk back toward the apartment, stumbling over the sand.

"She'll be fine," Jessica says to the group, loudly enough for me to hear over the waves and my head humming.

"You lookin' for somethin'?" Lori asks me at the locked gate, as I fumble for the key. Her makeup is everywhere, her hair tousled, her face a tumbleweed of movement and desire still scenting the air.

"Bed," I answer.

She points a finger to the hills.

"Things speed up here. Maybe it's the geography, the mountains," she says. "They know everything." And she stubs out her cigarette and walks away.

We wake at dawn to the sound of the ocean crashing. Jessica rubs her eyes and smiles a yawn, leaning in the doorway.

"Jacov has left," she says, sighing. "Today, we surf."

Heavy-headed and clumsily holding the board, I walk with the girls toward the shore.

"Breakfast," says Lori.

"Coffee," says Marta.

"She's a librarian, the girl he's been cheating on you with," says Jessica. "A student." She lights a cigarette and puts up her hair, the smoke snaking from her face.

"A what?" I walk faster to keep her attention, almost tripping over the sidewalk.

She exhales.

"I asked," she says. "We're on an island." She quickens her pace.

The beach is mobbed with camera crews, people in hats, sunscreen oily on their faces. A man with a microphone tries to talk through the wind.

"Today we will find out who is the strongest man in the universe." He gestures toward a line of athletes.

"Look," points Marta. "They're throwing Atlas Stones."

A dozen men, bigger than comic book icons, are lined up in the sand with giant slabs of concrete at their ankles.

"In the Dark Ages, they hunted people for sport." Lori says.

We walk past the spectacle, up the stairs to a balcony in a café. Jessica places a napkin in her lap while Marta lights a cigarette and Lori eats a sugar packet.

"She's of old money," Jessica says to me, hailing a waiter. "She's older than you."

I pick up one of the cigarettes on the table, light it, and start hacking again.

"How did you...?" But she touches my hand, shushing me before I can finish the question.

We sit on the upper wooden deck in the shade. My assigned surfboard begins to slip; I haven't leaned it properly against the railing. The man one table over from ours turns to catch it.

"He's a con," Jessica says, tapping my forearm quickly. "Let's get him to pay for our breakfast."

She stretches her arms just far enough for the man to smell her hair while he turns around to reposition my surfboard.

"You ladies want to join a surfer looking for a good time?" He has a thick Australian accent.

"Yes," says Lori, unblinking.

Two Bloody Marys later, the man is talking about Kiwis, New Zealanders, and the mysterious age-old beef Australians have with them.

"So I says to the guy, I says, 'This isn't the outback after all!'" Everyone laughs.

He asks us twice for directions to the northern part of the island for surfing, and if we think he'll be able to watch them filming television shows again, and which bus is safe to put his new board on, when Jessica, visibly irritated, suddenly touches his arm. "You pay for our eggs, man who is not really from Australia?" The man's face turns from tanned leather to sheet-white in seconds, and he stands, throwing forty dollars on the table. Grabbing his surfboard, he runs down the stairs without looking back, flip-flops clanging on the wood.

"Con artists," Jessica says. "Stay off my island."

"You don't appreciate their gusto?" I ask.

"No, I do not," she answers, sipping diet soda through a straw.

"Surf," says Marta.

We walk down from the restaurant deck, through crowds of tourists and past couture shops, stopping to talk about the dresses as if we could walk in and purchase any one of them.

"Jacov could buy me this," says Jessica.

"Why would you let him?" I ask her. I feel like I'm asking one of my students, *Why did you take that when it didn't belong to you?*

"Listen," she says to me. "Anything people do, they do it for love. Anything. Answer the phone, walk the dog. Women, we want a lot of things. But men, men want a reason to live. If Jacov wants to buy me dresses, why should I deny him that? Why should I deny him love?"

I pause to watch the way the strands of her hair are catching the breeze, trying not to hear the misguided hope in her voice, wanting to tell her it isn't right, but my eye goes somewhere else. My arms begin to twitch. I grab her shoulder, pushing her into Lori and Marta and our surfboards, till we're all backed against the shop window.

"It's them," I whisper.

There, crossing the road half a block up, my ex-fiancé and his wannabe student librarian. Taller than him, thin, blonde. Carrying surfboards, wearing bathing suits I've never seen, jogging in step like they've done it all along. My knees give out and I buckle onto the sidewalk, dropping the surfboard onto the concrete like the sheet of wood it is.

"He's supposed to be at the base," I say.

"I could kill them in the water," Lori says, unblinking.

Jessica grabs my arm, pulling me from the ground as she did the night before.

"Not here," she says. "Leave them to the sharks." We turn to head back to the apartment, my feet barely able to drag themselves away from him.

Staring at the roses in the vase on Jessica's table and the unopened envelope with her name printed on the front, I say, "You are not a prostitute."

She looks down at me from her loveseat and her beauty magazine as if I've just asked her to build me a boat.

"No, no I am not," she answers.

"And Jacov has a girlfriend, you said. In Spain."

"He doesn't really love her," she says coldly, plainly, ladylike, and paper-cut sharp.

"I am here because of a girl like you."

"No, no you are here because you *aren't* like me," she says, undoing and redoing her ponytail.

My eyes well up and my chest constricts and I leave her wilting roses, her months-old beauty magazines, and run out the door toward the beach.

"Nicolle, wait!" she calls to me through the window, but I'm halfway to the surf.

When I get to the beach, to the camera crews and the men sweating, I see the boats, football fields long, carrying containers like building blocks.

I walk to the street, to the bus stop. I have five dollars in my pocket.

"Will this go to the middle of the island?" I ask.

The one-lane roadway is thin and tortuous, the drive like something out of a movie about explorers in the tropics.

"The oldest tree," I ask the bus driver. "Where is the oldest tree?"

He points. "*Da kine*. One stop."

I get off at the macadamia grove and walk down a gravel dirt road covered in vines and branches, till I reach a stand. A woman beside a child in a folding chair asks, "Macadamia pack? Two dollars."

"The oldest tree," I ask her.

"*Da kine*," she says. "It's the baby of the older." She points above her head.

It's a tree grown from a sapling found in India that was moved to Oahu because of the land, because it can survive here. It was traced back to one of the oldest tree roots in the world. We'd talked about standing under it.

The toothless woman chuckles behind me.

"Well you ain't dead yet," she says.

I walk along the one-lane road, feeling the pebbles under my feet, my ankles swelling in the heat, until I see the grass. It used to be a pineapple plantation but now it's just miles of tall grass swaying in the hot sun. There's a shack alongside the road farther down, and a rooster is crowing beneath a worn billboard that reads, "We have ice in the God Room."

I walk through the field to the shack and realize when I see the cross that it's a church. Standing in the middle of a condemned pineapple plantation. Red arrows point toward a porch next to the huge wooden cross. Entirely alone, I go to it.

Graffiti covers the entire back wall, along with etchings of Jesus in different incarnations. In some, he is she, with long black curly hair and thought bubbles: "I have forgiven your sins." "Wichita Reservation Loves Jesus." "The Steins Love God!" I back away from the wall slowly, feeling a table for balance.

"Shave Ice?" the man asks me.

I jump, startled.

His head is shaven, monk-like. He is standing in the church doorway.

"Shave ice? Mushroom? We have."

I turn toward his blue eyes, bluer than the ocean, glowing behind the screen door I didn't see, looking like a squid under watery depths. I walk backwards, tracing my hands along the splintering picnic table, and I start to run. I jump down the steps, through the field. Tall grass crunches and slices my sweating skin.

I head farther down the road; a bus passes, blowing dust. Hot exhaust burns my eyes, and I look past the cliff toward the ocean below.

There are steps—hundreds of them, down hundreds of feet. They are tiny, steep, and carved directly into the rock. It takes an hour, maybe, and my muscles are seizing and I'm sweating every ounce of whatever I have left. Slipping, my skin grating against the stone. Finally I am at the beach, feeling faint, seeing colors, white spots, and I sit in the sand next to a lifeguard stand.

"Aloha, you gonna make it?" he looks down, asking me.

"Yeah," I answer.

I dust off my legs, walk to the outdoor showers,

and stand in my clothes under water, gulping, rinsing, breathing. The wind picks up momentarily. There is a preying mantis perched on the top of the showerhead, and I wonder for a second, *am I dreaming*?

I was here once, I think. We had a picnic. I step out of the outdoor shower, under the graying sky, and watch the waves at the rock formations along the shoreline, the people surfing. I walk back toward the lifeguard and knock on the bottom rungs of his stand.

"Is this," I ask him, "is this the beach in *From Here to Eternity*?"

"Yes," he says. "Yes, it is."

I also want to ask, "And do you know that kind of sigh where you half choke and your chest skips?" But he's busy. He jumps from ten feet up on the chair, yells at a group in bathing suits. They're all hunched, taking photographs, chattering, hands flying, running away, and then back again. I stand in the sand, then follow the boy in the red shirt toward the crowd. Five feet from the water, beached, is a black and white puffer fish, its quills outstretched, its body swollen to a perfect medicine ball. Its eyes turn and it looks at me, shaking. It spits water from its mouth, huffing. The lifeguard runs back to the stand, shouting, "Nobody touch the fish," adding that the quills are poisonous.

I take a towel from a man standing next to me. I point to the towel and then to the fish. I tell them to move back, and I scoop up the poisonous black and white creature with the cloth—a papoose. It doesn't shake, it doesn't sigh, it doesn't fight. I pull the towel in the sand toward the ocean. The lifeguard runs back with a pitchfork, shouting. But the fish is gone; I release it in the water, where it deflates and swims away.

"You could have killed it," he says. "I was going to lift it."

"It's O.K. now," I say. "It's fine now."

We sit and watch the waves and sip his water. It starts to get dark. The beauty escapes me here, and I feel terrible about it.

"What's your name?" he asks.

"Somebody else," I answer.

"There's a Filipino fable," he says to me. "A boy, who was named Boy, stood up on a surfboard with a paddle and said to his parents, his people, 'I am going to leave.' And he got pretty far out there, but then he ran out of steam, and his family, his people, they had to go out and get him. You see that man?" He points to someone paddling on a surfboard in the distance. From what I can see, there are at least ten people out—women with their hair long and loose, some going faster than others, some in a line, some in tandem. Silhouettes. They lift their oars, and they push.

"They go out there on this beach, and every night, they paddle. They paddle in his honor. So that nobody feels bad when it's time to go home."

I shiver and realize it's cold, that the sun has lowered.

We hear high-pitched buzzing coming from the air.

"Bombers," he says to me. "B-52s."

At night the beaches, the city, all of the island is infested with giant cockroaches. They don't mention that in the brochures. If you're at a beach anywhere near trees or the docks where they came from, you're going to meet a giant flying cockroach. They're like rats, but tropical, squealing, flying. They came here on boats.

"I have to go," I say to him. "It's dark, there are copper thieves."

"Let me drive you," he says.

We get into his rusted red truck and start making our way down the mountain.

"There's a monastery in the grass." He points.

"I was there before the stairs," I say to him. "I was running." I exhale out the truck window.

"When I met him," I say, "I was seeing someone else, and he was married to someone else. And I left that somebody else, I hurt that somebody else when I left. And he, my ex here, left his wife. And we didn't have sex then, when he was married, but we did when he was separated, so we might as well have. And now I'm alone." I lean my head into the back of his seat.

"He would have always cheated on you," he says to me. "He will always resent you for being in an affair, even if it was with him." He turns the steering wheel.

"I have been waiting here, for him." I push my hand to my forehead, telling the preying mantis, the entire beach, the road, the island.

"He will always resent you," he says.

Lights from the houses in the mountains are mirroring the sky. Tiny pagodas of white light and hope. We park in front of Jessica's. I look up at the apartment on top of the liquor store, at the windows with the lights on.

"I have to go," I say to him. "I can't stay here."

"*'Ohana,*" he says to me from the truck. "Island family."

"*Mahalo,*" I say back into his window, standing with my hands on the door.

I throw the keys on top of the pile of books under the coffee table and sit on the couch. The air is thick and smells like alcohol, and I rest my head on Jessica's leg, dangling off the couch while she reads a beauty magazine, twirling her hair in her fingers. She hands me a bottle of rum.

An hour later, I turn to Jessica, drunk, and say, "You have no idea how much I am like you."

She laughs into her knees.

We sit on the floor. I crawl on the carpet, closer to the coffee table. I reach toward the envelope under the vase, under the sweating roses. I open the paper and read: "*Aloha*, with love."

"Another man," says Jessica. "There is always another man."

I look at her from the dirty carpet, smile, shake my head.

"He'll come too, then he won't," she says. "They all come back, and then they never come back."

I reach for the keys under the table on the stack of books. I want to thank her, tell her to not be so loose with herself, with her heart. But the silence in the warm air takes me over, and I lean against the foot of the couch, remembering his face. Thinking about the mountains.

"What will become of us?" I ask her after a while.

She takes my chin in her hand. "Don't do this again," she says.

I go to the sink to wash my face and catch my tired, burning reflection in the mirror.

"I have to go," I say. I can only see her neck in the mirror behind me, and the necklace she's wearing. She stands up, takes my hand in hers, and presses hundreds of dollars into it.

"You send it back," she says. "It's Jacov's anyway, he's paying me not to call her." And she takes me into her arms, our terrible arms.

I wait downstairs for the cab.

Lori, drunk, leaning on the door, flicks out her red ash.

"Another day on the island," she says to me.

"*Aloha, da kine*, airport, *mahalo,*" I say to the driver. I roll down the window and try to catch the wind in my hand.

I watch a video of the other islands on the monitor while I wait in line for a standby seat. A volcano erupting, moonfish at night looking like tiny silver circles. I get to the desk at the international terminal and watch the tourists being frisked. I reach into my bag for my things, my wallet, and I realize my passport is gone.

⁊⁊ ⁊⁊ ⁊⁊

Nicolle Elizabeth is a writer for Words Without Borders. She is from a small town in New England and began her academic career at community college. This Hawaii excursion happened when she took a year sabbatical from her MFA at Sarah Lawrence. She returned to New York, graduated, and will never have an affair again. She has published more than thirty short stories and essays and writes a weekly column at fictionaut.com.

✿ ✿ ✿

Jersey Girl

For one souvenir seeker, shopping
becomes a sport.

$\mathcal{U}$pon arrival in Leticia, a steamy backwater in the Colombian Amazon, some visitors fear close encounters of the cartel kind. Others, strangulation by the town tourism ambassador, a geriatric anaconda periodically trotted out for gringo-swaddling purposes. Me? I feared souvenir failure.

In almost two weeks on the Mighty River, I'd found only the weakest of gift prospects for my neighbor, Max. And had he been just any boy next door, sure, I might have settled for the standby piranha statuette. But he happened to be my all-time favorite twelve-year-old—the kind of kid who cooked for fun, took up Italian in middle school, and always kissed both parents goodnight. A grinning wooden fish wasn't an option.

But what was? With only one day left on the Amazon—and no ideas of my own—I turned to a twelve-year-old California girl named Hannah who'd been traveling on the same ship.

"What would *your* guy friends want?" I asked as we were docking in Leticia. And after brief but careful consideration, the Gen-Miley oracle spoke: "soccer jerseys."

Of course!

No sooner had I turned off the port's muddy main drag—and into the local shmata district—than I unearthed the holy grail: a size L Colombian soccer jersey, a bit dirt-smudged, but otherwise perfect. And apparently, the best gift ever: three days later, Max tried it on, and more or less never took it off.

Pajama top, knock-around shirt, party attire—whatever his sartorial needs, this jersey seemed to fill them. So on all subsequent trips, I knew exactly what to get him. What I didn't know was how much I'd learn in the process.

Take Laos.

After days spent scouring markets that sold seemingly everything—from hair extensions to sportswear to "virginity-restoring" soaps—I finally spotted a local jersey on an unusually muscular, twenty-something guy in Luang Prabang. And without thinking, I made a beeline for him.

"Excuse me, sir," I began, feeling admittedly weird—but totally determined: "Do you happen to know where I could buy one of those shirts?"

He laughed. "You can't."

"But you must have bought yours somewhere," I countered.

"These are only for players," he explained. "The only way to get one is to be on the team, like I was."

Holy shit. Had I stumbled upon the Laotian Pelé?

But then came the even bigger surprise: "And we had to pay for our own uniforms."

Turns out Team Laos couldn't afford to outfit its own players, let alone mass-produce replica jerseys for fans.

Momentarily taken aback, but loath to surrender, I asked whether he knew of any former teammates who might be willing to part with their jerseys. At which point, for the first time in my life, a man literally gave me the shirt off his back.

Yes, he unhesitatingly stripped on the sidewalk, and I had no idea how to respond. Could I allow him to simply hand over his jersey? Clearly not, but what would a fair price be? In the past, I'd bought only replica jerseys—never the actual, game-worn variety.

Unable to come up with a price myself, I awkwardly asked him to name one.

Evidently surprised by the question, and perhaps realizing that he was leaving himself shirtless, he suggested that we make our way to his family's home while he pondered the issue. The walk was mercifully quick; I'm not sure I could have taken the looks we were getting—most of which conveyed some variation on the WTF theme—for more than a couple of blocks.

"Just over there," he said, gesturing toward a small, squat expanse of concrete façade that was almost indistinguishable from those around it. And when we reached the front door, he named his price: "One dollar."

Even having gotten a clear sense of Laos's poverty by then, I felt my heart sink at that number.

"How about twenty?" I countered, as I noticed the

eight or nine people who seemed to live in this equivalent of a New York "junior one-bedroom" apartment.

And in a bizarre display of reverse bargaining, he
tried to get me down to $10.

I told him I couldn't take the shirt for less than $15.

Sold!

Lesson learned: Soccer jerseys are an economic indicator.

My trip to Bhutan was an altogether different matter.
Once again, I found myself searching the country fruit-
lessly. In every town and village I visited, I asked the
same bizarre question at least once: "Do you happen to
know where I might be able to find a soccer jersey?"

But here, the shortage had nothing to do with a cash-
strapped government. The real issue was that no one
cared enough about the national team—nor, for that
matter, soccer—to create a demand for souvenir jerseys.

I eventually found out that if I really wanted one, I'd
have to commission a full set from the government's
official supplier—and pay for all twelve in cash. And as
crazy as this quest had clearly made me, even I had my
limits. Sadly, I conceded defeat.

If, however, I'd been in the market for an archery
souvenir, I'd definitely gone to the right place.

The official sport of Bhutan, archery not only trumps
soccer, but dominates the national landscape. Of all the
surprises I found there (and in a land whose patron saint
is best remembered for slaying demons with his magical...*member*, the wonders never cease), the ubiquitous
roadside archery contests took the cake.

*Lesson learned: Soccer isn't always the international
obsession it's cracked up to be.*

જ⁀ જ⁀ જ⁀

But then, there's Bolivia.

Soccer-crazed under any circumstances, the country had whipped itself into a full-blown frenzy during my first visit. The national team was on a hot streak in some World Cup qualifying series or other, and naturally, there was a run on official jerseys.

Everywhere I looked: sold out.

Though I might have resorted to the man-on-the-street trick again, my guide Mauricio was confident enough in his shopping prowess that he assured me I wouldn't need to. With each luckless day, he'd cheerfully reassure me that "tomorrow, we'll definitely find you that jersey."

And so we passed the entire trip.

En route to the airport on the morning of my departure, during a last-ditch sweep of La Paz's witch market, we even asked the ceremonial llama fetus vendors if they happened to have the magic polyester shirts. Alas, I went home empty-handed.

"Thank you anyway," said Max, who of course didn't mind. I was the one with the failure issues.

Several weeks later, however, a package arrived. It was from Mauricio, who'd enclosed a green Team Bolivia jersey with the following note: "Thank you so much for entrusting me with such an important mission. Sorry it took me a while."

After I recovered from my shock, I searched for a way to reciprocate—and within a few days, sent him an "I HEART NY" onesie for his newborn daughter. Several years later—though Max has gone off to college, I've moved out of the building, and the jersey quest has faded from my travels—Mauricio and I are still in touch.

Lesson learned: Whatever we're looking for, the real gift is the quest, and the people we meet along the way.

৯ৡ ৯ৡ ৯ৡ

Part beauty editor, part travel writer, Abbie Kozolchyk was likely the first person to file a story on Reese Witherspoon's hair from a yak-herding village in the Autonomous Tibetan Prefecture.

LAYNE MOSLER

𝒮𝒮 ﹐ 𝒮𝒮 ﹐ 𝒮𝒮 ﹐

Cab Fare

A traveling food lover refuels at
Michelangelo's Gas Station.

I slide across the back seat of the yellow and black
Fiat as the *taxista* pulls away from the curb, coasting
along the Avenida de Mayo. He takes a drag on his cigarette, asking me where I want to go.

Michael Jackson and Paul McCartney share a duet. A
white rosary dangles from the rear-view mirror, along
with ribbons in Argentine blue and white. I glance at the
laminated card hanging behind the passenger seat—the
name under the head shot of the silver-haired cabbie
reads: Miguel Ángel Vega. Michelangelo.

It is the week of May 25, the anniversary of the
Revolución de Mayo of 1810. Argentine flags blanket
Buenos Aires, and vendors walk the streets selling ribbons and pins in official colors. Restaurants are crowded
with customers indulging in *locro*, the hominy and

173

pork stew that is the country's dish of choice during *La Semana de la Patria*. I want to join the feast.

"So, where are you going?" Miguel Ángel asks again, turning on the taxi meter.

"I have sort of a strange request," I begin, tucking the stuffing back into a rip in the vinyl seat, "Can you take me somewhere good to eat?"

"Eh?"

"I'm new to Buenos Aires," I lie. "You know the city better than I do. Puerto Madero? No, I don't want to go to there. No, not Palermo Hollywood either. I'm not interested in touristy restaurants. I want to go to a place where you usually eat."

I am prepared to deal with Miguel Ángel's resistance—he isn't the first *taxista* I've enlisted on my food quests. Months ago I started jumping into random cabs and asking drivers to take me to their favorite places to eat. If you had to leave Buenos Aires tomorrow, I asked them, where would you go for your last meal?

Sometimes their answers thrilled me: there were fifty-year-old pizzerias where neighborhoods converged, road-side sausage sandwich stands where the *chimichurri* sauce had a kick, back-street steak houses where the grill masters were known and trusted and where heads turned when I—or any outsider—walked in.

Other times, the cabbies' responses wrenched my heart. I had more than one Buenos Aires *taxista* tell me that he cooked all his meals at home, that he couldn't afford to eat out, that despite working seven days a week, fifteen hours a shift, he didn't have a single peso left at the end of the month. *¿Que va a hacer?* They shrugged. What are you going to do?

The smell of *garrapiñada*, chocolate-covered peanuts cooked in copper bowls, wafts through the open windows of Miguel Ángel's Fiat, colliding with his cigarette smoke. We speed past art nouveau façades and wrought iron balconies, past the cupolas of the Palacio Barolo, past El Universo del Control Remoto and the Kingdom of Yarn, past hot dog vendors sporting Argentine flags. Our destination is still unresolved. I try to ease myself into the idea that we're headed for nowhere.

Miguel Ángel runs his hands through his silver hair and begins to tell me about his hatred for taxi drivers.

"They're liars and cheats," he insists. "You're lucky you got into my cab—another driver could have easily taken advantage of you."

So far none have, I tell him. I wonder how long he's been driving a taxi.

"It's been about a year. I used to sell lingerie—then people couldn't afford it anymore. Inflation, you know? After I left that behind, I knew I couldn't sit in an office all day. You put me in one of those buildings," he points to a steel and concrete high rise, "and I'll be dead in ten minutes."

He's not the first *taxista* I've met who's taken up driving in search of freedom. Maybe the Argentine novelist Adriana Romano is right: Miguel Ángel and his *compañeros* are the new *gauchos*. Their cabs are their horses, their passengers are the cattle, and their wild city is their pasture.

"Where are you from?" the *taxista* asks me.

Colombia? No. Venezuela? No. Mexico? No, no, I'm from California.

"What are you doing in Buenos Aires?"

I weigh my words before I respond to a question that I still have trouble answering after three years. When Bush won a second election, I knew that not even San

Francisco could shield me from the reality that I was out of step with my country.

"And do you feel in step with Argentina?"

"Not exactly," I tell him, "but Buenos Aires makes a good muse."

His shoulders shake as he starts to laugh. He relaxes his grip on the steering wheel.

"You're writing about Argentina? *Mirá,* if you tell people the truth about this place, no one will believe you. *¿Pero que se yo?*"

¿Que se yo? Translation: What do I know? Before choosing exile in Buenos Aires, I'd never listened to Spanish infused with so much *¿que se yo?, ¿puede ser? (can it be?),* and subjunctive, the verb tense used to express possibility rather than fact.

Eight years after the worst economic crisis in Argentine history, the subjunctive is more than just a verb tense—it's an acknowledgement of constantly shifting ground, a state of being I struggle to understand as food prices spiral out of control, the peso gets weaker, and the informal economy swells to bursting.

"Here, I expect things to fall apart every seven or eight years," the *taxista* says. "It's been that way my whole life."

His tone is neither fatigued nor resigned. Somehow, Miguel Ángel accepts the contingency of his reality. How? How can he—and so many Argentines—come to terms with this kind of precariousness?

"So where do you want to eat?" he asks. "How much do you want to spend?"

He takes another drag on his Marlboro, awaiting my answer. Rod Stewart yields to Stevie Wonder. The rosary swings.

"I want to go to the restaurant where you take your family on Sundays. Or the *kiosco* where you eat sandwiches with your *compañeros*. Or the café where you meet your lover. I don't care, as long as you've been there before and the food is good."

"Then I have to take you to the gas station," he announces, throwing his cigarette into the breeze.

I raise an eyebrow. He merges onto Avenida Entre Ríos.

"It's not actually a gas station. Eight months ago it stopped working as a gas station. But Marta is still running the restaurant."

"She's like Gardel.[1] She cooks better every day. She runs the place with her two kids. These are good people. From Chacabuco, in the province. They're like family."

According to Miguel Ángel, Marta's food is simple: steaks, house-made pasta, and *matambre* (tenderized beef wrapped around chopped parsley, carrots, peppers, and hard-boiled eggs). She always serves a daily special.

It is 12:30 P.M. when he brakes in front of the boarded-up gas station on the corner of Chile and Entre Ríos. After 1 P.M., it starts to get crazy, he tells me. Go in through the side door. Get the special.

He brushes off my thanks and my tip. I close the door on Stevie Wonder. His Fiat disappears into Balvanera.

Axl Rose greets me with a shriek when I open the door to the gas station cafeteria. The Crónica news channel broadcasts in mute from a wall-mounted TV. I take in gray formica, plastic chairs, and red signs advertising sandwiches and coffee. A snowy-haired woman watches me from behind the stainless steel counter.

---

1. "Gardel sings better every day" is a popular local refrain. It refers to legendary tango singer Carlos Gardel, Argentina's answer to Sinatra and Elvis. Gardel died in a plane crash in 1924, just as his career began taking off.

Plump, bespectacled, and dressed in all white, she exudes the power of a matriarch and the ease of someone who's exactly where she wants to be. The expression in her dime-sized brown eyes is that of someone realized, at peace.

I recognize that look of tranquility—where had I seen it before? In the gaze of a Franciscan nun who sat next to me on a bus to Rome. On the creaseless forehead of an ancient meditation teacher in Bangkok. What was that presence doing in a gas station café in Buenos Aires?

I line up behind the other customers—twenty-something workers from the TV station next door, elderly ladies in flowered dresses, taxi drivers on lunch break— and watch Marta Corsico work her magic.

She knows everyone who approaches the counter. Carefully wrapping empanadas, generous slices of quiche, and platters of fish in wax paper, she sends each devotee on his or her way with a few words of greeting, a question, a smile. She knows their stories, and they're important to her.

I study the menu pasted above the counter: hamburgers, *milanesas*, sandwiches, savory tarts, roast chicken, steak. This is soul food, Buenos Aires-style.

Today is Friday, and the *plato del día* is fish: fried hake served with french fries, mashed sweet potatoes or butternut squash. This is what I order when I get to the front of the line.

"Miguel Ángel sent me," I tell Marta, glancing at the tiny Argentine flag pinned to her collar. "He says you cook like Gardel sings."

She throws her head back and laughs from deep in her belly. I can see the questions in her eyes, but there is no time for my story. The man behind me wants his *matambre*. She writes my bill on a green scrap of paper and tells me to pay the brown-eyed girl at the cash register, who's obviously her daughter.

I hand over my twelve pesos. Despite Axl Rose, despite the growing crowd, and despite the muted shouts of Hugo Chávez on the news, the atmosphere is hushed, almost reverent.

A few bites into my breaded hake (moist and mild) and sweet potato puree (creamy and rich), I can feel the warmth in my stomach, and I understand the reverence and the reason Miguel Ángel delivered me here. Along with everyone else in the gas station cafeteria, I'm under Marta's nourishing spell.

I study the others, with their burgers, their *milanesas*, their fries and their mashed potatoes. No, I wouldn't include this food on a culinary tour of Buenos Aires—a temporary visitor probably wouldn't be looking for the gastronomic equivalent of a hug from grandma.

But for a lingerie salesman turned cab driver—and for many people in Buenos Aires who wake up to uncertainty every morning—Marta Corsico's cooking is a retreat into familiar. Her flavors—comforting, solid, and simple—are a direct response to all that's precarious in this city. Her food is solace, sustenance in a storm.

It's also an invitation to keep trying to find my way in a city laden with subjunctive, to continue communing with its flavors and decoding its neighborhoods, to go on roping the new gauchos into my journeys toward its center.

I finish my fish and empty my tray, and I'm reluctant to return to the streets outside. I cross Marta's threshold. A diesel spewing bus and a swarm of taxis roar past, defying lane lines and battling for space, beating a path to their destinations, determined to arrive.

Layne Mosler is a failed tango dancer and freelance writer who lived in Argentina for nearly four years before moving to New York City, where she drives a taxi. When she's off duty, she gets into random cabs, asks drivers to take her to their favorite places to eat, and documents the adventure at taxigourmet.com.

The Rhythms of Arezzo

Tuscany teaches a travel writer how to take it slow.

Ten ancient Italians with snow-white hair are lined up on gurneys in the corridor of San Giuseppe Hospital. Ten ancient Italians and me.

Hovering over the adjacent gurney, a man in his mid-forties strokes his mother's hair, "*Mamma, mamma. Madonna mia!*" Sobbing and soothing.

This was not part of my plan. I had jetted across the Atlantic to lead a weeklong writing workshop in Tuscany. After that I would grab an express train and travel the length of Italy's boot, from Puglia on the heel to Como on the cuff, to write a series of articles.

But when I arrived in Arezzo, I found myself soaking in fever-twisted sheets, staring at the hotel room ceiling. Fortunately, this being Italy, the ceiling was frescoed with flowers and birds.

Every morning, Franca, the hotel owner, knocked on my door. Shaking with effort, I would stand, put a shirt over my nightgown, and open the door.

"*Buongiorno,* Laura! *Come stai?*" she'd burst like a firecracker.

"*Molto malata,*" I'd gasp. Very sick.

"*Ma meglio, no?*" But better, right? Like she was at a pep rally.

I'd stayed with Franca the year before, racing from hill town to hill town, no time for a wave or a "*ciao.*" Gianni and Marco, owners of antique stores on the piazza, would call out as I flew past. "Laura*, come va?*" How are you?

"*In ritardo!*" Late! I'd shoot back, dashing to catch a bus or train.

Now Franca stared at a hollow-eyed ghost.

Franca's voice was raspy deep, the ashtray at her desk in the hotel lobby heaped with butts of Marlboros. I could hear her chatting in the street as she crossed the Piazza Grande to our hotel, her voice a slow whir and drone, like a machine that's stuck, an Army tank crawling over rough terrain.

She brought me liters of water, boxes of broth, pears and yogurt. And a house call from *il dottore.*

He didn't speak English, forcing my meager Italian in unexpected directions. *Ospedale, sangue, laboratorio.* Hospital, blood, laboratory. I told him I thought it was my *rene*, pointing to my kidney.

"Does this hurt?" I presume he asked, with a fierce karate chop to my right kidney. It did. I asked that he order lab tests, but "*molto difficile,*" he said. If I needed that, I should go to the hospital.

Two days later, Franca took me to the emergency room where I lay on a white metal bed awaiting my turn. After tests, the doctor mimed her concern, holding up photos of my inner organs, her mouth turned down in exaggerated sadness. I imagined hand-painted Pagliacci tears as she released me six hours later with a sheaf of prescriptions and admonitions, in operatic and incomprehensible Italian, about my kidney infection, and possible surgery if antibiotics didn't resolve the problem.

The next morning my workshop began. Five minutes in, my head dropped to the desk.

"Shouldn't you be in bed?" one of my students asked. I handed her my lesson plans and writing exercises.

Barely able to climb the stone stairs to my room, I felt my Type-A will had been surgically removed. I'd invested so much in this venture and now I'd have to cancel.

At the end of the first day, the students knocked on my door. "We're having a wonderful time and going ahead with the workshop as planned. Your lessons, your excursions."

They were moving forward and so would I.

"Tomorrow, do this exercise," I exhaled like Darth Vader, drawing a mind map on a sheet of butcher paper to illustrate. "See the Piero della Francesca frescoes, then write using this prompt."

So began our routine. *I will do my job*, I insisted to myself, pulling every ounce of energy into instructing students how to lead each other in the daily lessons. I wrote out exercises and drew maps of the towns they would visit without me.

I focused on each in-breath to punch out short phrases. "In Orvieto. Follow this lane. Twelfth-century church. Faded frescoes." I handed out a guided meditation. "Read this and sit for ten minutes. Then write, starting with this line."

They'd telephone to tell me of their breakthroughs. I'd issue edicts from my bed, then mentally draft my obituary. After classes they'd wake me from coma-like sleep: "Still having a wonderful time."

Each evening at 7:00, the men of our neighborhood gathered at the corner of the piazza beneath my hotel window. Echoing on the cobblestones, I could hear the basso profundo of *il dottore*, checking in with his friend Gianni.

I listened to their voices and I listened to the bells, the rhythms of Arezzo. The first night I thought, *surely the bells will stop at midnight*. The second night I thought, *surely this clanging will drive me insane*. The third, exhausted, I slept through the rings that alerted all of Arezzo to the fact that another fifteen minutes had elapsed.

I am a take-charge person, but I surrendered to the bells. Unable to sit, stand, or eat, I couldn't pack and get to the airport, let alone have a sit-down with the madman who'd programmed the bells. I emailed my doctor in the U.S. and called close friends back home. Lay low and recover, we decided.

Periodically, I dragged myself downstairs in the evening to speak to *il dottore*. With pen and paper, he drew a kidney so I would understand what was happening. With my dictionary between us, we "discussed" my latest lab results. Blocked kidney, infection, more tests required.

The students departed when the workshop ended. Frightened, I hugged my last ride to Rome goodbye. My week in Arezzo grew into a month. Trains left day after day without me, headed for the olive harvest in the south and tranquil lakes in the north.

I wanted to push on, and I wanted to stay. "Laura,

remain near the doctors and labs that you know," Franca said, granting the permission I needed to rest.

I graduated from liquids to gruel to solid food once a day. At a take-out place on Corso d'Italia, I found homemade soups, vegetables, and salads. My vocabulary blossomed with the bounty of the season: spinach, beets, green beans. At night I looked up words to fine-tune the next day's requests. *Latte scremato* (skimmed milk). *Pasta fatta a mano* (handmade pasta). I was learning to conjugate verbs. Soon I would have a past and a future, a trace of personality.

When I had the strength to walk across the sloping piazza, I limped uphill to the *biblioteca*, a fifteenth-century library that had been Wi-Fied for 100 Italian students and me. Together we marinated in the over-heated reading room while early winter storms beat against the leaded windows.

"*Lento, lento,*" slowly, slowly, Gianni called out as I thumped past his door, leaning on the walking stick I'd brought to conquer mountain trails. "*Piano, piano,*" slowly, slowly, Marco waved as I passed his shop. I paused to greet his eighty-year-old parents, seated on a bench overlooking the piazza.

"*Buona sera. Come state?*"

I sat with them as neighbors gathered for their evening stroll. Franca offered me a gelato. *Il dottore* ambled down from his office. My emails could wait. For now, I was living in Arezzo.

✒ ✒ ✒

Laura Deutsch has traveled the world in search of answers to life's big questions: Why did that guru give me a mantra that's the name of a high-end furniture store? If I eat foie gras without knowing it, have I really eaten foie gras? Along the way, Laura invented Conversational Yoga, mastered the Equine Experience to attain enlightenment by grooming a horse, and visited spas where she frequently found herself in hot water. Her misadventures have entertained readers of the Los Angeles Times, San Francisco Chronicle, More, *and* San Francisco *magazine. Laura is writing an irreverent memoir about her spiritual journey around the world and leads writing retreats from Tassajara to Tuscany.*

The Goddess of Wealth

A colorful festival takes a dark turn.

It is the last night of Tihar, Nepal's Festival of Lights—a five-day blowout honoring Lakshmi, the goddess of wealth. In Pokhara's lively tourist district, colored lights dangle from every roofline and candles illuminate the sidewalks, casting shadow puppets into the streets. Cows bedecked with marigold wreaths roam freely among the buildings, and rowdy bands of children run door-to-door, singing and dancing for coins. Sitting on the steps in front of their homes and shops, people chant and clap along with the roving performers. A few tourists, like me, thread tentatively through the crowds. When I try to sidestep a boisterous group of young dancers, a little boy reaches up and grabs me by the hips, spinning me in a clumsy circle. He is giggling, his plump smile pinned up by dimples.

"Dance me!" he orders, and how can I resist? I am quickly surrounded by a trio of small revelers, preening in their dress-up clothes, flaunting shiny black hair and gleaming faces. The little girls each wear a stick-on *bindi* between their brows. The boy's plaid shirt crackles with starch. Their eyes glitter in the dark, reflecting thousands of fairy lights and flickering candles, and the excitement of a festival night. The oldest one introduces herself as Laki, short for Lakshmi. My dance partner is her little brother Luksmin, and the shy, youngest girl is called Una. Laki is seven years old and speaks a few words of English, but mostly they communicate with smiles and hilariously exaggerated gestures. In the festival spirit, I start to dig into my pockets for a few rupees to give them, but Laki shakes her head, jingling her coin purse next to my ear. For tonight she is a rich girl, as prosperous as the goddess she was named for, and we are all her guests.

We wander together down the road, the children darting in and out of shops, touching everything, shouting to each other, and never letting me out of sight. Street vendors are doing a brisk business in snacks and sweets. Laki leads the way to a *chaat* cart and insists on buying us each a curry puff. The *chaat* carts are notoriously unclean, and since I can't explain to her that her gift could make me violently ill, I make a show of pretending to eat it and then chuck it into the gutter when she isn't looking. Her bright-eyed brother catches me, his gaze lingering on the delicacy I appear to have discarded without a second thought.

The children squabble good-naturedly to hold my hands, competing to show off their English words as we walk along. "Cow! Car! Tree! Dog!" they shout, and beam with pleasure when I understand. Their happiness is infectious, their smiles wide. It's a cool, starry night and when we laugh, our breath-clouds billow along behind us like smoke signals. The white razored peaks of Machapuchare, the Fishtail, loom under the Himalayan moon; the night feels eternal, magical. As we reach the end of the main drag, Laki tugs my arm toward an unfamiliar side road.

"YOU, me-house," she enunciates carefully.

I point the other way, toward the guesthouse where I'm staying.

"Yeesss!" she nods hard, tugging even harder. "You. ME-house!"

"Your house?" I ask doubtfully.

She nods again.

Following a group of children I just met into the outskirts of a strange town is not the sort of thing I'd likely do at home, but this is travel: a trusting, outstretched hand, an invitation to glimpse beneath the slippery surface of first impressions and second guesses—a chance for deeper understanding. Besides, what could go wrong? Not even the dreaded Maoist insurgents recruit seven-year-olds—or do they? Giving in, I allow myself to be towed along, trying to note a few landmarks so I can find my way back later on. We walk for another half-hour, stopping here and there so Laki can treat us to single sticks of gum, miniature paper cones filled with peanuts, and cheap boiled sweets—the local version of penny candy. I slip any suspicious-looking tidbits into my pockets, planning to give my candy to the kids, along with some small change, as my parting Tihar gift.

Our path winds farther away from town, along shadowy, unpaved roads, until there are no other foreigners around and no more signs in English. As we pass surprised locals, I join my palms together and raise them to my forehead with a hearty *"Namaste!"*—the traditional greeting that is also a prayer and a blessing. When they return the gesture, I see myself reflected in their bemused stares: an Amazon in their midst, anomalous as a walking Christmas tree and draped with smiling, gingerbread children. Our little group veers into a dim alley and Una, quick as a cat, slips over a fence and disappears.

"Bye-bye?" I ask Laki.

"Yes!" she confirms, delighted that we are communicating in English. "Bye-bye, Una!"

At last we reach a crumpled gate of corrugated tin, which Laki holds open for me. Stepping around it, and into a murky puddle of what I hope is only water, I enter a dark, barren courtyard. This is the Nepali version of poor urban housing: a single-story, poured concrete block studded with rusting metal doors. Somewhere in the dark, a television blares. No one is outside. The children kick off their plastic sandals and bound up the landing, dragging me along. As we approach an anonymous door, a loud moan rises from behind it and for the first time in the evening, I plant my heels in resistance. The door swings open to reveal a windowless box, lit by one buzzing fluorescent bulb and the dim light of a tiny, ancient TV set. Two adults are slouched together on a woven plastic mat on the floor, the woman emitting death-throe sounds while the man absently strokes her arm. Behind them, a child peeps out from the double bed, looking like a baby rabbit surprised in its burrow. Laki and Luksmin exchange some Nepali with their parents and urge me inside, but I am reluctant—the woman appears to be ill. *She probably doesn't want company*, I think, *and I don't want to catch whatever she has*.

As I waver in the doorway, their mother pulls herself to her knees, crying and beckoning. Feeling trapped, I slide out of my shoes, raise my hands to my forehead in greeting and kneel gingerly on the edge of the floor mat. The room is cold and reeks of kerosene. With a welcoming smile, the children's father asks if I speak Nepali. The half-dozen phrases I've picked up while trekking don't seem useful here, so I shake my head: *no, sorry.* He smiles again, pointing at Laki and Luksmin, then pats his heart. I nod and smile back warmly: *yes, they're lovely.* He then points to the toddler, who has crept over to inspect me at close range, and ruffles the blankets on the bed to reveal yet another baby, sound asleep. A family of six lives in this eight-by-ten locker, with one bed between them. A portable gas burner and a battered cooking pot comprise their kitchen. There is no heat, no toilet nor running water. Everything they own is in plain sight, and it isn't much.

Crouching awkwardly on the floor, I try to guess how old the parents are—late twenties, perhaps? Laki, who has lost her buoyancy like a small balloon left out on a cold night, retreats to a corner to count her coins and catalogue her treats. Her father continues to make polite gestures at me, mixing a few English words with Nepali and sign language: would I like a cigarette? A Coke? I decline as graciously as possible; I am desperate to leave. The children's mother is slouched over again, moaning piteously.

"Ti-haaar," her husband says slowly, noting my anxious expression. "She...*raksi!*" He points to his wife and pantomimes tilting a bottle into his mouth, repeating the motion until I understand: she's been at the festival drinking *raksi,* a traditional homebrew that smells like kerosene and produces roughly the same effect when ingested. I've heard the term "blind drunk" of course, but I can't recall ever seeing such an illustrative example. She clutches her hands together in her lap and rocks, sobbing. As five-year-old Luksmin reaches over to pat her with a chubby brown hand, her screaming and shaking reach an alarming crescendo. He recoils in fright, and the toddler bursts into tears, diving behind me and clutching my skirt. Not knowing what else to do, I catch Luksmin's eye and reach one arm around the little girl on my back, clucking softly in Nepali, "*Tiksha, tiksha*" (It's O.K.), although nothing about the situation seems O.K. to me.

Again their mother howls, tearing at her hair and convulsing. Luksmin cringes on the mat in front of her, seemingly hypnotized with fear. Across the room, Laki has checked out, lost in an imaginary world where she can buy anything she wants. The young husband shrugs and keeps smiling, helplessly. "*Ke garne?*" he murmurs several times—what to do?—the classic Nepalese response to any adversity. At that moment, several heads pop into the doorframe as the neighbors look in to see what's going on. One of them, a young guy in knockoff Western jeans, speaks to me in halting English.

"Hi," he says. "How. Are. You?"

"I'm O.K." I point to the raving woman on the floor. "Is *she* O.K.?"

He looks embarrassed. "She drink...too much," he replies shyly. "It is Tihar."

As if on cue, the mother goes into spasms. Her toddler whimpers, gripping my back like an orphaned primate. By now my heart is pounding and my mouth is dry. I want to do *something*, but this child clinging to me is not my child, nor is this my country. There is nothing to be done, and my presence is only adding to their discomfort. I should go. Gently unwinding the little girl from my skirt, I usher her back to the farthest corner of the bed where she tunnels into the blankets, sniffling, and curls around the still-sleeping baby. Luksmin scurries over to the bed, too, leaping aboard as if it is a life raft about to depart. As I rise to leave, the madwoman suddenly lunges at me, grabbing both my hands and pulling them into her lap, sobbing.

"*Tiksha, tiksha...*" I repeat breathlessly, locked in her drunken grip. "*Namaste, Namaste.*" When I speak the magic words, she robotically brings her hands together in prayer, dropping mine, and I slip out of her grasp to back toward the door. I turn to say goodbye to Laki, but she is Cinderella, lost in her own world and resisting the inevitable stroke of midnight. I say nothing, afraid to break the fierce concentration of her spell.

The neighbor boy follows me out and points the way back to town. "Come back tomorrow," he says kindly. "Tomorrow is better." Thanking him, I stumble off into the night. The streets are gloomy, deserted. The fairy lights have all gone out and the magic has evaporated with them. I find my way back to my room and collapse on the bed.

What to do, indeed? As the young man said, tomorrow will be better. By tomorrow, the young mother who keeps those four children so clean and well fed on so little will be returned to them. By tomorrow, I'll be on a plane to Kathmandu and this night will seem like a vivid dream.

Before crawling under the covers, I undress and empty my pockets, pulling out a handful of forgotten rupees and an uneaten milk caramel—the only tangible remains of my first Tihar. I wonder if I should stay in

Pokhara, try to do something for them, but I am about as useful in their world as the goddess Lakshmi herself, who accepts the gifts and adoration of the people but cannot grant their wishes. Like one of those tremulous, small-craft flights over the Himalaya that surge dizzily upward one minute and slam into a gut-churning tail-spin the next, my travels in Nepal continue to spin me from elation to horror, from envy to blame. I flounder between guilt and awe, empathy and humility, and in short order, I am beginning to understand the local saying: "You are not here to change Nepal; Nepal is here to change you." Like the Nepali pilots, I have to fly entirely on faith, hoping I'll end up wherever I am meant to land.

I know I will remember this encounter for a long time, and in some way, the woman in the tenement will always stay with me. For a moment, I glimpsed inside another world and, although our paths will probably never cross again, hers will run a blind parallel to mine, somewhere on the far side of a remote mountain. I will remember the word, the greeting, the prayer that linked me to her and freed me from her grasp. *Namaste*: the god within me salutes the god within you.

☙ ☙ ☙

Laurie Weed's stories and essays have appeared in three of The Best Women's Travel Writing *books and throughout the* To Asia With Love *guidebook series. When not careening across Mexico in her camper van, riding the rails through Burma, being shipwrecked in Laos, hitchhiking to Honduras, or bribing her way into Bali, she spins exotic tales and clever copy from northern California. You can always find her online at www.laurieweed. com.*

KELLY HAYES-RAITT

ဢ ဢ ဢ

Tongue-Tied

A fleeting connection survives in a war zone.

The one I want to wrap in my arms and bring home is Nebras.

I don't even know her name when I return to Iraq, shortly after the assault on Baghdad. I am armed with only a photo of a beggar touching her nose with her tongue.

I had met her a few months before, when I traveled to Iraq with a women's delegation, just five weeks before the U.S. bombings and invasion. Unfazed by impending disaster, the little girl, old enough to be in primary school, had begged for handouts in a popular market. I had taught her to touch her nose with her tongue. We'd teased; clearly she wasn't used to an adult making faces at her and delighting in her company. She followed me around the souk, nearly swallowing her tongue in laughter as she imitated my nose-touching stunt.

195

She was cold. The dirty scarf wrapped loosely around her neck neither protected her from the chill nor hid her calculating ability to work the shoppers. Without a translator, the most I gathered was a photo of a gleeful girl with laughing eyes and an acrobatic tongue.

When I return to Iraq five months later to find how war had touched the people who had so deeply touched me, translators are reluctant to take me to the souk. The mood in Baghdad has shifted; gunfire is heard nightly, and no one wants to be responsible for my harm. Finally, the day before I am to leave, I convince one translator to take me "shopping." We canvass the cluttered shops for hours, flashing the little girl's photo.

"Yes, that's Nebras." Finally, a shopkeeper gives a name to the girl whose deep brown eyes had humanized the smoldering CNN newscasts that absorbed my life back home. "But I haven't seen her in a while. Not since before the war."

I catch my breath. I just learned Nebras's name. She can't be one of the thousands of nameless Iraqis we dismissively call "collateral damage." I step out into the bright sunlight, and my translator catches my arm.

"We need to leave," he insists. The equally insistent gunfire across the river rattles my nerves. I feel conspicuous in the souk's crowded narrow alleys. People dart, avoiding eye contact. Shops close prematurely. Barricaded soldiers seem hyper-alert in the edgy heat. I stifle my creeping panic as we worm our way back to our car.

Behind me, a commotion erupts, and I turn around to see a crowd of men shoving toward me. I freeze. The shopkeepers part, revealing the terrified eyes of a familiar elfish girl they drag toward me by the scruff of her t-shirt.

Nebras doesn't recognize me at first. Not until I show her photos of herself does she smile. Backed against a shop and facing a tight crowd of curious men, Nebras shyly retreats, studying her photo intently. I shoo back the men who had treated this beggar only as a nuisance and, kneeling before her, I ask the interpreter to tell her I had come from America to see her. Without warning, the overwhelmed girl lunges forward and kisses me on the lips.

We buy her an ice cream from a passing vendor. She unwraps it and holds it out to me. My defenses melt. After two weeks of rigorous attention to all food and water that passed my lips, I lick the sweet street fare, sacrificing my intestines to this little girl's pleasure at hosting a visitor with all she can offer.

She's an only child who doesn't know her age. It is particularly ironic that we've met outside the Al Mustanseria University, the world's oldest science college, built in 1233. This schoolless girl's only education is learned navigating the streets outside the university's ancient walls.

I empty my purse of dinars, stuffing the oily bills into her plastic purse. She gleefully buys another ice cream for us to share.

Military helicopters zigzag overhead. Rumors that the American troops had closed bridges and jammed traffic make us jittery. Nebras escorts me out of the dicey souk, grabbing my hand and expertly keeping my skirt from being snagged by the ubiquitous wartime razor wire. As we pass a store being repainted, she mentions that it had been hit during the war's initial attacks. She tells me she spent the long nights of the early bombings in a nearby mosque.

I hug her harder than I intended. I feel her wiry hair

against my cheek, her grungy t-shirt against my shoulder, her warm, open heart so willing to accept mine.

And then I'm gone.

❧ ❧ ❧

Kelly Hayes-Raitt was press credentialed by the Jordanian government as she entered Iraq illegally in July 2003, three months after the U.S.-led invasion. She reported live via satellite phone to National Public Radio and other news outlets. Additionally, she wrote several columns for the Santa Monica Daily Press, *two of which were published in* Female Nomad and Friends: Tales of Breaking Free and Breaking Bread Around the World. *Hayes-Raitt is the author of award-winning articles and a forthcoming memoir about her work with refugees,* Living Large in Limbo: How I Found Myself Among the World's Forgotten. *A recipient of five writing fellowships, she's lived in writing colonies as far-flung as Bialystok, Poland. She is a college lecturer and public speaker and blogs at www.PeacePATHFoundation.org.*

.ॐ .ॐ .ॐ

Finding Gilbert

Fifty years later, a daughter seeks
to heal the wounds of war.

Gilbert Desclos sat in the tall grass on the cliff above Omaha Beach and shivered in the sea air. The sun rose over the trees as he hugged his bony knees tight to his chest and pulled his worn wool sweater around him.

Ever since the arrival of les Américains, his world had changed. Overnight, a military camp had sprung to life on the empty field just below his home in Normandy. For seven-year-old Gilbert, an orphan, it was a boy's dream. His caretaker, Mrs. Bisson, had to drag him in at night.

Now he watched, wide-eyed, as jeeps roared up the road and men in white caps scurried about, emptying trucks loaded with guns, ammunition, food, and giant duffel bags. He yawned as the smell of bacon, eggs, coffee, and toast wafted up from a massive tent. He tilted his small head back, breathing in the aromas. His stomach growled.

Donald K. Johnson, a lieutenant in the Seabees, the U.S. Navy's Construction Battalion, held a clipboard and checked off the morning's accomplishments. The infirmary tent was complete; now the medics and doctors had a decent place to treat soldiers. The showers worked.

Johnson and his men had been busy since dawn, and it was now noon. He dismissed them, then took a moment and touched the breast pocket that held the photo of his wife and two young sons. It had been more than a year since he'd seen them.

When the lieutenant turned to go, he spied something in the tall grass on the hill. Was that a child? He waved. A small hand waved back. Johnson beckoned. There was a moment of hesitation and then the boy, barely taller than the grass, made his way down. Johnson knelt to look into the child's thin face.

He tried out his high school French: *"Comment t'appelles-tu?"*

The boy's sparkly blue eyes shone. "Gilbert," he said.

Johnson shook his hand. This little guy looked like he could use a good meal, and the camp had more than enough food. In his halting French, he invited Gilbert to have lunch. When the boy nodded, Johnson lifted him onto his hip, as he might've done with one of his own sons, and headed for the mess tent.

Inside, dozens of young soldiers ate, talked, and clanged their cutlery. Gilbert's eyes grew wide. Johnson piled two plates high with roast beef, potatoes, carrots and peas, freshly baked bread, and apple pie.

The men at the officers' table smiled and made room for the two of them. Gilbert took small bites and, chewing slowly, ate everything on his plate. Johnson patted his head: "*Très bien!*" Gilbert smiled.

After lunch, Johnson held Gilbert's hand, and they walked into the June sunlight. He knelt beside the boy and explained that he had to go back to work. Gilbert nodded and ran back up the path to the tall grass, turning around to wave.

At 1800 hours, as Johnson was again heading for the mess tent, he saw Gilbert sitting in the same spot. He motioned, and Gilbert ran to him.

Dinner was fried chicken, mashed potatoes, corn, biscuits, and chocolate cake. Johnson again filled two plates, but Gilbert didn't eat as much as he had at lunch; it was clear that the boy wasn't used to so much food. But he sat close to Johnson and smiled his shy smile, taking big breaths between bites, as if willing himself to eat as much as he could.

After dinner, Johnson knelt close to Gilbert. "*Bonsoir,*" he said. "*A demain,*" till tomorrow. He watched the boy walk up the path and out of sight.

From that day on, Gilbert ate with Johnson, three meals a day, soon filling out from all the rich food. The other soldiers didn't mind; the boy helped ease their homesickness. Gilbert giggled when Johnson carried him around on his shoulders and soon began riding along in the Jeep down to the beach, where Johnson supervised the unloading of ships. When Johnson oversaw construction projects in the camp, Gilbert tagged along. If Johnson left camp with his crew to rebuild a road or a blown-out bridge, Gilbert waited for his return.

As the summer of 1944 passed, Johnson's French improved, and Gilbert learned to say hello, goodbye, thank you, Jeep, ship, and ice cream. He could also say Lieutenant Johnson.

In mid-October, when Johnson received orders to leave France, he drove to the local authorities in Caen to make some inquiries. He discovered that Gilbert had been abandoned at birth and had no living relatives. But when he asked if he could adopt him, the answer was firm: no.

Lieutenant Johnson was my father. Stories about the young boy and wartime France were an element of my childhood, as constant as the roar of Dad's motorcycle as he rolled in each evening at 5:45 after his commute from San Diego, where he worked as a civil engineer for the Navy.

At 6 P.M. sharp, my family gathered around the yellow Formica table that took up most of our small kitchen. Dad and Mom sat on each end, my sister across from me, our older brothers next to us.

My father looked straitlaced in his short-sleeved white shirt, skinny tie, and plastic pocket liner holding a pen, a notebook, and sometimes a slide rule. But his eyes were kind, funny, a bit mischievous. His stories made me laugh, and when he described his time in France, I could picture it all: the French countryside, the huge Navy ships, and Gilbert Desclos.

He always said Gilbert's name with a kind of reverence and the way the French would, with a soft "g" sound.

I knew he had tried to adopt Gilbert and bring him home. I thought about that sometimes, wondering what

it would have been like to have another older brother at
the dinner table.

As I grew up, Dad's stories seemed to belong more
and more to my childhood, put away with my dolls and
coloring books. After I married and had my own family,
he visited Europe again, stopping in Paris. He told me
how he tried to find Gilbert's name in the phone book
but couldn't. I remember how his shoulders slumped
and his head hung down as he recounted his failure.

In my father's old age, when he could no longer walk
and had lost his eyesight, I would sit with him as he
talked about his life. When he spoke about France, his
eyes shone. They glistened with tears when he mentioned Gilbert, pronouncing his name with that special
softness. I stroked his fragile hand, wishing there were
something I could do.

After Dad died, in 1991, I wanted to learn more about
World War II. I traveled to France in 1993 to tour the
beaches and write about the fiftieth anniversary of the D-
day invasion. I stood on the cliffs above Omaha Beach,
now the site of the American cemetery where nearly ten
thousand U.S. soldiers are buried. The air stung my face
as I wiped away tears, remembering my father, wishing
I could ask him more questions.

In my article for several newspapers, I mentioned
Gilbert Desclos. The press attaché at the French consul-
ate in San Francisco read the story and contacted me.
Learning that I was going back to Normandy to accept
a medal in Dad's honor, she insisted I try to find Gilbert:
"The French don't move around as Americans do. He's
probably still nearby."

After the medal ceremony, I placed an ad in the local

paper. Thinking it would take months, if not years, to find Gilbert, I listed my address in California, then left on a tour around France with Heather, my teenage daughter.

The next morning, Gilbert Desclos, reading his newspaper, wept when he saw my father's name. He called the paper and learned I'd left the area, so he wrote to my home address. My sister, collecting my mail, recognized the name, ran to a friend's, and faxed it back to France. I received it the night before Heather and I were to travel back to Paris and then home.

I called Gilbert and, stammering through my emotions, arranged a place to meet him that evening. As my daughter and I sat at a sidewalk café in Caen, waiting for Gilbert and his wife to arrive, I fidgeted in my metal chair, watching the passing faces. Could I possibly be meeting the boy from my childhood stories? And how would I know him?

Then a trim, well-dressed man walked up, smiled, and said my name. When I looked into his eyes, I recognized the same expression of kindness that my father always had. Gilbert actually resembled Dad somehow.

At his home after dinner, Gilbert uncorked a dusty bottle of Calvados. As we sipped the apple brandy and talked, I realized that all my years of studying French vocabulary and irregular verbs had been in preparation for this moment.

He asked questions about my father, about our lives, about how Dad had died. He told me how he'd struggled after Dad left France, living in an orphanage, lonely and sad—but that in his teens, a sweet woman had brought him to live with her family. Nourished by those years of love and caring, he went on to join the military, find a good job, and marry his wife, Huguette. Together they raised their daughter, Cathy.

But he had never forgotten Dad. He had always insisted to Huguette, Cathy, and later his two grandsons that he had a family in America who would come and find him one day.

I told him that Dad had never forgotten him either—that he had talked about him for the rest of his life, even at the end. I could tell that meant everything to Gilbert.

He told me the same stories my father had told, but from a child's perspective: his fascination with the military camp, the delicious food, Dad's gentleness. Remembering the lieutenant's arms around him, he wept again. We sat together, silent and moved, missing the father who had loved us both.

Gilbert took a gulp of his Calvados and told me his version of the October day in 1944 when he and Dad said goodbye on Omaha Beach.

Dad held him close. Gilbert hung on tight, burying his head in Dad's thick, wool Navy coat. Cold October winds whipped the sand around them as men rushed by, carrying their heavy seabags on their shoulders, excited to be going home.

"Do you want to come with me to America?" Dad asked.

"*Oui*," Gilbert murmured.

They boarded the ship. The captain, who'd been watching, shook his head. "Johnson, off the record, if you're caught, I know nothing about this." Dad nodded, shifting Gilbert's weight on his hip.

But within the hour, a storm raged. Twenty-foot waves lashed the hull of the ship. There was no way the boat could cross the English Channel until the storm had subsided.

As the sun set, the wind slackened and sailors prepared for departure. Moments before the ship was to sail, French gendarmes pulled up on the beach, demanding to speak with the captain; a Mrs. Bisson had reported that her ward had not returned home, and they were looking for him.

As Gilbert remembers it, the captain called for Lieutenant Johnson. There was a long, strained pause. The lieutenant appeared at the top of the gangplank, holding Gilbert in his arms. Gilbert sobbed and clung to him. "*Non!*" he wailed. "*Non!*" The gendarmes had to pull him away. The ship sailed without the boy, whom Mrs. Bisson placed in an orphanage the same day.

Gilbert put the cork in the Calvados bottle. "Your father said he would come back for me. I have been waiting fifty years for some word from him."

We sat in awkward silence until Gilbert's daughter asked, "Why didn't he? Why didn't he come back?"

I couldn't think of what to say in English, let alone French. Then Cathy answered her own question. "*Le destin*," she said softly. It was Gilbert's destiny to stay in France and have his family and his life there.

As we said goodnight, Gilbert took my hand. "I always knew that I would hear from your father, that someone would come," he said. "Thank you."

I didn't sleep that night, picturing the goodbye on that desolate beach, imagining the police pulling a part of my father's heart away. And how—why—had Dad carried that secret for the rest of his life? Was he ashamed that he hadn't fulfilled his promise? And why hadn't I helped him find Gilbert before he died?

As the clock ticked on the bedside table, I realized I would not find answers from the past. But we could go forward from here.

For the next two years, Gilbert and I wrote, phoned, and e-mailed. In 1996, my mother, my sister, Heather, and I traveled to France for a celebration that received coverage in the same newspaper I'd used to find Gilbert.

A year later, the Desclos family came to America, welcomed by forty members of the Johnson clan, spanning four generations. At dinner one night, Gilbert read aloud a letter he'd written for the occasion, as I translated into English. He shared memories of my father and told us what it meant to finally come to America. It was a dream, he said, that he had thought would remain a dream.

Other relatives and I returned to France many times through the years. Then, a few months before my planned visit last January, Gilbert was diagnosed with liver cancer. He died four days before my arrival.

I made it in time for his funeral. In his tiny village in Normandy, bells tolled as relatives and friends braved the cold to fill the church. The tricolor French flag draped his coffin, carried by an honor guard of fellow veterans.

I sat with Gilbert's family in the front pew and listened to the tributes to his life. During the service, the priest asked me to place on the coffin a photo of my father and one of Gilbert from 1944, together in one frame.

It was then that I realized that Cathy was right: it was *le destin* that the naval officer and the little boy had found each other and also that they'd gone their separate ways.

But I knew now, as candlelight flickered on the faces in the photographs and music echoed off the walls of the old church, that it was also destiny that had brought them back together.

❧ ❧ ❧

Diane Covington, an award-winning writer and photographer, lives on an eight-acre organic farm in northern California. Her work has appeared in many publications including Reader's Digest, More Magazine, The Sun, *and on NPR. You can follow her blogs at: dianecovington.com. She is writing a memoir based on this story.*

MARIANNE ROGOFF

Common Tongues

The night is restless, as is its beauty.
—Pablo Neruda

We see them move in with their big black duffels and wheeled bags—big guys! Speaking German? No? Dorothy spots the red-stitched word LATVIA on a black t-shirt.

"Divers," Liza says, noting their equipment.

We're all feminine and feminist, sitting around a wicker table on pillowed seats with colored pencils and notebooks, speaking of lust, poetry, restless urges, and *On the Road.* Everyone smiles. *Hello. Hola. Welcome.* They are noisy and fill up the space as they separate around us in search of their rooms.

That evening our writers' group meets in the ground-floor *sala* of Hotel California in Todos Santos, Baja, Mexico, on comfy couches and red-patterned rugs,

209

outdoors but in, lit by lamps and candles. The waiters bring margarita glasses and pitchers of ice; we
have brought our own limes, a knife, Cointreau, and
Reposada. We drink and the dialogue ranges and roams,
a tumbling roll of women talking. We never tire of it.
There is so much to say.

Suddenly Lana declares, "I think you write about sex
too much, Dorothy, I mean, really, we've all had it, we've
all done it, who cares? Enough already."

Too much writing! Not enough sex! I'm thinking, as
verbal shots volley between the two good friends. Liza
and Jade try to ease and smooth but the exchange only
accelerates.

"I've been following my libido around all my life."

"No one wants to hear about it!"

"Fuck you," Dorothy replies.

Ooh.

For a while the mood is mean, then Lana turns to me.
"As the leader of the group, you should…"

*What? It's happy hour! Nighttime. No topic taboo, that's
the rule.*

Today alone we'd traveled some territory. Who left
her husband? Who wishes she had? Who's gay? Who
wanted to be? Who's hosted more orgies? Who's had
more interesting characters in the room when everyone
was going down on everyone else?

"It was the times," someone says, "the era…."

More tequila and we are nostalgic for the era—all
except Jade, who wasn't born yet, whom Liza calls
"The Kid" because she's so fresh and pure and sweet.
As leader I squeeze limes for another round and nudge
us from wrangling and rehashing to focus on writing,
which brings up, "What do these characters fear and
want?" and moves the talk around to death and love.

By the time Jade and I retire to Room 4 we're drunk, stimulated, animated. We brush our teeth, don pajamas, slip under covers in twin beds and attempt to settle down by reading books in low light, when from the other side of the shuttered window we hear the giddy drunkenness of men stumbling with margaritas into chairs at the balcony table outside our door—they're staying in Room 3.

"The Latvians!" I whisper as I discern the Slavic rhythms of their banter.

Jade giggles.

"*¡Comprendo!*" we hear through the window.

"*¡Margarita!*" shouts the other.

Jade smiles. I laugh.

The men commence laughing in a Latvian way, a manly roll punctuated with single vocabulary words they must have studied on the plane.

"*¡Burrito!*" says one.

"*¡Sombrero!*" says the other.

Jade shouts, "*¡Guacamole!*"

"*Si,*" says a Latvian, slurring out a margarita toast, and all at once the gluey languor of their speech—so unwomanly, so pleasingly foreign after the day's intensity and confrontations—seems hysterically funny to us and we roar into fits of laughter.

The Latvians feel the same.

Through the shutters a dialogue of laughter commences: male guffaws, female giggles, male punch lines, female flirtations, Latvian come-ons, American responses. Howling like hyenas, like idiots, like there's no tomorrow.

"*¡Comprendo!*"

"*¡Hola!*"

"*¡Buenos noches!*"

"*¡Vodka!*"

Peals of laughter, belly laughs, till you pee, till you cry, till your stomach hurts and cheeks are sore. Then suddenly Jade is moved to throw open the shutters! I'm shocked! So are the Latvians! We put on our eyeglasses to get a look at them raising drinks to *señoritas mucha-chas* through the screen, profiles in silhouette on the other side of the window. I imagine they can vaguely make out the shadowy shapes of our chortling pajama-clad forms in the twin beds.

"*Margarita comprendo sombrero burrito,*" we hear.

"*Bienvenidos,*" I reply.

One has entered Room 3 and is tapping a beat on the wall behind my bed. I tap back and for a while we converse this way—no words, *tap tap,* rapping on the walls, call-and-response *are you there? yes I am* taps—all the while trying to bring the laughter under control. (Clearly it's out of control—it's been a half hour at least.)

Finally Jade reaches to turn off the lamp and shouts, "*Buenas noches.*"

"*Noches buenos,*" says the man, retreating to his room.

Tap tap on the walls, then an inspired bold move back outdoors to knock directly on our door, ask with words in several languages: *come play, vaya con dios, borrachos en Mexico, the night is young, nights are good.*

"*Buenas noches,*" says Jade.

"*Comprendo margarita*," says the Latvian.

Tap tap, says the other.

I am lulled to sleep by the hopeful taps that go on past midnight, inviting us to cease resistance, to devour and savor the night's restless beauty.

In the morning we'll learn it's true: there's no tomor-row.

The men will depart, wheeling their scuba gear back past our wicker-seated group, seeking eye contact: *Which ones were you?* we'll all wonder.

❧ ❧ ❧

Marianne Rogoff has had stories published in The Best Travel Writing 2010, The Best Women's Travel Writing 2008, *and* The Best Travel Writing 2006, *among others. She teaches Writing & Literature at California College of the Arts and leads weeklong writers studios in Mexico every January and August.*

ANGIE CHUANG

᪥ ᪥ ᪥

Vice and Virtue

A visitor to Kabul savors the durability
of childlike wonder.

*L*aila had just met me at the Kabul Airport when she
brought up the subject of ice cream. All around us
were cesspools, crumbling walls scarred by trails of bullet
holes, and amputee landmine victims begging for *bakh-
shesh*—but there was ice cream, she assured me.

Kabul was no place for trucks with tinkling music to
attract kids, though; here children worked, begged, or
starved, and a kid carrying an ice cream cone down the
street would soon find it coated in the mix of dust and
diesel residue that painted everything in the city—if he
didn't first get beaten up and have it stolen.

We'd been talking about burqas, a topic that in
Afghanistan segues to ice cream more easily than one
might think. As our driver steered his Volga sedan

down the unpaved roads, women in burqas—*chadori*, in
Afghanistan—moved alongside us like dusky-blue shut-
tlecocks, faces hidden behind small mesh ovals. It was
2004, and about half the women on the street still wore
chadori. They were no longer required, Laila explained,
but women still wore them because they felt safer and it
was more socially acceptable.

"What was it like wearing *chadori* here during the
Taliban time?" I asked. She had last visited Kabul in
2000.

Although Afghanistan was Laila's birthplace, she'd
lived in the United States for fifteen years, more than
half her life. She was born in 1979, the year the Soviets
invaded, her father was jailed, and her uncle was killed
by the Communists. That was the year that tore apart
the fabric of her family—and her country—forever.
As the Soviet War progressed, Laila's family had fled
to Pakistan. When she was twelve, her father's oldest brother, a university professor in the United States,
sponsored her, two of her brothers, and the three children of her slain uncle to live with him in Portland,
Oregon, which is where we met and became friends.
The trip to Kabul had been Laila's idea. We would stay
with her aunt, uncle, and cousins, who had been living
in the same house through the Soviet War, the civil war,
the Taliban, and now the U.S.-led war.

"It wasn't a big deal," she said, shrugging. "Just hot.
It was the other restrictions that made me mad. For
instance, we went to an ice cream shop in our *chadori*—
with male escorts like we were supposed to—but the
man wouldn't serve us because we were women."

The Taliban's infamous Department for the
Prevention of Vice and the Promotion of Virtue—the

same government agency responsible for beating women who showed their ankles or polished their fingernails— had also outlawed selling ice cream or French fries to women. The religious police scoured the city in their Toyota pickup trucks, shutting down stores or beating shopkeepers if they suspected them of having served female customers. The man who refused to serve Laila was probably alarmed to encounter a woman openly ordering ice cream. He wasn't taking any chances.

Ice cream and French fries. I found it puzzling that Vice and Virtue, as they were known, chose to outlaw these particular foods. Was it the phallic nature of a French fry? The suggestive quality of ice-cream licking? Did Taliban leadership hold a *jirga*, a traditional tribal council, to discuss the vices and virtues of certain foods before deeming ice cream and fries worse than, say, peaches and cucumbers?

Eve Ensler, the playwright and activist, wrote about a group of women in Taliban-ruled Jalabad sneaking behind a wall of hanging sheets in the back of an abandoned restaurant, lifting their burqas, and taking a few furtive bites before the roar of pickup trucks sent them fleeing—abandoned bowls tipped over, spoons akimbo, melting rivulets of cream providing evidence of their crime. A woman caught with ice cream could be punished by flogging or even execution, Ensler's guide told her.

Similar stories are never told of French fries.

"It's like no ice cream you'll try anywhere else," Laila said.

"What's so special about it?" I was sweating in the un-air-conditioned Volga sedan and felt cooler just hearing about it.

"It tastes like it came straight from the cow," she said, her voice quickening against the lethargic, stale air. "Every shop makes its own right there in the back, and it doesn't have flavors; it's just pure sweetened cream. Then there are little extras—rosewater, pistachios, cardamom—to make it interesting but not cover the rich taste. It glides on your tongue like butter." Her large, round eyes took on a dreamy softness.

"Plus, there's just something about it that takes me back. It's part of my childhood."

In the summers of her youth, when it was hot enough, Laila's father would take her and her brothers and cousins to the ice cream shops. "The kids need to cool off," he'd insist. And seeing the way he devoured his own ice cream—so fast it didn't have time to melt even a little—she knew that he did, too.

"This time," Laila said, "I'm going to find some ice cream."

Outside the car window I saw cratered concrete and buildings flattened like cardboard boxes. Two wiry men pushed a vegetable-laden cart being pulled by an emaciated donkey too feeble to contribute noticeably to the men's efforts.

It suddenly struck me that there was something necessary about discussing ice cream while driving through a war zone. Laila's quest became my quest: I would not leave Kabul until I tasted that ice cream.

It was hard to leave the house. We went out for official purposes and sometimes accompanied Laila's relatives on errands or to school (activities only Americans would find interesting), but a purely social outing was another matter.

First, we'd have to take a cab, which required a male

escort—not because of the former Taliban decree, but for safety's sake; two women traveling alone would garner unnecessary attention, and with the Taliban gone, some men were exercising their newfound freedom by sexually harassing women on the street. Also, desperate poverty and the post-September 11 influx of wealthy foreigners had spurred a cottage industry in kidnapping for ransom.

Finding a male to escort us wasn't terribly complicated; Laila's cousin Asad could take us. The problem was that if we brought him, it would become an outing with family members, in which case it seemed unfair to leave Nazo and Nafisa behind. The two young women of the household were always eager to go out but had little opportunity to do so. When Laila and I first broached the idea of finding ice cream, Nazo's green eyes lit up, and a smile crossed Nafisa's elegant, serious face. Then they hesitated and looked at each other cautiously—Nazo's mother would expect one of them to stay home and help prepare dinner.

"No, no, you go," Nafisa said to her sister-in-law.

"No, no, you go," Nazo said. They were sisters, a bond that in gender-segregated Muslim countries was as important as that of a husband and wife. One could not openly act against the interests of the other, yet it was clear they both wished the other would yield and offer to stay home.

But even if both Nazo and Nafisa managed to get away, with a male escort there would be five of us, and we wouldn't fit into a cab. We'd have to take two, which would necessitate two male escorts, not to mention skillful coordination through Kabul's unmarked, congested roads to ensure we ended up at the same place. Nobody had cell phones. Finally, there was eleven-year-old Ihsan, Nazo's nephew from Kandahar who was living at his grandparents' house for the summer. He'd be crushed if we all went for ice cream without him.

"I'm beginning to think this is going to be another trip to Afghanistan without ice cream," Laila said, sighing. Her narrow shoulders slumped under her bunched-up scarf, which she had allowed to slide off her head inside the house. As a guest, I was far too intimidated by Laila's traditional aunt to test the limits of propriety. After I saw how she looked at her westernized niece's exposed, pony-tailed hair, I dutifully kept my scarf on my head.

Laila wasn't so relaxed about other rules, though. The first time I met Asad, she muttered through clenched teeth as he entered the women's sitting room, "Do not...make eye contact...with my cousin...in front of his mother." I studied the slightly frayed cuffs of his cargo pants against his dark socks as he and I made small talk in English, which he'd learned in a Pakistani boarding school.

As the post-Soviet civil war and the Taliban had rendered secular education in Afghanistan nonexistent, Asad's family had sent him to a ragtag boarding school for Afghans run by refugees in Peshawar. Although the living conditions were abysmal and students often went without enough to eat, they did learn English, thanks to the postcolonial British influence.

It seems silly, looking back now, that family politics—not the Vice and Virtue Department—would have prevented us from fulfilling our goal. But within the high, white plaster walls of the family compound, those obstacles felt as real as Taliban rules.

"It's O.K.," I told Laila. "There are more important things than ice cream."

Laila disagreed.

One night, Asad ducked into the women's room during dinner and announced that he'd been told Laila and I would want to buy souvenirs and gifts before we left. He could take us shopping on Chicken Street tomorrow if we'd like. Souvenir shopping hadn't even crossed my mind.

"That would…" I said, looking at his mother—her nod was barely perceptible—"be nice."

We left the house the next day with little drama; no one was very interested in souvenir shopping, though Ihsan joined us. When we reached a busy intersection, Asad asked the taxi driver to stop. We climbed out, stepping over open sewers to the sidewalk, and rounded the corner onto a bustling street of shops. Each storefront on Chicken Street was full to bursting, wares dangling from overhangs and doorways—a richly loomed rug here, a patina-coated goblet there. Every centimeter of the window displays was filled with lapis, turquoise and silver jewelry, tea sets, miniature maps of Afghanistan carved from semi-precious stones, decorative boxes of every imaginable shape and style. Some were coated with a thick layer of dust that must have dated to the Taliban days.

Still, the most distinctive part of each store was the shopkeeper himself. Often wearing a certain cap or turban to indicate his ethnic and tribal affiliations, he beckoned in sweetly intoned Dari for passersby to come in and behold his wares. Crowds of men, women, and children walked quickly in all different directions, jostling each other but never losing pace. We moved much more slowly than them, stopping to look at everything.

People bumped into us from behind and sidled past, exasperated.

After shopping and bargaining for hours, we found ourselves laden with bags of jewelry, knickknacks, and a small carpet, blindly following Asad, who had inexplicably picked up the pace. Without warning, he'd become one of the jostlers. Finally, we stopped in front of a nondescript storefront, and Asad walked in, motioning for us to follow. Ihsan became very animated, practically skipping inside. Asad exchanged brief words with the man in charge and ducked past the crowded main room, poking his head into an empty back room painted electric blue. He said a few more words to the man, who nodded and motioned for us to sit back there.

Asad had been searching for a table where the four of us, a mixed-gender group, could sit together comfortably without coming under scrutiny. In the main room, only men sat with men, or women with women.

We settled in—Laila and I on one side of the table, Asad and Ihsan on the other. Laila pulled out her camcorder for the first time that day, grinning so widely that the skin around her big, brown eyes crinkled.

"What?" I asked. I still didn't understand that we were in an ice cream shop.

"I'm so happy," she said. "Just wait until you try this."

As if on cue, waiters arrived and set four glass dishes in the center of the table. The ice cream, a vanilla color, was molded into shapes: two portions looked like donuts standing on end with crushed pistachios and cardamom sprinkled over them, and the other two were cylinders covered with moist strands of fresh coconut.

Laila paused for a beat, then almost reverently sunk her spoon into hers, careful not to topple the perfect donut shape. Then she wedged a bite out of the frozen concoction and tasted her first ice cream in Afghanistan in more than twenty years. She closed her eyes and smiled, nodding her head.

"Mmm," she said. "That's even better than I remember."

Awaking from her nostalgic reverie, she suddenly fired up her camcorder and pointed it at me. "Eat, eat," she commanded. "We have to document your first Afghan ice cream."

I too had the pistachio and cardamom. I carved out a small amount, and the cold steel of the spoon hit my mouth before I tasted the surprising flavor of pure, sweet cream. I had been expecting vanilla because of the color—a cultural assumption. The texture was impossibly dense but smooth, rich and delicate, buttery and fatty, and quick to melt on contact. It had the heft of Devonshire clotted cream with the fragility of panna cotta.

After savoring a few more bites, I wrested the camcorder from Laila's hands and turned to the boys' side of the table, filming Ihsan as coconut shreds and melted ice cream dribbled from his mouth. Unlike the rest of us, Ihsan gobbled his treat, eating it the way any eleven-year-old boy would—quickly, and with equal amounts gusto and mess.

As I raised the camera to Asad, I realized that, through the small-screen viewfinder, I was seeing him face-on for the first time. The absence of an audience—whether other restaurant-goers or his mother—and the shield of the camera afforded me this brazenness. I studied his face in ways I hadn't dared before. He had dense black eyes fringed with long, straight lashes, a toasted-wheat complexion, and thick, arcing eyebrows. His left eyebrow was bisected by a hair-thin scar. I wanted to ask what had happened and how old he'd been, but I stopped myself. He looked back directly into the lens, unflinching, and I felt heat rise to my face, despite the cold buzz of the ice cream.

Suddenly, a small, cool hand slipped under the camcorder and I turned to face Laila.

"Your ice cream is melting," she said into the camera, raising her eyebrows. Then she added, "We're never going to forget this."

She was right. I wouldn't be forgetting any of it. But this time, it wasn't just about seeking out and tasting a national delicacy, the way I'd sought out gelato in Italy or durian in Vietnam. I understood now what was necessary about ice cream in a war zone. The luxury and impracticality of this food—so transient by nature—demanded attention. It was the taste of being fully in the present.

But for Laila, it represented the past as well. For her, an outing like this—not war, death, nor the Taliban—defined her childhood. Ice cream was the Afghanistan she wanted to remember. And on that afternoon in Kabul, she found it again.

***

The names of the Afghan and Afghan-American characters in this piece have been changed because the family has been threatened for cooperating with the author, an American journalist. Angie Chuang is a nonfiction writer and educator living in Washington, D.C. She was a newspaper journalist for thirteen years and is now on the faculty of the American University School of

Communication. She is working on a book-length work centered on a 2004 trip to Afghanistan and the family with whom she stayed and traveled. Excerpts have been published in the anthology, Tales from Nowhere, *and in the online magazine,* InTheFray. *She has been awarded residencies at Jentel, Virginia Center for the Creative Arts, and Caldera.*

CAROL REICHERT

🐚 🐚 🐚

Contratiempo

Finding balance on the dance floor.

My train rolls out of the Granada station, and I smirk like a fugitive. I feel I've gotten away with something, even though my husband and two small children know I'm on board.

For the second time in two years, we've swapped our suburban east coast American life for a rural one in Albuñuelas, a scruffy, white-washed village in Andalucía. The children attend the village school, my photographer husband takes pictures, and I dance. Our trips to Spain are long enough to push us from tourist to temporary resident, and we carry a card just to make it official.

With my flamenco *profesora* in Granada, I learn the firecracker footwork and florid hand movements, but I still can't hear the beat. There's no one-two-three about this fusion of Arabic, Indian, and African rhythms, and without learning it, I'll never be able to dance. So I head to Seville for flamenco boot camp: five days of undistracted study at a school that teaches the "beginner with experience."

The train chugs into the countryside; panoramas of sunflowers tilt toward the sun, and fiery orange poppies shimmy as we pass. My husband is fathering solo for the week and expects nothing but lots of sex when I return. I've struck a good deal.

I arrive in Seville in early afternoon on the last day of *feria*, the celebration that occurs just after Semana Santa. I assume the Spaniards will be weary from weeks of partying, but there is relentless vitality. Men swagger down the streets in their wide-brimmed bolero hats and tight, high-waist pants. Women swish past in brightly colored flamenco dresses that cinch their torsos then flare out mid-thigh in tiers of wide ruffles. They sweep their hair up with *peinetas*, combs decorated with flowers. Everyone is on display.

But I have no time for parties. I roll my suitcase over the cobblestones to my hotel and swear the wheels beat out the rhythm of a tango: *uno, dos, tres, cuatro*. Breathing in the air of yet another Spanish city that claims to be the birthplace of flamenco already helps my rhythm.

When I arrive at class the next morning, the school is closed. I wonder if the employees are still sleeping off their hangovers. Eventually, the office manager arrives and introduces me to my teacher, Antonio, and my classmates, Trina from Belgium and Emma from Australia.

Antonio is bleary eyed and unshaven, with wild, uncombed hair that falls in black ringlets around his shoulders. He has the strong body of a dancer: powerful thighs, broad shoulders, and a narrow waist. We start with *plantas*, striking the soles of our feet on the ground—left, right, left, right, over and over again. Antonio shows us how high he lifts his leg back, until his heel almost touches his butt, and then he brings it down to the ground in a snap. "*Alta, alta*," he says. "Higher, higher. That's how you get the sound."

Antonio seems annoyed with the entire class, but my Spanish teacher in Albuñuelas warned me that most flamenco teachers are mean. They belittle you, beat you down. Thankfully, my classmates and I are about the same level, so Antonio hates us equally.

I walk past the school office after class, where the flamenco teachers gossip and smoke. My Spanish is good enough to understand that Antonio and his colleagues are complaining about poor pay. I meet my rhythm teacher, David, also known as *La Gamba de Jerez*, The Shrimp from Jerez. We sit in the tiny classroom, and David turns on the music.

"Do you know this rhythm?"

I listen hard but can't recognize it.

"A tango."

A tango. Easy, I think. I know this. Four beats. But it isn't easy after all. Bing, one, two, three, four. Bing, one, two, three, four. I've never noticed the bing before, an extra beat in the rhythm. David nods his head at the bing then claps on one, two, three, and four. I ask him about the bing.

"No, no, no. The bing isn't in the beginning. It's between the two and the three. *Contratiempo*. Do you know what that is?"

"No." I learn later that it's the offbeat between two whole beats.

David doesn't talk to me. He barks.

"You're not holding your hands correctly. Look. *Sordas.* Quietly."

He cups his palms and extends and spreads his fingers. He grabs my hands and turns them at a diagonal to each other. The sound is deep and soft. Then he slaps the fingers of his right hand on the palm of his left hand. It makes a loud crack. "*Fuertes.*" I try it. Sometimes I make the cracking sound and sometimes I miss. David turns on a metronome and startles me by shouting, "Tango. *Fuertes.*"

I try to clap the four beats with the popping technique he just showed me.

"Cup your hand a little."

I try again and again until my hands sting. There are people, *palmeros*, who are hired just to keep the beat for the singer, the guitarist, and the dancer. The *palmero* glues the whole show together rhythmically, clapping with the precision of a metronome.

"O.K. Now rest," he tells me.

I rub my hands together.

"What do you do for a living?"

How was I going to explain this complicated job in Spanish?

"I started a company that writes medical education programs for the pharmaceutical industry. I don't run it anymore, now I consult for the new president."

"You're a doctor."

"No, I'm not a doctor. But I work with doctors, and they help us know what to write and make sure it's correct."

"You're a doctor."

"O.K. I'm a doctor," I smile and turn myself over to David's authority. I'm no longer a CEO or mother but a student, a beginner. The music whirls its bewildering melody around me, and I try again to hammer out the four beats.

"That's enough. Now go to your hotel and practice."

I have three hours until my next round of disgrace. I comfort myself at a nearby café with spoonfuls of the most delicious gazpacho I've ever had, the color of a terra cotta tile.

How easy it would be to give up. No one would care if I just walked away and spent the rest of the week as a tourist in Seville, going to museums, eating tapas, reading in my canopy bed, playing it safe. Five days of rejuvenation instead of the humiliation of studying an impossible rhythm. But I can't. I'm inexorably hooked, not just to the movements and the beat but to the *duende*—those moments when the dancers and singers and musicians expose what it is to be human. They reach out to the audience with tenderness, but as the Spanish poet Garcia Lorca once said, it's a tenderness behind volcanoes. It caresses and it burns.

More is at stake for me with flamenco than when I founded my company on two credit cards. I know in this dance is the possibility of giving myself over to my bliss. I let the music touch me, claw at me with authentic feeling, truer to me than running a company ever was.

At four o'clock, I begin my private class with Laura.

"We're going to work on how you hold your body," she says. "Beginners do this all wrong."

At least we're starting on a positive note, I think. Laura gives me a set of instructions fit for a contortionist.

"Sit into your butt, lift your chest. Drop your shoulders. You have to carry the emotion in your chest."

I try to follow her instructions, but I arch my back and my shoulders rise.

"No. No. No. Like this." Laura walks behind me

and pushes her hand flat on my upper back between my shoulder blades. "Let your shoulder blades crawl down your back. If you arch, you'll get back problems."

I let my shoulder blades fall like weights.

"Good. That looks good. Now stay like that."

Laura turns on the music, and I stand in my form, a concrete flamenco statue. Posture good, posture bad, back and forth, until I ache, until I'm sure I have done it all wrong.

After class, I ask the office manager to recommend a flamenco show. She gives me a list, and I decide on *Casa de la Memoria*, a museum dedicated to preserving the memory of the long period in Spanish history where Moors, Jews, and Christians lived together, mostly amicably, in Andalucía. It doesn't seem possible that the world will ever again know such peace.

I buy a ticket, then call my family to learn that my kids have spent the afternoon careening over a dry riverbed filled with boulders on the zipline that our neighbor set up for his son's birthday party. Only in Spain, I think, where there aren't as many lawyers.

I'm relieved that my children sound happy, but I still feel guilty. I tell myself that maybe my friend is right when she says, "It's good for your kids to see that you have your own dreams." I want to believe this, but I know the truth is different. My kids want my life to revolve around theirs. They want me home where they can be sure of where to find me, inert on the couch like I'm hatching an egg. They can't help it. Their job is to survive, and to do this best they want me available on demand to provide affection, read a story, witness their greatness.

Isn't this just what I wanted from my own mother? To come home to her soft hugs and a refrigerator stocked with Twinkies and parfaits of chocolate pudding swirled around cubes of strawberry jello? I resented any sign that she had her own life; I hated it when she started working as a reading teacher, and I was forced to come home from sixth grade to an empty house. To convince myself that leaving for five days will be good for my kids is pure rationalization.

Inside *Casa de la Memoria*, I sit in a courtyard draped with ivy. A guitarist and singer come on stage and perform a few songs, then the dancer walks on and begins to clap. She wears a tight white dress with red polka dots and enormous, dangly red and white earrings. She dances a *llamada*, attention-getting footwork that calls to the guitarist and singer and tells them something is about to happen.

I listen hard as the music plays. I think I can hear the rhythm of the *siguiriya* the way my teacher in Granada taught me to count it: one and two and three and a four and a five. Yes, I hear it. I clap softly in my seat, but then the feeling slips away. The dancer rolls her hips back and forth in the outline of a crescent moon. She bends forward and shrugs her shoulders to keep the beat, raw and earthy like a gypsy. I study her style, how she sits into her legs but doesn't stick out her butt, how she keeps the rhythm with her hands as she circles them in the air. The tension she creates is almost unbearable. It builds and then explodes in a thunder of footwork.

The show ends and I feel humbled to have seen the real thing. I head to a restaurant nearby for dinner and eat the tapas that Seville is famous for: fried squid, grilled pork in a spicy sauce, spinach and chickpeas, a shot of gazpacho. I wonder what would have happened to my life had I discovered flamenco much earlier. Who would I be now? Would I turn myself over completely to dancing, forgoing marriage and children? Guilt tugs at me because I can imagine such a life.

The next day in class, Trina says, "I don't remember a thing we learned yesterday." When Antonio arrives, we freeze like schoolgirls, afraid to be chastised by the headmaster for doing it all wrong. He turns on the music, begins the footwork, and as usual, seems deeply inconvenienced by our presence in the studio. He yells at us for stepping too lightly instead of dropping our heels with a clean snap. He's right, we're hopeless.

"Carol," Antonio tells me, "your problem is that your elbow flips back when it should be forward and your left hand is in front of you when it should just stay close to your body."

Emma sometimes laughs out loud as Antonio berates us.

"Just imagine he's a tiny fly standing at your feet," she says, "and if he isn't careful, you'll drop your heel on *him*. That's what I do,"

I try to embrace his scolding as a valuable lesson not only in dance, but also on how to remain centered in the presence of a bully. I want to keep my two flamenco shoes firmly planted on the ground and stay radiant even around Antonio's negativity. Maybe I'm becoming more like a gypsy, able to use the dance to rebel against indignity, to let the movements and music wring out the pain so I can soak up the ecstasy.

In rhythm class, David and I clap the *bulería* again and again until I hear the accents. Then he plays the music and asks me to clap with it. When I do it right, he smiles and his eyes sparkle.

Later, in Laura's class, she grabs my bra between my breasts and pulls it up toward the ceiling. "That's the correct position for your chest. Stay like that and walk to the middle of the room."

I am stiff, not sinuous like the dancer I saw two nights ago. The hour speeds by, and Laura pulls and twists my body, shaping me like a lump of bread dough. "O.K., for now you're doing it right. But tomorrow you'll have it all wrong again."

I vow to practice in my hotel room and prove to her—and to myself—that I can do this.

On Wednesday night, I take Trina and Emma to *Casa de la Memoria*. A man and woman dance together in a romantic duel. "I want you—but my family thinks you're a bastard," she suggests with her body. "When can I see you again?" She lures us into her drama of desire and obligation.

Each day seems to shave five years off my age. By Thursday night, I'm in my late twenties. As I walk to my hotel after a show, a young man asks me out for drinks. Can this be happening? I'm decades older than he. I'm flattered but not tempted. My life this week beats out its own *contratiempo*. I am the definition of the word: literally "against time." I am at once young and old, radiating youthful energy and in middle age, racing to learn the rhythms of flamenco before it's too late—hoping that the dance will age with me, that what a former teacher told me is true: "When you're old you have more *duende*." I remember once watching an old gypsy dancer in Granada. She no longer had the fiery energy and suppleness of the younger performers, but with the slightest gesture of her hand, the languid rise of her arms, and the fragile look in her eyes, she flooded me with the feelings of anguish and hope.

During my last class with Antonio, I picture him as a fly on the floor and try to stomp on him. His words don't sting as much, and just as I'm beginning to actually absorb some useful instruction, the office manager pulls him out of class. His wife is in labor with his first child. Antonio runs out the door like someone caught on fire, and we laugh so hard we can't dance. We replay the past week with the new piece of information that our tormenter is about to become a father. I imagine Antonio coaching his wife through labor, yelling orders at her and telling her she's doing it all wrong.

But Antonio has toughened me up. They all have because they've taken me seriously.

During my last class with David, he sings for me. He holds out his arms and seems to pluck his vocal cords with his breath. He has the *duende* I want, and I feel it surging over me, an expression of grief that makes me feel alive. We continue to work on the mysteries of the rhythm. He tells me I've learned a lot but have a long way to go.

At the end of my final class with Laura, I ask her, "Do you have children?"

"No, I'm not married," she says, turning her eyes away from me. She seems practical about what she's had to sacrifice for her art. But I sense wistfulness, too. "You can't get married and be a dancer. My friend got married and her husband made her quit dancing." I don't tell her that I know of married flamenco dancers, some who are even mothers. In Laura's world, maybe this is her truth.

With the workshops over, I walk back to my hotel. On the way, I drop into a flamenco shoe store. A pair of red leather flamenco heels with thin straps crisscrossing in the front calls to me. I slip them on and try a few steps when the storekeeper isn't looking. Funny how shoes play a part in the feminine fairy tale: ruby red with magic powerful enough to transport a girl back home, glass in a size that allows a prince to find his wife, and shiny red leather that condemns a girl to dance until she finds herself.

I feel most like the girl in the red leather shoes, the one who's told, "Be careful what you wish for." Like her, I want it all—the dancing, my family, my work, to be needed and independent at the same time. I slap down ninety euros.

My family is heading to Seville, and I'm impatient; I stand in front of the hotel until I see them turn the corner. The kids run to me and we hold each other. They yell, "Mommy, mommy, mommy." I never want to let them out of my sight again. My son buries his head in my shirt.

"Mommy, you lost your smell."

"What smell?"

"Your mommy smell. You don't smell like you."

The mommy smell. Maternal pheromones, sweat, and perfume all mixed up in a fragrant stew, overpowered now by five days of dancing and drinking around swirling cigarette smoke. By tomorrow, with my family around me every minute, my mommy smell will return, but for now, I inhale what's left of my independence.

ॐ ॐ ॐ

Carol Reichert is working on her first book, a memoir of her family's travels in Spain. She continues to study flamenco in Boston and Spain and anywhere the flamenco rhythm moves her. And speaking of moving, she plans to pack up her family again in a few years and live in Argentina. But shhhh. She hasn't told them yet.

ᔪᓐ ᔪᓐ ᔪᓐ

In Lardo We Trust

Only in Italy can lunch be considered
an endurance sport.

The first time I tried it was in Umbria, at a tiny trattoria in the medieval town of Gubbio. It came on a crostini with just a trace of honey drizzled on top, and it was close to a religious experience. I closed my eyes and placed it in my mouth as if I were receiving communion. My eyes rolled back in my head and I let out a deep, unladylike groan of pleasure—a sound you might expect to hear during moose mating season. It had a rich buttery quality, salty with hints of sage, clove and rosemary, but subtly sweet too, courtesy of the honey glaze. The crostini gave it balance and texture without intruding on its delicate flavor.

Although I'd never tasted lardo prior to that moment in Gubbio, I'd read about the town of Colonnata and the struggle to defend their right to produce *Lardo di Colonnata*. For centuries the villagers used marble from the nearby quarries of Carrara to cure the lardo, but this method was in danger of being outlawed in the name of cleanliness and hygiene, until the town put up a fight to preserve their lardo heritage. Personally, my rule of thumb is that if the health department doesn't want you to eat something, it must be worth trying.

Lardo is exactly what it sounds like—pure fat. But it's a special fat not easily found in the states. Pork lard aged in salt brine, rubbed with herbs, pressed under slabs of marble, and left to cure for several months, Italian lardo looks like the wiggly white part of bacon and is commonly served raw and sliced paper thin. The flavor is divine, almost mythic, as if it has been cured between the creamy white thighs of fifteen-year-old virgins instead of mere marble. Pure fat heaven.

Lardo di Colonnata is now protected under the *Arca del Gusto di Slow Food*, and all ingredients must be sourced locally for it to be authentic. But residents claim it's actually the mountain air from the quarries that imparts a distinct flavor during aging and prevents their lardo from being replicated elsewhere.

My own relationship with lardo was love at first bite. So when my Italian friend Fabio offered to take me on a pilgrimage to Colonnata, I jumped at the chance. Set high above the coast of Marina di Massa alongside the marble quarries of Carrara, Collonata's main square features several shops selling lardo. We stopped in one store no bigger than a closet that had been making it for a hundred years. The shop had a slow food designation decal and magazine articles posted on the door touting the family for its authenticity and longevity in the business. A refrigerated case displayed hunks of lardo sealed in plastic. Not unlike what you might find in a marijuana buyers club back in California, they were carefully measured packages of pleasure, and not cheap: we bought three small bricks for just over U.S. $150. I tucked them into my backpack and zipped it tight.

After our shopping spree in Colonnata, Fabio, his girl-friend, her dog Lucca, my husband, and I drove a few miles north to Castelpoggio, a tiny berg perched along the ridge next to the Parco Naturale delle Alpi Apuane. We planned to hike a short way and then lunch at one of the rustic mountain huts called *refugios* that offer bare-bones lodging and meals to long-distance hikers.

The *Refugio Carrara* was set between a spread of oak, with a large veranda from which the Gulf of La Spezia could be seen in the distance. Red flags strung between the trees flapped in the breeze, and Lucca darted about sniffing for rabbits and squirrels. We took a seat at a table on the portico. A harried man with intense dark eyes and a blue apron tied snugly around his thick waist appeared with four glasses of Prosecco and toast points with lardo. He quickly recited the menu for midday *pranzo*. We couldn't agree what to order. "*Non importa*," he said. "I will decide for you."

He returned with a carafe each of red and white wine, some frittata, *carciofi fritti* (fried artichokes), a plate of cheeses and—to my delight—more lardo. But that, we would learn, was just the antipasto. We were still eating the frittata when he brought out five more dishes: capel-lini pasta with pesto, *pappardelle con corniglio*—thick flat noodles with rabbit ragout, a bowl of *pollo cacciatore*—a fragrant stew of tender chicken with carrots and onions, a dish of sautéed spinach with garlic, and a plate of grilled peppers glazed with olive oil. The scent of the roasted peppers was intoxicating, almost intimidating. It was as if they were *daring* me to eat them.

Serving dishes covered very inch of the table, and we dug in, a clatter of cutlery our musical accompaniment. As we passed food around the table, overwhelmed by the array of hearty fare, a second platter of salumi and cheese arrived, followed by a plate of grilled tomatoes stuffed with seasoned breadcrumbs and a ramekin of sautéed wild mushrooms.

"Excuse me," I said to the waiter. "Please tell the cook this is wonderful, but we can't possibly eat all this food."

The waiter glared. "*Mi chiamo Carlo. Sono cuoco.*" My name is Carlo. I *am* the cook, he said. "*Mangi!*" And he moved the mushrooms toward me.

This is ridiculous, I thought. I had Italian grandmothers; I knew what it meant when someone said *mangi* in that manner: "Eat! No excuses." His was not an invitation to dine; it was a demand.

But the mushrooms had a deep, woodsy aroma, a creamy, nutty flavor, a texture that was almost meaty. I couldn't slide them away.

In between bites, I covertly pulled a Ziploc bag out of my pack, filled it with the remaining salumi from the cheese platter, and put it back in my sack. Carlo returned then and eyed the empty plates suspiciously. "You have been feeding the dog?" he asked.

"No, we didn't feed the dog."

He disappeared and came back with a bowl of kibble. He set it before Lucca, who took a sniff and walked away.

"*Ah, il cane non ha fame!*" The dog is not hungry! he declared and stomped off.

"Fabio," I said, "maybe you should explain to Carlo that we did not hike fifteen miles to get here. Tell him we drove up. Maybe he thinks we're famished hikers in need of the calories."

In an attempt to solve the problem, I resorted again to my backpack. In one small bag I carried a host of crucial items: Advil, matches, flashlight, hand sanitizer, corkscrew, earplugs, and duct tape. Emergency inflatable life raft containing two weeks of provisions for four adults? Quite possible.

My ability to produce any item at any time had led Fabio to nickname me Eta Beta, after a Disney character from the 1950s still popular in Italy. Eta Beta was a space alien with a magic bag that held everything, no matter the size. Out of my bag I pulled a pair of novelty store gag glasses—black owl-eye Le Corbusier-style frames with huge fake eyes painted in the center of the lenses.

"Why on earth would you have something like this?" asked Fabio.

"I always travel with these. I wear them on the plane when I don't want to be bothered. Trust me, it's effective."

I had put them on when our food taskmaster returned to clear dishes.

"*Mi occhi piu grande da mio stomache*," I said. My eyes are bigger than my stomach.

"*Beh!*" he grunted, unfazed. It was Carlo's primal duty to feed his guests, and he would not be distracted. It was like we were in the midst of some sort of extreme food brinkmanship—a game of chicken. First person to swerve away loses. And our host was in it to win, driving straight at us with more food.

He returned with another bottle of wine and grilled eggplant sautéed with capers and olives. Eggplant! How did he know it was my weakness? I felt like I was caught in a Chinese finger trap, a toy I played with as a kid. You stuck your index fingers into each end of a woven straw tube and when you tried to pull out, the tube would constrict and lock your fingers in place. The harder you pulled the more it tightened. The only way out was to offer no resistance. I decided to reverse my tack: I would submit.

I became one with my fork and ate the entire dish of eggplant by myself. My gaze drifted over to the remaining mushrooms. After I finished them, I polished off the tomatoes and grilled peppers. My tablemates were impressed; I had entered into the altered state of *scorpacciata*. Although Italians don't really have a word for pigging out, *scorpacciata* is close—it's used to describe a sort of seasonal feeding frenzy of foods that are only available or ripe for a short period of time.

Poker-faced, the cook nodded silently as he cleared the plates. I nodded back. Ha! I had looked the eggplant in the eye and refused to blink. Who's playing chicken *cacciatore* now?

But then, out came the desserts—torta, biscotti, fruit, and more cheese followed by a bottle of grappa and espressos all around. My stomach felt like a gas line close to rupturing. *Impossible*, I thought. Although *maybe some grappa would help—it is known for its digestive properties, after all*. Fortified by the grappa, I managed to eat a few biscotti. Slowly and with great focus, I raised the espresso cup to my lips and took a tiny sip. And with that sip, four and a half hours after we first sat down, the meal finally came to an end. Just at that moment, a weary group of hikers showed up.

"Umm...*pranzo?*" Lunch? they asked.

"*Ah si, subito,*" said Carlo.

The hikers spread out around the wooden tables in front of the *refugio* and Carlo returned with two bottles of Prosecco.

"Someone should tell those folks what they're in for," I said.

"This is Italy," said Fabio. "Eating is what hiking is about."

With new guests to stuff, Carlo eased up and reluctantly brought our check. The bill for four and a half hours of Chef's Choice topped 125 euros. Not unreasonable considering the spread, but still unexpected given our remote location. The real problem was that Carlo only accepted cash, and between the four of us we had less than fifty euros.

Then it hit me.

I pulled one of the precious bricks of vacuum-sealed lardo from my bag and placed it on top of the little cash we had.

When Carlo saw the lardo, a smile flickered across his face. Payment accepted. *Lardo di Colonnata*, it turns out, is not just an important part of regional custom, culture, and cuisine; it's also currency—with a very favorable exchange rate.

ॐ ॐ ॐ

Marcy Gordon's travel essays have appeared in several Travelers' Tales anthologies, including The Best Women's Travel Writing 2010, 30 Days in Italy, *and* More Sand in My Bra. *She is a contributing editor for* Authentic Italy, *a guidebook series published by Touring Club of Italy. She writes a blog about wine, food, and travel at www.comeforthewine.com.*

જ્જ જ્જ જ્જ

Ex Marks the Spot

Freedom's just another word for nothing left to lose.

*B*efore I leave, my friends and family offer survival tips.

There's the helpful: "Call me if anything goes wrong."

The suggestive: "Don't drink—with him."

The nostalgic: "Try to remember why you liked him."

The bitter: "Try to remember why you broke up with him."

And the righteous: "Who you travel with will influence the trip more than where you go."

I have my retorts. It's a matter of convenience, a gesture of goodwill. Adam and I are no longer a couple, but we still have mutual friends, and we've both accepted teaching positions in Slovakia. We'll attend a wedding in Ireland, then backpack through Spain and France before reporting to our new jobs. The trip will forge our friendship.

It won't be that bad, I reassure myself. *The worst thing that can happen to the relationship already has; I have nothing to lose, no one to impress. Who cares if we stop trying to make small talk, if I smell or if we set off in the wrong direction? Who cares, really, if it's any fun at all? Won't it be wonderful when it's over, when we've forgotten all about it?*

In that case, why are we even taking this trip? There is no good reason. I don't need any more scenic photographs of us together—I was the one who split us apart, after all. Yet my mother adores Adam. The ponytailed tennis player I'm pursuing doesn't. And I can't confess my own doubts to either of them.

The streets in the Irish village of Ballinakill remind me of the French Quarter after Katrina: bright walls, dark windows, empty. No one looks back at me when I look through the glass. No one sees me snooping.

Weddings here last three days, like Easter. Adam and I will join Noel and Marissa at the party tonight. Today, Saturday, I'm determined to leave him behind as I walk to a pond outside the village.

I would like to escape. I would like to be able to take a picture of something without him there beside me, angling for the better shot. I want my golden memories of monastery ruins and cows behind fences and puddles in lanes for me and me alone. When I say I'm going to take a walk, Adam says kindly, "What a great idea. I think I'll take one, too." At the front door, he turns left and I turn right.

We meet each other a mile outside of town. I'm sitting on a rock, writing, and around the curve of the path he appears. Behind us are trees, beneath our feet are leaves, and beyond, the pristine pond. A ring of tangled water lilies floats in it, a great green and white crown with a blue hole in the middle. The plant moat protects the small circle of reflected sky.

"I just want to be left alone," I say, eyes on my journal.

"I'm not bothering you."

I stand. He sits.

"Here's an idea," I say. "Let's split up when we get to Spain. We're both smart. We'll be happier left alone. Why don't we just meet up back in Slovakia in a few weeks?"

"Aubrey, that is ridiculous. For one, it's unsafe."

As he reminds me why I couldn't have made it here without him—I flew in without knowing Marissa's phone number or Noel's last name—I try to walk away. He throws my journal uphill after me. All the scraps of paper I hold dear flutter in the air before settling on branches and grass like the feathers of a shot bird.

Adam jumps to free the poem the tennis player had written for me from its perch in the tree.

"Can't we just get along?" he asks.

At "the afters" of the wedding, following the Mass and the four-course meal with three kinds of potatoes (roasted, scalloped, mashed), there are more drinks, a live band, and sandwiches at midnight. Older women wear neon ruffled dresses and pluckings of whole birds on their hats, and everyone stands in a circle while the bride and groom dance to a techno mix of Trisha Yearwood's "How Do I Live" and kiss. Unabashed passion with tongues.

So we drink, and take breaks to dance. Not with each other. I meet Peter, who swings me around and takes me out on the balcony. We talk about soccer; like me, he doesn't know anything about tennis.

"Is that lad there your boyfriend?"

"Who?"

"That guy you came in with."

"No, no, he's not my boyfriend." I actually haven't seen Adam in a while, and as I turn and squint at the distorted bodies and skirts and tuxedo jackets, I can't pick him out. I realize I'm watching for his signature dance move, The Puppeteer: one hand lifts his hip with an invisible string, then the other snips the string so the hip swings back into rhythm.

I feel a jolt at my own hip, Peter's hand.

"So can I kiss you then?" he asks.

I'm turning my cheek to him when I see a flush of people moving toward the exit. Although I can't see Adam, somehow I sense his involvement in the commotion. "Be right back," I say.

He had pushed on a glass-paneled door that said, "PULL." The door shattered.

Days later, as we fly to Barcelona, he's nursing cuts on his left arm with gashes along his lower palm, close to the prominent blue blood vessels. He has a puncture wound in his hip. His wrist is bandaged like an outpatient's, and his clothes are wrinkled. We soaked them in cold water, but there wasn't enough time to let them dry under the cloudy Irish sky.

Spain, beneath us at sunset, looks washed with warmth. And it is. We feel it up close, though we keep a careful distance between us. We tour museums, take day trips, walk unfamiliar streets. At first I am mindful of old pains, cautious in conversation, but it doesn't take long for the distant tennis player to dissolve in my memory. It's just us here now.

Every night we sit on the beach, heat seeping into us through the sand. We find things to say. As we recover and rehydrate after Ireland, the past crusts and heals into a scar. We squint at the sky and try to make out stars through the smog while the couples around us noisily lock lips and limbs. We don't say we were once like them, or could be again.

One night the wind comes up, and we don't make it back to our covered balcony in time. It starts to rain. We run for shelter, huddling in the dark underneath the ledge of a building on Barceloneta. Adam removes his passport from his pocket and hands it to me.

"It's getting wet. Put it in your purse," he says, and we make a covert transaction under the cover of my jacket.

"Let's go back home," he says.

A few nights later, Adam and I and our two backpacks sit on a bench in a park by the zoo, watching for night to come, and our train to Paris. I unfold a poem I wrote on the back of a receipt so I can copy it into my journal. When I'm finished, I zip the receipt back into my purse and set it on top of my pack.

The poem and its singular intended reader are still on my mind when a haggard man walking with a bicycle approaches Adam's side of the bench. I stifle a yawn. When I tune back in, the man is crouching, pointing at the ground. He draws two lines in the dirt. Adam and I both glance down, but there's nothing there. The man and his bike are soon gone, and Adam leaves to join the line for the bathroom. I decide to get back to my poem.

By the fountain is a pigeon with one leg. Sensing a symbol, I reach for my camera. It's not there. I rustle,

then rifle, through my bag. Where did Adam put it?
He stands nonchalant. When he glances over, I squint
one eye and position my fingers like pincers, snapping
a photo. My bag, he mouths. I find his camera and take
the picture. Adam still stands. Time to start a new story,
I think.

When I reach for my purse, it's not on top of my pack
where I left it. My eyes flit back and forth, replaying the
events. I had looked in one direction, at the man digging
in the dirt. I had not watched the other half of the scene,
where my bag sat.

Adam is next in line. I jump up, raise my eyebrows,
gesture wildly. He shrugs and hurries into the bathroom.

Besides our passports, in my purse were cash, credit
and debit cards, my driver's license, my digital camera,
and a vintage bead necklace. After filing a police report
and canceling our train reservations, we're back on the
street—we'd checked out of our hotel that afternoon.
The concrete we sit on is cold.

"Did you see the bike that guy had?" Adam asks. "It
was a Trek."

"No, just his missing teeth. He looked like a starving
writer in a Knut Hamsun novel—you know, you feel
sorry for him, and then he strikes."

"What was he drawing in the dirt, anyway?"

"An X," I say.

We both laugh.

"I don't think I want to spend tonight on the street.
But maybe I should have mentioned that earlier."

"I figured you'd say that," he replies, without a trace
of impatience.

It's one A.M., and there's one hotel room left in the city.
The cost of a room is about what we expect to earn for a
month of teaching in Slovakia.

"I assure you, this is the only room you will find," says the mustached man at the desk. We must look skeptical. "And it has a wonderful view."

The room also has NBC Nightly News in English, a heated towel rack, and a tiled terrace. We drink cheap wine and have a last look at Barcelona. Up here, liberated from the unceasing forward flow of the streets, I relax.

I'm weary and delirious, without any form of identification between the familiar and foreign. But for the first time, I see the spot we're in.

And I see the beach in the distance where Adam and I sat back to back for the last three nights, gossiping about people on the other side of the planet, looking a long way down the sand in different directions. The tide coming in and going out, like the silences and bad jokes, steady and separate, soothing without end.

I feel free, disarmed, as if it's my emotional baggage that has been stolen.

Tomorrow, we'll take a train to Paris and spend the night outside the station. Adam will drink wine and smoke with an illegal Hungarian immigrant; I will doze off with my legs intertwined in the straps of my backpack, then wake again with a start and try to kick it off.

By the time we get to Slovakia, we will again have been hungry, smelly, irritable, and bitter. We will be carrying new passports when we cross the border, and we'll both be wearing our only jackets, ivory-colored with the same dirt. We will turn and go our own ways. We will meet again. After a number of years we will marry.

Tonight, though, we're too tired to see our future waiting for us in the dark, back over the ocean. There is only one bed in our room. I get under the covers. Adam lies down on top of them. I roll to face the wall. He flips to face the door.

I whisper to the wall, "Adam."

Nothing.

"Adam, can you please . . ."

He exhales.

"No," he says. "I will not check. I'm sure I set the alarm. Goodnight."

I fall asleep to the sound of his breathing, in and out, sure as the tide.

ぷ〜 ぷ〜 ぷ〜

After teaching in Slovakia, Aubrey Streit Krug came home to study and write about the Great Plains. Her creative work has appeared in the Land Report, Identity Theory, Visual Communication Quarterly, *the* Tipton Times, *and* Precipitate. *She now lives and bicycles in Lincoln, Nebraska, with her husband, Adam. The two decided to marry while on a return trip to the Low Tatras in Slovakia.*

LAURA FLYNN

♫⟩ ♫⟩ ♫⟩

Carrefour

A writer's first visit to Haiti
leaves an indelible mark.

The first time I went to Haiti was with the nuns. I was twenty-five years old, green and scared and driven, and younger in some ways than anyone has a right to be. It was February 1992—five months after Haiti's first democratically elected government was overthrown by the military. The president, Jean-Bertrand Aristide, was in exile; anyone who supported him was a target for violence. Since the poor had elected him, and since nearly everyone in Haiti is poor, the whole population was frozen in terror.

My memory of that first arrival is blurred now by the imprint of dozens of subsequent landings, one imposed upon the other like so many passport stamps. But surely as we flew over the island from the north I was struck by the green rib of mountains, which appear so suddenly,

so unexpectedly after miles of dazzling Caribbean blue,
ninety minutes into the flight from Miami. And then
the first outposts of the city: bright green hillsides giving
way to shantytowns, or popular neighborhoods as they
are known in Haiti, fingering their way up through the
ravines, stretching the limits of the city, which is suddenly in full view, a sea of concrete and rebar, brilliant
in the sunshine. A flash of white from the Palace, the
faded pink wedding cake of the Cathedral, the lavatory
blues and greens of the cemetery, and just before landing a long low view of Cite Soleil: ramshackle houses of
cinderblock, mud, cardboard and corrugated tin, heaped
together, brown and dusty from the air. At the last possible moment, the single runway, dust and goats right up
until the wheels touch down.

Our little delegation—a Methodist minister from Los
Angeles, four Catholic nuns from the Midwest, and me,
of no particular faith, representing a secular solidarity
organization from California—had come to listen to
stories, to collect testimony and information about what
was happening here as a result of this coup, a coup which
we, along with all our contacts in Haiti, believed had its
roots in Washington. The six of us had met for the first
time the night before at a guesthouse of the Catholic
diocese in Miami. Several weeks earlier an OAS fact-
finding mission had been greeted at the same airport by
paramilitaries wielding guns sent by the generals running the country. We hoped to slip in and out of Haiti
unnoticed, and had agreed the night before to pass ourselves off vaguely as missionaries, nuns and a minister,
which of course we were, except for me.

As the plane landed, the tension in my body rose.
Perhaps to distract myself from the real terror below,
I fastened my anxiety on my attire. The contents of

my suitcase–tank-tops, knee-length skirts, flat but stylish sandals—had all seemed restrained in California, but the sisters wore a near uniform of modest blouses, calf-length skirts, muted colors, unrelentingly sensible sandals. Would I pass?

The humidity hit like a blow as I stepped out the cabin door: a moment's pause to blink in the sun at the top of the stairway, and then the descent to meet the upswell of heat from the tarmac below, which felt soft underfoot. There were soldiers everywhere in oversized uniforms, pants tucked into black lace-up boots—skinny men who looked more sleepy than fearsome, dangling automatic weapons under their arms.

At immigration I exchanged a tense look with the soldier who stamped my passport. Did I make a plausible nun, as I'd written under "profession" on my immigration form? He paused only a moment before stamping my passport, and releasing me into the chaos of the baggage room, where I waded through redcaps, ten to a passenger, each trying to cut a private deal to carry bags. Once the single carousel began to move, our bags were easy enough to locate, large duffels loaded with medical supplies and batteries to give to people we would meet, but still the smallest luggage on the carousel. Haitian suitcases leave the country sagging and empty and come back straining at the seams, roughly the size of houses in Cite Soleil.

Claudette, our host in Haiti, had instructed us ahead of time to keep hold of our bags—not out of fear they would be stolen, but to avoid having to pay a relay of porters who would pass them hand-to-hand, carousel to customs, then out the door and to the car, with perhaps a few extra hands to lift them into the trunk. I lost this struggle—I would always lose this struggle—and had to pay. But somehow the van from the hospice was waiting in the parking lot. We loaded ourselves into it, paid everyone who had to be paid, rolled the windows up over all the remaining hands and voices, and got on the road.

The days were filled with meetings. A priest in hiding who came to see us at the hospice laughed when we asked if he was afraid for his life: "In Port-au-Prince today," he said, "we all carry our coffin under our arm." Peasant leaders slipped in from the countryside to tell us of the carnage they were witnessing, whole towns burned to the ground, murders, arrests and beatings, on mere suspicion of sympathy with Lavalas, the movement that had elected Aristide. We traveled north to Cap Haitian, the second-largest city, and met with students at the University. The repression aimed at young people was so intense, they said, "It is a crime to be young in Haiti today." While we were there a two-minute demonstration erupted as people left the Cathedral after Sunday Mass. The crowd briefly unfurled signs and erupted in cries of *Viv Titid* (long-live Aristide), then fled and waited for the crackdown. It was the first public protest the city had seen since the coup four months earlier.

But it was the visit to Carrefour, the southernmost neighborhood of Port-au-Prince, through driving rain on the second day of our trip, that marked me most and marks me still. I'd heard enough by then to bring me near nausea each time I saw the mustard-brown of an army barracks. There was one where we turned off the coastal highway and drove up into the mountains, into the avalanche of houses that is Carrefour.

Off the main road our oversized Toyota 4Runner was hopelessly conspicuous on the winding dirt roads. When we parked and got out, the people in the streets seemed shocked. They struggled to look away, as if even looking at us might invite trouble. Claudette took us to the home of an old man and his son who'd been beaten and arrested after the coup. I say old because he appeared so to me—weathered skin, tall, thin, well-muscled, with a long sculpted face and a scraggy beard—but likely he was only forty, or fifty. He spoke in a hushed voice, but with an authority that made us strain to catch each word. The son, who was perhaps twenty, possessed a younger version of that sculpted face, but none of his father's calm.

In the dim light of their one-room house—it was late afternoon and clouds were gathering—Sister Grace and I, the two *blan* (whites or foreigners, synonymous in Haiti), sat on wooden chairs set out for us on the packed earth floor and listened to their story. The son did most of the talking, his body jumping and twitching, the light from the open door animating the planes of his face.

He spoke Creole, but I caught a few stray words from my four years of high school French: *militè, militan, Aristid*. The old man fixed his eyes on me and then on Sister Grace, gauging our reaction. Claudette translated, but I had a hard time following. Somehow the tenses and time sequences were confused, everything looping around into a present in which all events seemed to happen again and again and at the same time.

On the night of the coup and every night since, the soldiers drove up from their base to patrol the neighborhood, to shoot randomly into the houses from the backs of their trucks. The old man and his son were arrested. Were beaten. Were released. Were arrested again. The soldiers returned. They fired bullets into the houses. On that night and every night.

We asked the questions one asks on human rights delegations—or in my case the questions I imagined one asks. I was bluffing my way through, having never done this before. I focused a great deal on dates, charges, the specifics of abuse—none of which I remember now.

What I do remember is that at the end the old man stood in the doorway, silhouetted by what was left of the afternoon light. He waved his hands as if to indicate we were missing the whole point. "The soldiers come at night to stop the people from putting up posters of the old President on the wall." He paused and then said, "We will continue to do it anyway."

I was wearing a wooden cross the size of my palm around my neck. The sisters had given it to me in Miami. The cross was so ridiculously large that when my hand floated up to touch it as it did at moments like this, my gesture was as outsized as the terror and courage of the people I met.

As we left, the old man reached out and touched my arm. I've been told my face does not hide much, and surely fear had registered there. "God is on our side," he said, as if to reassure me. "*N'ap reisi.*" We will succeed. Or perhaps more literally: we will overcome.

We traveled farther up the mountain, winding our way through ravines and gulleys. The sky opened up and a warm, fierce rain fell. The windows fogged, the road before us turned to dirt, then mud, then disappeared, but the driver kept on, calm, unperturbed by the slick ground or the wipers beating at the windshield. Eventually we stopped and the driver got out. I wiped my window with my sleeve and saw a ravine dropping steeply to the right of us with a tiny house clinging to its side. Our driver was offering his arm to a woman scrambling up over the rim of the ravine to meet us. She reached for his arm, clutching at roots as the mud gave way under her feet.

She climbed into the back seat next to me—her feet in flip-flops, caked with mud to the knees. As she got in I could see that the water on the road was running several inches deep.

She spoke quickly as she told her story, elbows to knees, looking straight ahead, while Claudette translated.

She had lived down below, in an area of Carrefour just off the main road near the military base. On the night of the coup she was home with her five children. When the shooting began, she put the children under the bed, where they huddled for hours listening to the trucks traveling back and forth on the Carrefour road. Then a few jeeps drove up to her neighborhood, and she heard the soldiers going house to house. The older children were all quiet, but the baby would not stop crying. A soldier threw the door open and without even looking for them shot a few rounds into the house. When he left, everything was silent; the baby wasn't crying anymore.

Later, much later, she took the dead infant in her arms and walked down the hill to the main road toward the city. She saw bodies in the street and people streaming past her in the other direction, some wounded, some hysterical. They pushed at her and told her to go back, told her that many people would perish in the city that night. But she didn't listen to them. She had to take the baby to the morgue in the city.

Then her sister's brother was before her, talking loudly and shaking her. When finally she came to, she heard him say she couldn't go into the city, it was a coup d'etat, the soldiers were everywhere, they were shooting people, and then trucks came and took the bodies away. She let him turn her around and lead her back to the house where the children were waiting.

Together they wrapped the baby and buried her in the yard. Her brother-in-law had to go back to his own family but he told her to take her children into the hills, where the soldiers' trucks couldn't go. She took what little food she had in the house, gathered up the remaining children, and turned toward the mountain. She got only as far as this abandoned hut in the ravine below us, because her feet were swollen and she couldn't walk. And the milk was still coming. Here Claudette lifted a hand to ask a question and turned to us to clarify: the baby was six days old. She couldn't walk any farther because she'd just given birth.

When the woman stopped speaking there was just the rain. It was dark out now, and there was no world beyond this car. Sister Grace, better trained for moments like this, reached across to pat the woman's knee and thanked her. "We will tell your story back home," she said. I wrote down everything I'd heard in my notebook, but said nothing. I worried, as I worried with every person we met, that they risked their lives for nothing. That we raised expectations we could not possibly meet. That even though we didn't look like much, she might think we were—something, an advance team of the United Nations, some harbinger of justice, with a big organization behind us. Claudette spoke quietly to the woman for a few moments and discretely gave her some money, then the woman slipped away as quickly as she'd come, out the back door of the car and over the edge of the ravine.

On the long ride back to the hospice I leaned my head against the cool window. At the main highway, which was just a few feet above sea level, water rose to the bottom of the doors of the 4Runner, but it did not come in. Music played quietly on the radio, and none of us spoke. My mind looped around, trying to find an adequate vow to rest upon: to tell her story, to make it worth her while, to not rest until...

It's nearly twenty years since that first trip to Haiti. I don't know if the old man and his son or the woman who lost her child are still living. The earthquake that devastated Haiti on January 12, 2010 was centered ten miles south of Port-au-Prince. Carrefour was the hardest hit area of the city—no two-story buildings survived, and the death toll, like the death toll from the 1991 coup d'etat, will never be fully known. In 2010, this worst of all years of Haitian history, I am still searching for an adequate vow. I come to this: repeat the story, don't measure *worth*, set down the words that will not rest.

All along the route that night smaller cars were stalled and blocking traffic. A man in front of us was driving with his head out the window because he had no wipers. In the city the streets had all become rivers. People moved quickly, ducking in and out of *tap-taps*, dashing for cover with bags held over their heads. Plastic juice bottles gathered and bobbed in the gutters. But the rain seemed to cut through the terror.

Claudette turned in her seat to say, "The soldiers will not go out tonight."

In the darkness, people moved through the mountains, the old man and his son tacked posters to the wall, the hut clung to the side of the ravine, and water carried refuse through the city to the sea.

◈ ◈ ◈

Laura Flynn is the author of Swallow the Ocean. *She lived in Haiti from 1994 to 2000 and remains deeply involved in the struggle for Haitian democracy and human dignity, and in the recovery from the 2010 earthquake. She is the editor of* Eyes of the Heart: Seeking a Path for the Poor in the Age of Globalization *by Jean-Bertrand Aristide. She teaches creative writing in Minneapolis where she lives with her husband, son, and daughter.*

EVA TUSCHMAN

* JS, JS, JS,*

Without Knowing I Had Ever Been Lost

A dancer is moved by the magic
of a temporary tribe.

I wait for the number 60 bus, the Egged line heading south. In the Be'er Sheva Station, young women
with bleach-blond hair and miniskirts strut the walkway
in plastic stilettos, past the shawarma stands and the
vendors selling neon-colored toy guns and fake tattoos.

The "line" for the bus is now a collection of mulling
teenagers in army uniforms carrying overstuffed backpacks and M-16s slung across their shoulders. As the bus
pulls up, the crowd surges toward the open door. The
seats quickly fill and it doesn't seem to matter that there
are no more spaces: a group of young Ethiopian girls
settles in, cross-legged, in the aisle. I sit next to an older

woman wearing a leopard-print blouse who proceeds to
talk nervously in Russian. I somehow understand that,
like me, she doesn't know where and when to get off
the bus. In broken Hebrew I tell her that I don't speak
Russian. She doesn't speak Hebrew.

We ride through the open desert as the driver, who
navigates this surreal route everyday, speeds around
every bend on the empty road. Little schoolboys with
shaved heads and long twisting side-curls get on the bus,
and two Filipina women with a crying baby and plastic
bags full of Coke bottles and bananas get off. Although
there is nothing but vast desert all around, everyone
seems to know their destination through this landscape
of invisible pathways. A soldier stands in front of me,
the barrel of his gun pointing an inch above my open-
toed shoe. I slowly pull myself upright, slipping my foot
under the seat.

The bus suddenly brakes to a halt and the driver
announces over the intercom, "Hangar Adama." As
quickly as it stops, the bus skids off again—a caravan
of immigrants and refugees tumbling through the open
sandscape—and there I stand in a cloud of dust. I have
seen this scene in movies before—the foreigner with the
little suitcase left on the side of the road. The desert cannot help but amplify the absurd.

I've come to this failed industrial town in the Negev
on the recommendation of a Fulbright fellow who's
researching contemporary dance in Tel Aviv. She gave
me the phone number of her friend who's directing a
dance company in an abandoned hangar. When I spoke
to Lior on the phone, he ended the conversation by saying, "Most Israelis create problems. We create dance." If
he was smiling on the other end of the line, I couldn't
detect it.

From where I stand, there are no signs of life—the warehouses are vacant, and even the few bare trees seem to wish for their own death. Spotting a curtain flowing out of a doorway, I walk toward it, pulled closer by the steady drumbeat of what sounds like a funeral dirge.

Exactly one week ago I approached another doorway much like this one in a residential quarter of Jerusalem, but it led up a flight of stairs to an Orthodox synagogue. There was dancing there, too, though I didn't actually see it. I could hear the flamenco-like stomping and clapping of the men on the other side of the white partitions. The women, wearing headscarves, sat in folding chairs with their strollers and children, as though they were waiting in the silence of a hospital lobby.

As I part the curtain to enter, a young woman with a wild mane of wavy auburn hair and a white linen tunic runs past me and up onto a stage at the end of the long hall. She embraces another young woman in an urgent gesture of grief, and both begin to mourn what appears to be a corpse played by a fidgeting little boy. A troupe of bohemian musicians and actors are strewn about on couches, resting on each other's bodies, stretching and rehearsing songs. No one takes note of my presence.

When Lior finally appears, he gives me a tour of the hangar. His professionalism starkly contrasts with the dingy dance studios and mangy yard where there are more couches, rugs, a petting zoo with chickens and rabbits, and a native herb garden. He proudly explains that everything has not only been envisioned by his dancers but also constructed by them. My "teepee," where I am to sleep, is like a life-sized cardboard diorama, the kind I made in middle school, complete with pink stucco, exposed two-by-fours, and lopsided mobiles of yarn, twigs, and pinecones.

Like all Jews who wander the desert, we eat tofu and curried mung beans and drink chai from glass jars under a canopy of palm fronds and stars. I fall asleep that night to the fading rehearsal of the elegy and awaken the next morning to the same chorus and beating of the drum. In the first class, a young woman named Orit leads us in sensory-awareness exercises. As we roll around the carpet, we are told to imagine floating on a cloud, peacefully balancing in mid-air. Suddenly, there's a loud sound overhead: an airplane's engine followed by echoing booms. No one seems to notice as, eyes closed, they continue to roll on their clouds listening to Orit's melodic voice.

Earlier this week I was lying on a beach chair in North Tel Aviv watching old ladies inch carefully into the Mediterranean. I wondered how many of them were survivors and how many miles from this glorious sprawl of sunbathing teens gunfire and suffering—the stuff of common news—occurred in real time. Across the pure blue sky, a jet swerved to a landing pad nearby. Teenage boys continued to play paddleball in the sand while their sunbathing girlfriends shut their eyes against the sun.

In the hangar, I open my eyes to see Orit standing above me. "I'm sorry," I say. "I don't understand what to do."

"You should really learn Hebrew," she responds in English. "It is, after all, *our* language."

I am still getting used to the idea that I am part of the "our" to which she refers. Since arriving in Israel, I have found myself staring at strangers in shopping malls and cafes, wondering what an Iraqi-Polish waiter has in common with a Moroccan grocery clerk or a Bulgarian taxi driver. Judaism has suddenly become a perplexing term as its representatives pass before me in every possible color and from every culture the world over. How, after thousands of years, did they all end up reunited together in this strange desert? I'm not even ready to begin considering how I fit into this enthralling mosaic.

That night the dancers congregate and follow Lior's lead in several cooperative exercises. At a certain point there is a linguistic cue—which I miss—that the directives are over, and people begin to move freely to the sinuous sounds of an oud. Everyone dances alone, yet there's a synergy across the floor as each person enters into a private flow of expression: a pale redheaded girl spins in circles while an olive-skinned man with a raven ponytail swivels his hips and sways from side to side. I suddenly feel, amid the whirl of movement, like I am an animal who has come upon its herd without knowing I had ever been lost. All night I pretend to dance, but really I am watching them dance, studying their faces, believing they have been living secret magical lives all these years without me.

The last note of the oud disappears, and with it the dancers retreat into the night. Before tucking into my tee-pee, I drink tea with a soldier on short-term leave from his base. In his thick Russian accent he tells me, "If you learn one thing about Israel, remember this: we are an army with a country. Not a country with an army."

Next year many of Lior's dancers will practice different routines, but their costumes will be near identical: green or tan fatigues and felt berets with plastic pendants pinned on. They will learn to stand upright in straight lines, to memorize patterns of running and ducking through desert terrain, and they will be trained to aim and shoot a combat rifle. All culture is ultimately a matter of choreography. For now, though, they continue to twirl on trapezes, sew their own tunics, and lounge tranquilly late into the night playing Bedouin drums and smoking cigarettes under the stars.

      ॐ ॐ ॐ

Eva Tuschman was born in the San Francisco Bay Area and is an alumna of Stanford University, where she earned a degree in Cultural and Social Anthropology. As a freelance writer, she has produced texts for several ethnographic projects, and her publications have appeared in New York Jewish Week's Text/Context *and the anthology* What We Brought Back: Jewish Life After Birthright. *She was also a main contributor to the* Tassajara Dinners and Desserts *cookbook, after having cooked for several years at the Zen Buddhist monastery and retreat center in Big Sur, California. Eva continues to explore the world through culinary endeavors from her kitchen in the Bay Area where she is currently completing a Master's degree in Clinical Psychology.*

JACQUELINE LUCKETT

❧ ❧ ❧

Traveling with Ghosts

A mother follows in her son's footsteps,
searching for the way back to him.

_T_he ghost of my son—my boy now man—appeared
as my airplane descended into the twilight surrounding Siem Reap. His profile etched the rays of the falling
sun. He was not dead, physically. He was not dead spiritually, either. Just gone. From me. He'd traveled to the
Kingdom of Cambodia six months before me, alone. A
celebration of his early college graduation, a celebration of
independence. I, too, was traveling alone—no celebrations
of independence or otherwise. Merely another trip to quell
my restlessness, to be someplace other than where I was.

I'm told my son sent long emails to many—adults
and peers—detailing his travels, but I wasn't included
on that list. Spite, a desire to punish, or a young man's
penchant for privacy, the reasons didn't matter. The lack
of connection did. From my seat, I watched his spirit

grow stronger as the plane neared the ground, and I
understood the message—I would find the link to him
in this foreign land.

The airport resembled a holy place—arched roofs,
edges dabbed with gold—a sacred gateway to another
world. The air was clean, the humidity palpable. Insects
droned their welcome. A young Khmer woman stood
beneath a pointed arch and requested, with a courteous
bow, boarding passes, passports, and shiny, holographic
visas. I sensed my son there in the din of the crowd and
goose bumps danced on my arms.

At all of three years old, my son headed confidently
toward the gate on his first flight. With the authority of
an adult, he held his own boarding pass and approached
the purser. I'm positive that he walked through this
gateway with the same assuredness. Like many twenty-
somethings, he seemed more mature than young adults
were in the sixties—my generation. Some of us were
bold; many of us helped change the world—free love,
free speech, free Huey. My son's generation appears to
have a handle on where they want to go and how to
handle themselves once they get there. They are aware
and sophisticated. I took my first plane ride at the age
of twenty-two. My son took his first at the age of three
and, even by 1988 standards, he was old. Here in Siem
Reap, he'd continued his four-month trek around the
world, gifted with the freedom of adventure at such a
young age.

When had he become that mature, that worldly? I
like to think of my son as spontaneous and whimsical in
planning the steps of his journey. I like to think of that
carefree look on his face, the same one he wore when he
was nine and told me, without a thought to the barriers

that could stop him, that it was time for him to practice his driving.

My skin evokes Africa, Mississippi Choctaws, and a drop of Europe from way back when. My brown hair is streaked with blonde highlights, and I like to think of my 5-foot-6½-inch frame as tall. All in all, characteristics of a foreigner in Cambodia. Too tall. Too brown. A stranger in a strange land. Not one person looked like me, not one word could I understand without an English translation. How must my son have felt as he stood here? Black man. Young. Alone. Tall, handsome, backpack and duffle bag, name brand jeans hanging off his narrow hips—an easy American target. The assumption of wealth. But I was full of pride for his ability to navigate, to get from point A to B—he seemed more a grownup at twenty-one than I, at well past fifty.

My trip was comfortable, preplanned. A travel agent arranged my itinerary and the services of a guide. What had my son thought of this place, or the fact that the cost of his vacation could have fed many Khmer families for months? What would he think if he knew the cost of mine could feed them for years? At the sight of Sokha and my name on his printed sign, tension dropped from my shoulders. I released my anxiety and my need to multitask, to be in charge and on guard. Sokha's English was good, and he was as caring as someone could be to a stranger.

On the way to the hotel, my mental camera snapped picture after picture: a wide and bustling boulevard, left-side driving, two and three people, young and old, lined on mopeds like nuts on an Almond Joy, no helmets, fearless faces; cement stalks of buildings going up and coming down; open-air restaurants and picnic tables clustered under single light bulbs; a massage palace parking lot crowded with tour buses; vendors selling spiky orange and green fruits the size of bowling balls. Men huddled in the well-lit doorways of souvenir shops. Like a view lit by a strobe light, a staccato of mini-stories flashed in the headlights' white glow.

Lotus blossoms decorated tables, niches, desks, and pillowcases at the Hotel de la Paix, their leaves folded back like sleeves on a hot day, revealing luscious pink centers. The building was American and European in texture and style, with straight and modern lines, sleek slate floors, a well-lit pool, and an attentive and accommodating staff. The breeze of air conditioners followed me everywhere. Where did he stay, that son of mine, so accustomed to the comforts his father and I once provided? Was his bed soft? Was there a discreet can of spray beside it to protect him from mosquitoes? Did his door lock not once but twice, its edge flush with the floor, keeping out hallway light and hot-weather critters?

For all its acres of treasured temples, Siem Reap felt small. Spirits surrounded me: the ghosts of civil war, news flashes of death, skulls piled high in the killing fields—all hovered in the haze. The boulevard outside my hotel teemed with sad-faced redheaded street boys, cars, and *tuk-tuks*—a hybrid of tricycle, open carriage and moped named for the sound of their tiny engines scuttling through the streets. Dust flew; exhaust fumes tainted the air. Moped drivers and passengers stared at me from behind surgical masks.

Camera in hand, determined to capture the beauty of Siem Reap, I headed in the direction of the Old Market. I searched for the logic of the streets, neither perpendicular nor parallel to one another; they seemed to feather out at various intersections and this provoked in me a new feeling—a hesitancy to explore. I was nothing like my son, so eager to drive at the age of nine, so sure of his ability to navigate empty streets and parking lots.

Feeling lost and conspicuous, I came across a troupe of four boys who looked to be around eleven years old; the tallest one asked for money in perfect English. I tried to ignore him, tossing a few French phrases his way. He repeated his solicitation in French.

"You speak French?" I asked.

He shrugged, "Español, Deutsch—"

"—Stop, stop!" I laughed, handing him my pocket change. "You win, now tell me how to get to the market."

The Old Market had multiple personalities: cheerful outside, dark and moody inside, bustling in both places. The exterior shops teemed with a combination of practical and tourist paraphernalia: Buddha heads, silk pillow covers, flip flops, laundry detergent, brooms fanned wide like palms, plastic buckets in rainbow colors. Inside, the market was dim and full of unexpected turns—a city within a city. Vendors huddled inside six-foot wide cubbies stacked with floor-to-ceiling goods in perfect symmetry of color and size: blue scarves, orange shawls, pink skirts, embroidered handbags. Deep in the center of the market, I saw squiggling eels, battling crabs, skinned chickens and pigs. Fish flopped wildly in raffia baskets, some managing to make their way to the slick floor.

I asked each vendor permission, pointing in a sign language of my own invention to my eyes, my camera, and them. *Can I take your picture?* More often than not laughter accompanied assent. I wished I understood.

Of course, take the picture, you idiot, this is nothing but my work. The men and women smirked behind hands cupped across their mouths. If I ever saw my son's pictures, would I find he'd captured these people, too? I snapped in the same way I had those summers when my son ate wedges of watermelon in our backyard and spit the seeds on the lawn. *Why are you taking pictures, mom? I'm just eating watermelon.* Snap.

Later that day, our van crept past small houses on the way to the Siem Reap River, where villages of families lived their entire lives on the water's edge. The road to the river wound through a neighborhood of wooden houses on stilts—fortification against floods. Looking at the dry bed of the river behind the structures, though, the tide seemed not out but permanently gone—no water, just sludge—but this was winter, the rainy season over.

The villagers seemed lifted from 1960s TV—Dan Rather reporting war up close and personal. Those images blended Southeast Asia into a stereotyped blur of squatting people. Now bare-chested men, women in long traditional wrapped skirts, children young enough not to be embarrassed by their bare bottoms—all squatted in darkened doorways, in the dirt yards among the chickens, hats and hands their only protection from the sun.

Off to the side of many homes, ornate, miniature houses sat atop thick posts painted vibrant pinks, reds, and golds. The "spirit houses" were detailed with windows and doors, more elaborate than the homes they guarded. Spirals of thin smoke wafted from incense sticks, bright fruits honored the spirits; this was where good spirits lived and protected against mischievous and disruptive ones. Could I take one home, set it beside my front door and lure good spirits to chase away the ghosts of divorce, rehashed arguments, mistakes and misinter-pretations? Could I send one to my son?

The river was wide and full at the point where we stepped out of the van, its beach muddy and crammed with brightly colored long boats to carry tourists, all of us with our fancy cameras hoping to capture pictures of the floating people's privacy. Our boat putt-putted down glassy water, past everyday life: men changed shirts on boat decks, fishermen beat nets overflowing with small luminescent fish, boys and girls ran full-court presses on a floating basketball court, women paddled to the grocery store in long canoes. Water hyacinths choked the shore and eased up the trunks of trees rooted in the river's mud, and sprouts of sparse water grass peeked from the smooth surface, broken only by the occasional wakes of boats. Tourists photographed tourists.

We drifted to the juncture where the river fed into a larger body of water. Lake Tonle Sap was almost infi-nite. Phnom Penh and Battambang were beyond, much farther than my eyes could see. Suddenly, swarms of long paddleboats rushed to our side, hulls brimmed with bananas, bottled water, and orange Fanta sodas jammed into red coolers. *One dollar, one dollar!* Wrinkled old women, a few with snakes around their necks, teeth rot-ted by betel nut, and cataract-covered eyes stared into my camera's lens. Children, hustlers by speech, innocents by face. A smile did not bring a smile. *One dollar, one dollar!* They posed, made the "V" for victory sign, begged with their eyes—please, American woman, if you can be here, then you can pay. *One dollar, one dollar!*

When my son was five or six, about the same age as the longhaired boy staring up at me, he was obsessed with cars. Names, makes, and assorted automotive trivia fell easily from his tongue. His favorite question was,

"What kind of car do you drive?" Whenever I stopped by the toy store, he begged for a new model car to add to his collection until I gave in—and I always gave in. Manipulator of mother, gentle negotiator. His eyes fixed on mine, the softened gaze of a child who wants something extravagant. These children in the long boats did not beg for the sake of extravagance, they begged to live. Did my son succumb to the eyes, the plaintive pleas? Did he hand over one dollar, one dollar? I did, in his name.

Angkor Thom, Angkor Wat, Ta Preah, and Preah Khan—I'd visualized these sacred places amid steamy and vine-filled jungles, quiet, meditative, hours from the city, with clouds of swarming mosquitoes and monkeys screeching overhead. But they were not. The temples had an unexpected commonality: gray stone etched with the soot of time, Buddhas sculpted into tower facades, small bunches of fresh flowers, incense sticks poked into sand-filled cans, smoky perfume swirling in the light breeze. Chants, loud and soft—prayers of gratitude and pleas for divine inspiration—drifted into high towers pointed like lotus buds with wind-softened edges. Holy flowers perfect in form, height, and majesty. Narrow steps led to unseen altars amidst hundreds of squared stones wide as my arms and long as my body, piled upon one another like a child's discarded building blocks.

I had studied European empires in college and explored ruins in Italy, Greece, and France, but stepping onto these ancient stones, I was overwhelmed by Angkor Thom's magic. These ruins were different, mystical.

Once a royal city, the last capital of the Angkor Empire, more than a million people are speculated to have lived in the area surrounding Angkor Thom.

Unlike today, all its gates were open then, each with a special significance: the North was the spiritual entry used by monks; the West, the entrance of the dead; the East, no longer open to the public, the portal of victory and ghosts. This was the entrance that fascinated me. How I longed to walk through that eastern doorway, obscured by the jungle and time, and join the ghost of my son. Reunion in spirit better than none at all.

Instead, I crossed the bridge over a moat filled with blooming water lilies and walked through the south gate with the other visitors.

We tourists came from many continents, our languages as varied as our countries of origin. As I wandered the ruins, I eavesdropped, catching snippets of conversations here and there, listening for English— eager to share the moment. Weren't they equally awed by the immensity, the history, the timelessness of these structures? But there seemed no time for questions. Like busy ants we scampered up the steep steps, marveled at the carvings, the windows within windows. I walked through narrow passages and squatted beside emptied pools, amazed at the simplicity, imagining the rituals that took place there. People passed on my left and right, chattering, laughing, rushing to get to the top. I sat still, trying to conceive of the quiet sacredness that must have once pervaded the air.

Outside the temple, I separated myself from the crowd and stepped back, taking in the full view. Suddenly, I was struck by the towers and the faces covering them. I let the tenets of each sculpted image of Mahayana Buddhism—*Lokesvara*, the principle of compassion, and *Prajnaparamita*, the principle of wisdom—infuse me; they were what I needed to appreciate, what stood before me—these structures and my future.

In my head, I talked with my son like we used to when he was younger. I whispered the story of the bas-reliefs: Jayavarman's attacks, the monkey kings at his side, driving back the *Cham*, the Vietnamese, from Cambodia. I stared at the lovely Sita, holding the wounded Rama, protecting him from the chaos of war.

Minutes away, the mighty Angkor Wat stood beyond a moat almost as wide as the Siem Reap River. A broad, bumpy causeway led to an outer wall, dirtied with the silt of centuries. Pillars pitted with bullet holes from the Cambodian Civil War marked this west entrance, and oversized doorways and massive columns stretched left and right as far as I could see. At last, I was where I had dreamed of being, as thrilled as the French explorer Henri Mouhoot must have been one hundred-fifty years before when he made this discovery, hacking through the Cambodian jungle in search of beetles and giant butterflies.

Beyond the outer wall, another wide pathway led past the ancient library to the temple. Palm trees lined the way. A white horse grazed a rolling lawn. Five lotus towers rose like turrets from the temple. Streams of orange-swathed monks passed by, the straps of small silver cameras peeking from their cloth-draped arms.

On the second level of the grand temple, I came across two Buddhist nuns, silent and wizened, their faces gaunt and their heads shorn, praying before a twenty-foot Buddha. Yellow chrysanthemums garlanded the altar, and buckets of incense lined the floor around it. In a profane moment, I zoomed my lens to capture their reverence. When the nuns rose and turned toward me, I asked permission to take another picture. The women, their faces serious, stood side-by-side and looked directly at my lens. I snapped, yearning to breach the forbidden and touch them, arrange them in softer poses than the formal upright ones they chose.

After, I bowed as I had been instructed: thank you. The taller of the two women put her hands together in the prayer position underneath her chin and bowed. *Akun*. Her voice commanded me to imitate her words and perfect gesture. *Akun*, I repeated, without her force, once, twice, three times, until my intonation matched hers. *Akun*. Then she raised her joined hands over her head and gave thanks to Buddha. Perhaps she saw something in my eyes. Her instruction was more than an age-old bow, it was a life lesson: say thank you; be grateful for what you have, not what you have lost. Satisfied that I had learned my lesson well, she walked away, leaving my spirit lifted.

Akun. Akun. The ghost of my son—my boy now man—came alive in Angkor Wat. Had he paused at the lithe images of the Apsara dancers and wondered at the symmetry of the carved figures, the perfection of their curved hands and thick lips? Had he bowed before Buddha, lit incense and prayed for divine guidance, as I did?

On that temple's smooth stairs, I saw him taking two at a time and imagined his unending curiosity, his hands pressed to the walls and the intricate messages carved into them. I sighed, thankful for the splendor of the past around me, thankful for my own past, for the happier years with my son, for the foundations that would surely support this ancient place far beyond my years, for the foundations of love that my son did not understand, that would carry him into his future.

Ghosts, dating back to the tenth century, inhabited the temples of the Kingdom of Cambodia. Angkor Thom granted them a special gate, but in Angkor Wat they

lurked in waterless pools, sought their bodies, waited
for rescue from the netherworld between life and death.
They had been conquered, tortured, shot. Murdered
in the killing fields. Blown apart by land mines. They
skulked around the roots of banyan trees, in the market,
and in bullet-ridden columns. In those temples, among
those ghosts, I believed in the future and its connection
to the past.

Before I left on my trip, I'd argued with my son. Our
relationship, once so close, fell apart along with my marriage, and although the state of California helps adults
navigate the technicalities of divorce, there was nothing to help this mother with her child. My son's deep
voice had trembled with anger when he told me he was
cutting off all communication with me—no hugs, no
pinching his cheeks, no him.

Standing in the ruins of Ta Preah, those memories returned as I entered the temple built by King
Jayavarman VII in honor of his mother. A son's devotion
in the lushness of the trees and the unseen, squawking
parrots. Smaller than the other temples, pretty and feminine, its massive stones had fallen into lichen-covered
piles. Banyan tree roots dripped, sinuous like enormous
snakes, into the hard dirt below.

Before another Buddha, I lowered my forehead to the
ground. On my knees, comfortable among strangers,
tears washed my face. On my knees, I asked for connection and reunion and freedom from my ghosts. For
peace with my child. I listened for the somber sounds
that once flowed through these walls—a gong for dinner, the call to prayer, a monotone chant of gratitude.
The rustle of silk, the whisper of prayers, the padding
of bare feet.

Akun.

𝕤 𝕤 𝕤

Jacqueline Luckett is a former sales representative. After leaving the corporate world, she took a creative writing class on a dare, from herself, and began writing short stories and poetry and never looked back. The Bay Area native loves living in Oakland but travels frequently to nurture her passion for photography and learning to cook exotic foods. Her first novel, Searching for Tina Turner, *was released in January 2010.*

ﻬ ﻬ ﻬ

Missing Paris

What can you do when the city of love
won't return your calls?

I'm homesick for Paris, although that's where I am.
It happens to me every time I visit. I grieve for this
great city I have lived in and left, precisely because I'm
only visiting. Like having a drink with an ex-lover: we
don't belong to each other anymore.

Becky and I have been here for three days now. This
is usually when it strikes me, on Day Three, after I've
recovered from the stunned blur of jet lag and the thrill
of landing (the melodic French tones that accompany
flight announcements at De Gaulle); after the dazed
ride on the RER, silently rushing on its rubber wheels
into the city; after the arrival at l'Hôtel Saint Sulpice, a
sliver of a building jammed into a corner of the square,
our *chambre à deux personnes* a little shabbier than it was
on our last stay.

After breakfast—breakfast in Paris!—after the first bite into the freshest baguette, sweet with butter and strawberry jam; after pouring coffee from the porcelain pot and, simultaneously, hot milk from the pitcher into a bowl so ample it might hold heaped fruit; after we kiss our French friends on both cheeks and they cry, *"Mais vous n'avez pas changé, vous êtes toujours aussi jeunes!"* although they demonstrate, beloved mirrors, just how much we've changed since we last met.

It's after we cross the river, breathing in the newly washed sidewalks, and leave behind the Left Bank to head toward l'Île Saint Louis, and walk and walk for three days straight, ignoring anything indoors, suspended in the gray grace of these streets, these shimmering buildings topped with red clay chimney pots, around us everyone speaking French.

On the third day, at last, my homesickness swoops in: I don't live here, this is not mine.

I no longer know which bus to take to get to l'Opéra. I have no idea how to find out which films are playing, or what they are once I've found them (except those still showing after forty years in the same dilapidated *cinémas* where I first saw them at age twenty). I have three friends left in Paris, and one is fading fast. Once, I had a universe. I knew my way around it, owned it. What's the name and address of that tiny restaurant where we used to eat soufflé au Grand Marnier when I was married to Michael? I remember we had to order it the minute we walked in, before we'd even read the menu. Then hours and many courses later, when we'd forgotten all about it, suddenly the waiter placed before us a dish that held a toasty, puffed-up, fragrant hat—but when we sank our spoons in, we discovered it was warm, sweet, eggy air.

I lived in Paris for nine months that time. I was

Michael's wife, and I truly thought we were married forever, even though I was in love with someone else, the second of my two great Parisian loves. They were both women—as Paris is to me. My heart has broken twice here, the first time when I was twenty on my junior year abroad, the next when I was thirty-five. But neither of those women was fully mine: one was straight, the other absent at the deep heart's core. They were no more mine than is the culture of this city or its language. Though I'm fluent, I will never speak French as immediately and naturally as I speak English. Perhaps it's recognizing this always already present absence that overcomes me on Day Three.

I am homesick for Paris, even though that's where I am. Now, on the third day of our trip, my French friend Amie has decamped to her boyfriend's for the weekend, leaving us her garret on rue de la Bûcherie, which looks out over rooftops, chimneys, and the spires of Notre Dame. I'm plunged into depression. (Amie suggested to me once that this is precisely why Americans come to Paris: you travel here, you get depressed, then you go home and write a novel about it.)

Life feels so bleak at the moment that I've lost my sense of humor. "Becky," I say to my lover, "I need to be alone. Do you mind? Would you mind just—leaving? For a while?"

She doesn't speak French, but I've taught her how to say *s'il vous plaît: une omelette mixte et un café au lait*, which guarantees that she won't starve out there. And why should I feel guilty about asking her to walk the streets of Paris at twilight? She grabs a handful of euros and slams out, leaving me to my mood.

❧ ❧ ❧

A short while later, I hear the key turn in the lock. "There's Bach around the corner," she says, out of breath. She has run back to get me. She knows how I love Bach. "In that church. In fifteen minutes."

She has come back hopeful, bearing gifts.

Becky is a generous woman. We share a life in that other great city across the ocean where I was born and grew up. We live together in its huge cluttered verticality, near my grown-up children, my aging parents, our friends, our work. France is the only thing that isn't in New York.

I look at her. She's not missing Paris, she's enjoying it. Or trying to, in the face of my doleful self-imposed exile. I pull myself up out of the uncomfortable Louis Something armchair I am sunk in. "What church?"

"You know, the one along the river, in the park."

We squeeze into the minuscule French elevator, rush out in the silver twilight, and race to St. Julien le Pauvre, the little medieval chapel two blocks distant.

The doors are closing as we arrive; we're the last inside. The ticket taker leads us to the only two empty seats, in the front row, immediately facing the young woman cellist who, perhaps four feet from us, begins to play Bach's unaccompanied cello suites.

The church is lit by candles, its walls bear faded frescoes, and the single line of melody is all that we can hear. Its resonant simplicity fills up the space, ungraspable, entirely present. I am seated next to Becky, whom I love. We're listening to Bach. And I am in Paris, which belongs to me, sometimes.

Nancy Kline's articles, essays, short stories, and reviews have appeared in The New York Times, The Boston Globe, San Francisco Chronicle, Playgirl, *and numerous literary magazines. She has published six books, most recently, a new translation (with Mary Ann Caws) of René Char's* Furor and Mystery and Other Writings.

Fish Tale

Annie Nilsson

It's true.

There's a piranha on the end of my fishing pole, and I haven't showered in an entire week, and my hair has begun to change its texture, possibly for good.

How did I get here?

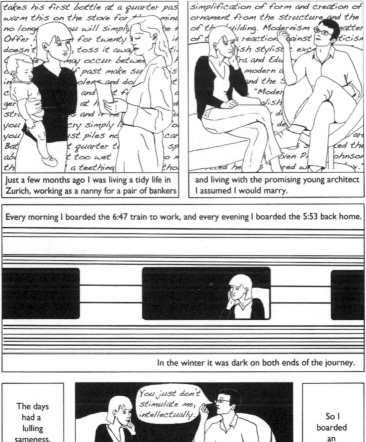

Just a few months ago I was living a tidy life in Zurich, working as a nanny for a pair of bankers and living with the promising young architect I assumed I would marry.

Every morning I boarded the 6:47 train to work, and every evening I boarded the 5:53 back home.

In the winter it was dark on both ends of the journey.

The days had a lulling sameness,

right up until the day that they didn't.

You just don't stimulate me, intellectually.

So I boarded an airplane

at 7:58,

I began working on a farm at the edge of the jungle,

rising before daybreak

pulling up weeds from the untidy rows,

to slop the pigs,

trekking into the field to hack down sugarcane with a handleless blade.

There was a rhythm to the days here as well.

But it was different somehow.

But now I'm standing in this boat with my catch on a wire.

And I haven't showered in an entire week,

but I've bathed in a river.

For now the bugs are humming thickly all around me.

And I don't know where I will go tomorrow.

Tonight I'll roast a piranha over a small, wet fire.

I wonder what it will taste like.

෯ ෯ ෯

Annie Nilsson is an MFA candidate at the University of Iowa's Nonfiction Writing program. Her work has appeared in Fourth Genre *and* Fugue, *and has been nominated for a Pushcart Prize. She has settled, for now, in Iowa City with her husband, four chickens, and a Siberian reindeer-herding dog named Loki. She is currently at work on a memoir.*

ACKNOWLEDGMENTS

Being asked to edit this anthology is an enormous honor; therefore, my first words of gratitude go to the brilliant minds behind Travelers' Tales: Larry Habegger for entrusting me with the project and helping me see it through (and sorry again about your car), James O'Reilly for offering wise and thoughtful counsel along the way, and Sean O'Reilly for providing valuable input and carrying 150 stories on the plane to Germany instead of watching back-to-back in-flight movies like I would do.

Stephanie Elizondo Griest, you have been my saving grace, and "thank you" doesn't even begin to cut it; I am eternally indebted to you for always answering the phone, even when you knew it was me. Christy Quinto, you are a marvel, and I hereby dub you Queen of Tireless Effort and Infinite Patience and Long Hours. A huge thank-you also to Natalie Baszile: your work is so appreciated!

I am lucky beyond measure to have some tremendously smart and kindhearted people in my corner. For encouragement, feedback, and steadfast support, thank-yous of the highest order go to Dan Prothero, Dolly Spalding, and Jen Castle. You all complete me. A big group hug also to Elizabeth Barrett, Rolf Potts, Amy Flynn, Susie Protiva, Blake Spalding, Anthony Weller, and Steven Prothero.

Jim Benning and Michael Yessis of *World Hum* were kind enough to nominate some marvelous essays, as was Tim Leffel of *Perceptive Travel*. Meanwhile, Jeff Lebow, April Orcutt, Boyer Rickel, and Jen Leo helped spread the word that got the stories rolling in.

Mary Oliver once wrote, "Instructions for living a life: Pay attention. Be astonished. Tell about it." With that in mind, I reserve the final and most significant acknowledgment for the several hundred women who traveled, paid attention, and told about it, putting pen to paper and sharing their experiences with Travelers' Tales. Every last story stays with me, and for that, I am deeply thankful.

About the Editor

Lavinia Spalding is author of *Writing Away: A Creative Guide to Awakening the Journal-Writing Traveler*, chosen one of the best travel books of 2009 by The Los Angeles Times, and coauthor of *With a Measure of Grace: The Story and Recipes of a Small Town Restaurant*. A regular contributor to *Yoga Journal*, her work has also appeared in a wide variety of literary and travel publications, including *Sunset Magazine*, *World Hum*, *Post Road*, and *Inkwell*.

She spent her bohemian childhood in Kensington, New Hampshire and Flagstaff, Arizona, climbing trees, writing poetry, and playing the classical guitar. Upon graduating from the University of Arizona's creative writing program, she took a one-year position teaching ESL in Busan, South Korea, and stayed for six years. An incorrigible nomad, she has traipsed through more than thirty countries on five continents, a blank notebook and a clutch of pens her constant companions. She is a practicing Buddhist, a Scrabble junkie, an avid kimchi maker, and an amateur knife thrower, but her greatest sense of accomplishment comes from her ability to say, "I love you" in twenty-five languages.

She currently lives in San Francisco and can always be found at laviniaspalding.com. Visit her there to see more of her work, including interviews with the contributors of this book.